IO152242

Twenty-Four Signs of the End Times

Marc Wheway Ph.D.

Ark House Press
arkhousepress.com

© 2022 Marc Wheway Ph.D.

All rights reserved. Apart from any fair dealing for the purpose of study, research, criticism, or review, as permitted under the Copyright Act, no part may be reproduced by any process without written permission.

Unless otherwise stated, all Scriptures are taken from the New International Translation (Holy Bible. Copyright© 1996, 2004, 2007, 2013 by Tyndale House Foundation. Used by permission of Tyndale House Publishers Inc., Carol Stream, Illinois 60188. All rights reserved.)

Some names and identifying details have been changed to protect the privacy of individuals.

Cataloguing in Publication Data:
Title: Twenty-Four Signs of the End Times
ISBN: 978-0-6454926-3-7 (pbk)
Subjects: End Times; Revelation; Christian Living;
Other Authors/Contributors: Wheway, Marc. Ph.D;

Design by initiateagency.com

This book is dedicated to Sharyn who asked if we (Kingdom Seekers Fellowship) could do a week or two in Matthew, chapter twenty-four. We agreed, a little over six months later, we completed the series.

CONTENTS

Prologue...vii

Introduction...xi

CHAPTER ONE: 'Birth Pains'...1

Israel Reborn (Matt. 24:32-35)..2

Led Astray / Falling Away (Matt. 24: 4-5) 11

Rumours of war, Famine and Pestilences

(Matt. 24:7 (KJV) (cf. Lu. 21:11) 20

Earthquakes (Matt. 24:7) 28

Days of Noah (Matt. 24:37) 35

Days of Lot - Homosexuality (Matt. 24:38, Lu. 17:20-37)..........46

Drunkenness (Matt. 24:38, 49) 56

Faithfulness Vs. Faithlessness (Matt. 24:45-51).............63

Love Growing Cold (Matt. 24:12)....................................70

False Peace (Matt. 24:15)..79

CHAPTER TWO: 'Commencement of the Tribulation' 87

Great Oppression (Matt. 24:21) 88

Persecution (Matt. 24:9)...95

Increase of False Prophets (Matt. 24:11) 108

The Gospel Proclaimed throughout the Whole World
(Matt. 24:14) 116

CHAPTER THREE: 'The Great Tribulation' 126
Abomination of Desolation (Matt. 24:15) 127
Flee (Matt. 24:16) 136
Tribulation like Never Before, or will be Again (Matt. 24:21).......145
False Prophets and False Messiah's (Matt. 24:24) 152
Armageddon (Matt. 24:28) 162
Vultures Will Gather (Matt. 28:28) 170

CHAPTER FOUR: 'Immediately After the Tribulation' 180
Powers of Heaven Shaken (Matt. 24:29)..181
The Sign of the Son of Man (Matt. 24:30-31) 189
The Angels are Sent Out (Matt. 24:31)..196
The Thief (Matt. 24:42-43) 204

CHAPTER FIVE 213
The Ten Virgins (Matt. 25:1-13) 213

CHAPTER SIX 222
The Talents (Matt. 15:14-30) 222

CHAPTER SEVEN 230
The Final Judgement (Matt. 25:31-46)..230

Conclusion...239

PROLOGUE

The book of Matthew, chapter twenty-four, provides vital information about the close of this age (Matt. 24:3), compiling a prophetic list of twenty-four identified things to come. By referencing the things to come, Jesus provides signs of the time, commencing as birth pain, which are irreversible and unstoppable when begun. As with labour pain, contractions start small and then intensify over time. The contractions also move closer together, with intensification, until birth occurs. So likewise, will it be for the signs leading into the tribulation. Once commenced, the birth pains Jesus referred to cannot be stopped, or be avoided, leading to, and only ending after the prophesied great tribulation to come (Matt. 24:8).

The twenty-four signs identified in Mathew, chapter twenty-four, as follows:

1. Rebirth of Israel (vv. 32-34)
2. Led Astray / Falling Away (vv. 4-5, 11, 23-26)
3. Wars, Famine and Pestilences (v. 7 (KJV) (cf. Lu. 21:11)
4. Earthquakes (v. 7)
5. Days of Noah (v. 37)
6. Days of Lot - Homosexuality (v. 38, Lu. 17:20-37)
7. Drunkenness (vv. 38-49)

8. Faithfulness Vs. Faithlessness (vv. 45-51)
9. Love Growing Cold (v. 12)
10. False Peace (v. 15)
11. Great Oppression (v. 21)
12. Persecution (v. 9)
13. Increase of False Prophets (v. 11)
14. The Gospel Proclaimed throughout the Whole World (v. 14)
15. Abomination of Desolation (v. 15)
16. Flee (v. 16)
17. Tribulation like Never Before, or will be Again (v. 21)
18. False Prophets and False Messiah's (v. 24)
19. Armageddon (v. 28)
20. Vultures Will Gather (v. 28)
21. Sun Darkened. Moon not giving Light. Stars fall from Heaven (v. 29)
22. The Sign of the Son of Man (vv. 30-31)
23. The Angels are Sent Out (v. 31)
24. The Thief (vv. 42-43)

The above list of twenty-four signs of the times is concise, and is most evident in the present day, reported daily through the news; still, most remain ignorant. And then those who do have some prophetic knowledge yet remain largely ignorant of scripture. The ignorant include the date setters, stating dates as to when Jesus will return. They are unaware of scripture due to Jesus saying, no one knows the precise day and hour of His return. Five times (Matt. 24:36, 42, 44, 50, 25:13), Jesus said that we do not, and will not 'know the day and the hour' of this His appearing. The reference to 'day and hour' narrows in on a specific date and time (which we should never do). Despite not knowing the exact day and hour of Jesus' return, we are to understand and decern the 'season' (cf. 1 Chron. 12:32; Luke 12:56), through the signs of the times.

An example of knowing the season is with Daniel, who perceived in the books the number of years that, according to the word of the Lord to Jeremiah the prophet, must pass before the end of the desolation of Jerusalem, namely, seventy years (Dan. 9:2). Following a significant sign of the times, Daniel turned to the books (cf. Jer. 25:11-12), seeking to understand the event through the lens of Bible prophecy. The sign of the time for Daniel was the end of seventy years of captivity, marked with the death of Belshazzar, the last Babylonian King.

Although Daniel knew about the signs of the times (Dan. 2 & 7), he did not understand the timing regarding the biblical prophetic calendar. Therefore, at the time of Israel's seventy years of captivity, he incorrectly assumed God would judge the nations and set up His Messianic Kingdom. Daniel's reference to God's holy hill and city (Dan. 9:16, 19, 20) refers to his understanding of the Messiah ruling from Jerusalem (Isa. 65:17-25, esp. v 25). Daniel saw Jesus taking dominion over the earth in chapter seven (Dan. 7:9-14, 26-27), causing him much anxiety (7:15, 28), over the signs of the times. The reason for Daniel's concern was that his people were not ready for the coming King, therefore, they were likely to face judgement.

Although Daniel misunderstood the timing of the coming events, prompting an angelic visitation from the angel Gabriel to clarify (Dan. 9:24-27), he was aware of the signs. His awareness motivated him to look for and live for the Messiah, always seeking to be ready. And likewise, so must we be, promoting the words of Jesus, YOU MUST STAY AWAKE, YOU MUST BE READY (Matt. 24:42, 44). Mark's account says YOU MUST BE ON GUARD, KEEP/STAY AWAKE (Mk. 13:33, 34, 37), and Luke's account says WATCH YOURSELVES, and STAY AWAKE (Lu. 21:34, 36).

In addition to the warning to be ready, be on guard, stay awake, and watch yourself, Luke provides more in chapter twelve, warning the church to keep their lamps burning (Lu. 12:23, cf. Matt. 251-13). Next, the church must keep its lamp burning, to be ready (Lu. 12:40), faithful and wise (Lu. 12:42), doing and acting according to Jesus' will (Lu. 12:43, 47), or else (Lu. 12:45-48). The 'or else,' or consequences of failure are self-explanatory (Lu. 12:47) and are taken to another level in the concluding parable of Matthew, chapter twenty-four (Matt. 24:51).

INTRODUCTION

Matthew, Twenty-Four and Revelation, Chapter Six
"The one who endures until the end shall be saved" (Matt. 24:13)
"Here calls for the endurance of the saints"
(Rev. 13:10, 14:12, cf. 1:9, 2:10, 3:10, 12:17)

Matthew's incredible parallel future events, chapter twenty-four and Revelation, chapter six, were foretold by Jesus when asked, "What will be the sign of Your coming and the close of the age?" (Matt. 24:3). While Jesus rattled off some twenty-four signs, the list below is a condensed summary of the top ten end times signs. The number one sign of the end times is deception through false teachers, teachings, and lying signs and wonders. So deceptive will false teachers be, even the elect could be led astray (Matt. 24:24).

Birth Pains	Event	Verse	Where	Prediction
1	False Teachers, Led astray, apostasy	24:5, 10, 11, 23-26	Catholicism, Prosperity Peaching, Hyper Faith/ Grace, NAR, Ecumenicalism	Every book of the NT, bar Philemon (cf. 2 Thess. 2:3)

2	War / Conflict (Technology)	24:6-7 (Dan. 12:4)	Middle East, South, Far North, and the East	Ps. 83, Isa. 17:1, Jer. 49:24-27, Ezek. 38-39, Dan 11:40-45, Rev. 6:4, 9:12-19, 16:12-16, 19:11-19
3	Famine/ Sickness	24:7a (KJV)	Global	Lu. 21:11 Rev. 6:5-8
4	Earthquakes	24:7b	Global	Rev. 6:12 11:13, 16:18
5	Delivered Up, Persecution	24:9-10	Global	Lu. 12:12-18 Rev. 6:9
6	Days of Noah	24:37	Global DNA Corruption	Gen. 6
7	Lawlessness, Love of Self & Money	24:12	Global Sin Forsake Law	Matt. 7:21-23 2 Tim. 3:1
8.	Peace Treaty	Isa. 28:14-16,18	Israel	Isa. 28:15, 18 Dan. 9:27
Tribulation	Last Call	24:9-28	Whole world	Rev. 3:10, 6-19
Three Woes	Remaining Three Trumpets		Global	Rev. 8:13, 8:13: 1). 9:1-11, 2). 9:13-19, 3). 11:15-19
9.	Third Temple, Abomination of desolation Great Trib.	24:15-23 24:21	Jerusalem Global	Dan 9:27, 11:31, 12:11, 2 Thess. 2:4

10.	Signs Wonders	24:24	Two Witnesses Third Temple Antichrist	Rev. 11 Rev. 11:1-13 Rev. 13:14-15
Days of Lot Armageddon Jesus Returns	Judgement	Matt. 24:39-41 24:28 24: 29-31, 36, 42, 44, 50	Global Megiddo Mount of Olives	Lu. 17:28-37, Dan. 12. Rev. 16:12-16 Rev. 6:12-17, 11:15-19, 19:11-21
Before and Following Jesus' return	Sun, Moon, Stars	24:29-30	Heaven and Earth Shaken	Joel 2:30, Acts 2:19-21, Rev 16:14

Comparing the Olivet Discourse from the synoptic gospels confirms the same events and orders of things to come, with some minor differences. Matthew's account is the most comprehensive. Nevertheless, throughout each account, the gospel is proclaimed (Matt. 24:14, Mk. 13:9b-11, Lu. 21:13-15), debunking the idea that God has abandoned humanity, exchanging grace for judgement. A comparative chart is below.

Matthew 24	Mark 13	Luke 21
False teachers/teachings (vv. 24:5, 11, 23-26)	False teachers/teaching (vv. 5-6)	False teachers/teaching (v. 8)
War and rumours of wars, nation rising against nation (vv. 6-7)	Wars and rumours of wars, nation rising against nation (v. 7)	Hear of wars and conflicts (v. 9)
Famine (v. 7)	Earthquakes (v. 8)	Nation rising against nations, and kingdom against kingdom (v. 10)
Sickness (v. 7 KJV)	Famine and troubles (KJV) (v. 7)	Earthquakes (v. 11)

Earthquakes (v. 7)	Beginning of birth pain (v. 8)	Famine (v. 11)
Beginning of birth pains (v. 8)	Delivered up and beaten (v. 9)	Pestilence (v. 11)
Delivered up to tribulation (v. 9)	**Gospel proclaimed (v. 9b-11)**	Terrors and great signs in heaven (v. 11)
Falling away, betrayal, and hatred (v. 10)	Betrayed, and hated (vv. 12-13)	Before this (above) persecution first, delivered up and imprisoned (v. 12)
Lawlessness (v. 12)	The abomination of the desolation (third temple) (v. 14)	**The gospel will be proclaimed (vv. 13-15)**
The gospel will be proclaimed (v. 14)	Awakened Jews will flee Jerusalem (vv. 15-18)	Hated (v. 18)
The abomination of the desolation (third temple) (v. 15)	Commencement of the great tribulation (v. 19)	Not a hair will perish, by endurance gain lives (v. 18-19)
Awakened Jews will flee Jerusalem (v. 16-20)	Those great tribulation days are cut short (v. 20)	Jerusalem surrounded by armies, desolation near (v. 20)
Commencement of the great tribulation (v. 21).	Antichrist and the false prophet (vv. 21-22)	Awakened Jews will flee Jerusalem (vv. 21-23)
Those great tribulation days are cut short (v. 22)	Lying signs and wonders (v. 22)	Jews slain; Jerusalem trampled (v. 24)
Antichrist and the false prophet (vv. 23-27)	After the tribulation, signs in the sky, heavens shaken (vv. 24-25)	Fearful signs in the sky and on the earth (vv. 25-27)

Lying signs and wonders (v. 24)	Jesus appears and judges the nations (vv. 26-27)	
Jesus returns (v. 27)		Jesus appears (v. 27)
Armageddon (v. 28)		When these things (above) begin to take place, straighten up, redemption draws near (v. 28)
After the tribulation, signs in the sky, heavens shaken (vv. 29)		
Jesus appears and judges the nations (vv. 30-31)		

Following the removal or rapture of the church, who endured this side (Matt. 10:22, Rev. 3:10), marked by verse nine, the tribulation commences. Having failed to heed the warnings, such as recorded in each of the letters written to the seven churches (Rev. 2-3), the loveless, compromising, corrupt, dead, sleeping, and lukewarm churchgoers now must go through and endure the tribulation until the end (of their lives) to be saved. Foretelling this event, Matthew chapter twenty-four is an exact fit, set in the precise order of Revelation chapter six.

The chart above shows the sequence of events from birth pangs to the signing of the peace treaty, which will trigger the tribulation. The tribulation will not happen before the church is removed; therefore, the signing of the peace treaty and the rapture will coincide. The tribulation is then split into two parts, the first and second half, each three and a half years long, or forty-two months - 1260 days each.

After the second woe, the second half of the tribulation, known as the great tribulation, will commence. The great tribulation is referenced in Matthew's account (24:21), and the book of Revelation (2:22) and (7:14.) Satan is cast to the earth between the second and the third woe - and the antichrist announces himself to be 'God' from the rebuilt third temple. At that point, all hell breaks loose on the earth, literally. Revelation, chapter six, introduces the events unfolding throughout the seven years.

Matt 24	Matt 24	Matt 24	Matt 24	Matt 24	Matt 24	Matt 24
Deception vv. 5, 11, 24	War vv. 6-7, 22	Famine vv. 7b-8	Pestilences v. 7	Martyrdom v. 9	Earthquake vv. 7	Cosmic events vv. 29
Seal 1	Seal 2	Seal 3	Seal 4	Seal 5	Seal 6	Seal 7
White Horse 6:2	Red Horse 6:3-4	Black Horse 6:5-6	Pale Horse 6:7-8	Martyrdom 6:9	Earthquake 6:12	Cosmic events 8:5 (cf. 6:12)

When Jesus was describing the tribulation, He was not just referring to the first part but the entire seven-year period. Matthew, chapter twenty-four, and Revelation chapter six cover the period. Matthew, chapter twenty-four (Matt. 24:4-8) are the signs leading to the tribulation. The first half of the tribulation starts with increased persecution, following the signing of the Middle East peace treaty. Once the tribulation persecution commences, the gospel will spread like wildfire (Matt. 24:9-14). The midway point was marked with Jesus' words, "For then there shall be great tribulation" (Matt. 24:21). Verse twenty-one refers to verse fifteen, being the abomination of desolation (v. 15). The abomination of desolation is where the antichrist announces that he is God.

The seven seals of Revelation, chapter six, are the first of three sets of judgements yet are ongoing for seven years - still even within, the midway point is marked with the opening of the fifth seal. Persecution followed by martyrdom, the fifth seal follows the antichrist's announcement that he is God and must be worshipped as God by all. Anyone refusing to worship the antichrist and receive his mark (666) shall be slain (Rev. 13:10, 15).

The seven seals are followed by the seven trumpet judgements, concluding with the seven bowl judgements, before Christ returns to the earth. However, they are the same judgements repeated three times over, only intensified with each retelling. Evidence for the above mentioned is seen in Matthew's account, chapter twenty-four, where Jesus provides a detailed description and outline for the entire book of Revelation. The following chart illustrates the pattern discussed above. Also, the event, the Olivet Discourse, is split up into four parts, being 1). Before the tribulation, 2). Commencement of the tribulation, 3). Midway through, commencing the great tribulation, and 4). After the great tribulation.

Section	Matthew 24	Revelation	Events
Introduction	Verses 1-3	Chapters 1-5	Opening scene
Part 1	Verses 4-14	Chapters 6-8a	Seals
Part 2	Verses 15-28	Chapters 8b-14	Trumpets
Part 3	Verses 29	Chapters 16-17	Bowls
Conclusion	Verses 30:52	Chapters 18-22	Be ready / Come

In conclusion, when His disciples asked Jesus, "Tell us, when will these things be, and what will be the sign of Your coming, and the end of the age" (Matt. 24:3), Jesus answered both questions. Jesus answered them 'what will be the signs,' question with what has been covered above, and the 'when will these things be' question within verses thirty-two to thirty-five. Verses thirty-two to thirty-five refer to Israel becoming a nation again, which happened in 1948. Jesus said the generation that saw that event would be alive to see His return (Matt. 24:34). Israel, the nation, is now seventy-three years old; therefore, the youngest living person who saw Israel reborn is seventy-three years old today. The scripture says we can expect between seventy and eighty years of life (Ps. 90:10), on average. Therefore according to the prophecy (Matt. 24:34), if we have understood it correctly, we have seven years left. If there is another interpretation, time is still short due to humanity not generally living more than one hundred years in the best-case scenario.

Although we do not know the 'day and hour' (Matt. 24:36, 42, 50), we know the times by the signs, and the seasons, as discussed above. Of the signs, no other is greater than the rebirth of Israel. Going by the above mentioned, the rapture could happen as soon as 2021, but no later than 2022, if the interpretation is correct, leaving seven tribulation years before Jesus returns. Narrowing in further again, the month the rapture is likely (but not conclusively) to occur in September, during the feast of trumpets, or Rosh Hashanah.

To escape the trial coming upon the whole world, you/me must endure now and until the end (Matt. 10:22, Rev. 1:9, 2:10, 3:10). Or else, in failing, the left behind must endure then, in and through the tribulation (Matt. 24:13, Rev. 12:11, 17, 13:10, 14:12).

CHAPTER ONE

'Birth Pains'

(Matt. 24:1-8)

The last days commenced with Jesus' first appearance (Heb. 1:2) and will conclude with His next. In-between, the last days are the days known by the outpouring of the Holy Spirit, which begins with tongues, prophecy, visions and dreams, and end with judgement (Acts 2:17-21). Throughout the last days, lasting some two-thousand years, the primary work of the Holy Spirit is leading humanity to Jesus for salvation. When John wrote his letter (1 John), in the late first century, he used the term, last hour (1 Jn. 2:18), indicating the nearing of Christ's return. James writes, "The Judge is at the door" (Ja. 5:9), Paul wrote, "He (Jesus) is at hand" (Phil. 4:5, 1 Cor. 16:22), and the author of Hebrews says, "The day is drawing near, and He (Jesus) will not delay" (Heb. 10:25b, 37).

In-between the resurrection of Christ and His return (for the church), the church can expect tribulation (Matt. 10:16-25, Jn. 16:33). Leading up to the tribulation, deception, persecution, and rumours of wars, nation rising against nation, and kingdom against kingdom will become more common. The two primary signs leading into the tribulation are deception and conflict, accompanied by famines, pestilences, and earthquakes. All these signs are the beginning of birth pains, they must first take place, but the end is not yet.

Israel Reborn
'A Lesson from the Fig Tree'
(Matt. 24:32-35)

When the disciples asked Jesus about His coming and the end of the age, two questions were raised, 1). When will these things be? And 2). What will be the signs? (Matt. 24:3). Interestingly, Jesus answered the second question first; however, due to living in the age Jesus spoke of and connecting the dots, the first question will be addressed first, "When will these things be?"

The first question: "When will these things be?" The question of when these things will be was answered through the fig tree lesson, which applies the signs to the times. The 'when' question was addressed where Jesus taught the disciples, 'when' the branches of the fig tree become tender and put out its leaf, (then) you will know summer is near (24:33). Twice Jesus said near (24:33, 34). Included with the sign of the fig tree, Jesus said, "When you see ALL these things (signs), you will know that He (Jesus) is near, at the very gates" (24:33). Jesus' reference to 'all these things' includes everything mentioned from verse four onwards.

Included in the list of signs is the lesson from the fig tree. The fig tree is a significant sign of the end times, commencing the visible prophetic countdown. Jesus went on to say, "This generation will not pass away until all these things take place" (24:34). It is also important to note Jesus' reference to 'you'. Four times Jesus said, "You will know and see by the signs of the times; you (being the generation that sees the signs) will not pass away until all the prophecy is fulfilled." All of it!

From the lesson on the fig tree, several questions are raised:

1. What does the fig tree represent?
2. What timeframe, and generation does 'ALL' these signs refer to?
3. What does summer refer to?
4. What is the gate?

Jesus' teaching about the fig tree was recorded by Matthew (24:32-35), Mark (13:28:31), and Luke (21:19-33). Matthew and Mark's accounts are the same; however, Luke adds, "Look at the fig tree and ALL THE TREES" (Lu. 21:29). Jesus said, as soon as THEY come out in leaf, you see for yourselves that summer is already near (Lu. 21:30). Luke also adds, "So also, when you see these things taking place, you know that the kingdom of God is near" (Lu. 21:31). Again, Luke concluded by connecting the reference to 'you' with 'this generation.'

Identified above, with Luke's account, two more questions are raised:

5. Who are the other trees?
6. What kingdom is nearby? (Kingdom Now versus Kingdom Then)

The first of six more questions in need of answering is: What does the fig tree represent? To answer, the reader must first consider the context and apply the principles of systematic theology. There is no other reference to the fig tree within the context, but it is undisputable a significant sign of the end times. Contextually, the fig tree answers the 'when' question. The fig tree is one of many signs that must be fulfilled but is also a significant sign commencing the visible prophetic countdown. From the immediate context, we know that Jesus is not talking about a regular tree but rather applying something more.

Due to not having any other reference of the fig tree within the immediate context, the next step is to identify a reference to a fig tree elsewhere, which is not too difficult. A few chapters before (Matt. 21), Jesus cursed the fig tree for not bearing fruit (Matt. 21:18-20). The fig tree that Jesus cursed was a sign or harbinger of summer. The signs Jesus spoke of indicating His return would also serve as a harbinger; summer is near (Matt. 24:32).

In Matthew, chapter twenty-one, Jesus cursing the fig tree is essential for identifying the symbolism used in chapter twenty-four. Lessons to learn from the previous connection of the fig tree are that fig trees produce fruits, then leaves follow, or at least, both simultaneously. The tree Jesus approached had put forth its leaf, but no fruit (Matt. 21:19a). Due to not bearing fruit, Jesus cursed the tree, and it withered at once (Matt. 21:19b). The lesson taught through this event is on faith. If you have enough faith, you will do the same, and more, even moving mountains (Matt. 21:21).

Common sense should be enough to suggest the faith Jesus spoke of was not in the ability to wither trees and move mountains with a spoken word. That would revolve the message around man. The point of the lesson is to have faith in Jesus, the Son of God. Having faith in Jesus refers to repentance and the forgiveness of sin. Israel failed to bear the fruit of repentance, whose fathers were the first fruit on the fig tree (Hos. 9:10). Jeremiah also references Israel to figs, both good and bad (Jer. 24:5-8). The good ones have saving faith by obeying God, and the bad do not, producing no eatable fruit, as illustrated with the fig tree's withering (Matt. 21:18-20).

Israel had no faith in Jesus, therefore, bore no fruit, so the kingdom was taken away from them (Matt. 21:43). The fig tree refers to the nation of Israel, which might appear to be fruit-bearing at first glance, yet with closer inspection, they were found to be fruitless, at least bare any eatable (good) fruit. In support, Luke (13:6-9) offers a connecting parallel of the fig tree that did not bear fruit; therefore, it was in danger of being cut down.

The warning is to the religious who do not bear spiritual fruit, starting with the fruit of repentance (Matt. 3:8). For their fruitless condition, the warning was they would be destroyed unless change came. Contextually, the passage from Luke follows the call to repentance (Lu. 13:3, 5).

Due to being fruitless (none-repentant), Jesus cursed that generation, stating no fruit would ever come from it. A few days later, that cursed generation of Jews rejected Jesus, even pronouncing a curse on themselves (Matt. 27:25) when calling for Christ's crucifixion. That pronouncement led to that generation's judgement with the destruction of the second temple in 70. A.D.

Again, the cursing of the fig tree is symbolic of Israel for their fruitlessness. Due to rejecting Jesus, the nation of Israel has been set aside until the church is removed (Rom. 11:25). However, once the tribulation has commenced, a remnant of the Israelites will recognise Jesus and be saved (Rom. 11:1-5, 14b, 26-27). Although a remnant, still many Jews will come to faith in Jesus. Evidently, God has not done away with Israel; the call to salvation is irrevocable (Rom. 11:29).

The second question: What is the timeframe where all these signs will be seen? Although Israel's spiritual eyes will not be opened until the tribulation, the visible prophetic time clocked, and the countdown commenced with the nation of Israel being reborn. The fig tree putting out leaves is symbolic of the rebirth of Israel, partly fulling Ezekiel's prophecy (Ezek. 37). The nation of Israel was no longer after being desolated in 70 A.D. Not until 1948, when Israel once again became a nation, did the Jews have a homeland.

Following the destruction of Jerusalem in 70 A.D., the Jews were scattered to the uttermost parts of the world. Again, in 1948 Israel was reborn, in a day, fulfilling Isaiah's prophecy (Isa. 66:8). Jesus said the generation (of Jews) that sees all these signs would also see His return. In 2021, the youngest living person today that saw Israel become a nation was73 years old.

Great care must be taken when calculating the time remaining on the prophetic time clock, yet sadly and often, it is not. The term 'generation' is widely misused when calculating the time remaining before Christ returns. For example, some say a generation amounts to forty years, calculated from Matthew, chapter one, which would mean Jesus would have returned in 1988. Clearly, He did not. And, if He did, the rapture would have occurred in 1981, leaving seven years of tribulation.

Date setters failing with their 1981/88 interpretation reset the date to 2006/07, forty years after the six-day war (1967). Again, Jesus did not return in 2006/07; therefore, the generation that witnessed the rebirth of Israel does not apply to the forty-year theory. As mentioned above, the youngest of the Jews alive today, witnessing Israel's rebirth, are 73 years old, and they will still be alive to see Jesus' return.

Before Jesus returns, the church will be removed (2 Thess. 2:6-7, Rev. 3:10), leaving seven years in-between the rapture and Second Coming of Christ. Of Interest, elsewhere referencing the fig tree is Solomon (Sol. 2:13). Song of Solomon reads very similar to the rapture story where the Groom (Jesus) returns for His bride. When the bride sees the fig tree ripening, blossoming, and giving forth fragrance (summer is near), she (the bride) is told to arise and come away (cf. 1 Cor. 15:51-52, 1 Thess. 4:16-17, Rev. 4:1).

As mentioned above, the timing of ALL these signs is essential to note. Yet, some have said the prophecy was already fulfilled, pointing to 70 A.D, known as preterists. Preterists take a historical view of prophecy instead of a futuristic one. By doing so, they overlook the obvious, Jesus has not physically returned in the same way He left (Acts 1:9-11). If He has returned, then I would suggest His ruling rod of iron (Rev. 2:27) is too short, and Satan's lease (Rev. 20:1-3) is too long.

Furthermore, if Jesus has returned, several questions need an answer, such as: Where is He now? When did He return? Who saw Him return? When did the resurrection take place? And what judgement followed? (Zech. 14, Matt. 24:30, Rev. 1:7, 20:4-5). The preterist position is flawed and foolish. Paul addressed similar fools by saying, "And the talk of such men will spread like gangrene. Among them are Hymenaeus and Philetus, who have deviated from the truth. They say that the resurrection has already occurred, and they undermine the faith of some" (2 Tim. 2:17-18).

Amillennialism, like the preterist, also overlooks the obvious when dealing with the signs of the end times by stating the millennial kingdom commenced at the cross, spiritually speaking. Therefore, according to their theory, Jesus is not literally coming back, despite the angel saying He was (Acts 1:9-11), and John says that every eye would see Him when He does (Rev. 1:7). Amillennialism's interpretation of Bible prophecy was best described as exegetical gymnastics.

Despite prophecy snubs and scoffers (2 Pet. 3:3, Jude 1:18), Jesus will literally return before the generation that saw Israel's rebirth pass away. Before Jesus returns, however, birth pains must occur first (Matt. 24:6), leading into the tribulation, which is split into two parts. The latter part is described as a time like never before or seen again (Matt. 24:21). That statement alone debunks the preterist and millennial argument. Furthermore, if Jesus has returned, then why is the church still being persecuted? Persecution for the church is a birth pain, increasing until removed. Once the church has been removed, those coming to faith in the tribulation will also be persecuted. Most will lose their natural lives in exchange for eternal life.

The pre-tribulation birth pains commenced with the last days and will continue until the church is removed, and then the tribulation commences. The first half of the tribulation is addressed in Matthew, chapter twenty-four, verses nine to fourteen. The second, is the great tribulation and is addressed in verses fifteen to twenty-eight. As mentioned above, the second half will be a time never seen before or will be again (Matt. 24:21, cf. Jer. 30:7, Dan. 12:1).

The commencement of the midway point of the seven-year tribulation is identified through the abomination of desolation. The abomination of desolation does not refer to the destruction of the second temple in 70 A.D., but to the antichrist proclaiming to be God from the rebuilt, third tribulation temple (Dan. 7:8, 24, 9:27, 11:36, 12:11, Matt. 24:15, 2 Thess. 2:4, Rev. 13). Again, those that 'see all these signs' will also see the return of Jesus Christ (Matt. 24:34). So confident of this, Jesus said it would be easier for heaven and earth to pass away than for His words to fail to predict the coming events (Matt. 24:35, cf. 5:18).

Question number three: What does summer refer to? While summer is a time to look forward to for most, particularly those living in cold climates, the biblical meaning is not what most would expect or be looking forward to if they understood it. The word 'summer' in Aramaic is in Daniel (2:35), which means 'to cut off' or 'to pluck' or 'to gather fruit'. Here, Isaiah should be considered (Isa. 18:6), in context (read the entire chapter), referencing ravenous birds feeding on the carcasses of the slain (cf. Lu. 17:34-36, Rev. 19:17-19). Contextually (Matt. 24:32, Lu. 21:30), and systematically (Isa. 18, Lu. 17:34-36, Rev. 19:17-19), summer point to the time of trouble.

Keeping within a Jewish context, the summer period applies from May to September. September again is when the feast of trumpets, or Rosh Hashanah, takes place. In 2021, the dates were 6th – 8th of September, and in 2022, the feast will take place on the 25th – 27th of September. The feast of trumpets is often (but not conclusively) connected to the rapture trumpet (1 Thess. 4:16-17, Rev. 4:1).

The fourth question: What is the meaning of the gate? To understand the reference of the gate, the book of Samuel (2 Sam. 19:8) should be considered. In biblical Israel, 'gates' were not just a doorway into the city, but where prophets cried out and kings judged, and people met. The word 'gate' and the word 'door' can be used interchangeably. Some Bible translations use the word gate; others use the word door. James also used the word door, referring to a warning, "The Judge is at the door" (Ja. 5:9). When considering the meaning and application of the gate, another passage should be compared (Matt. 7:13-14). There, note the reference to the narrow gate, which is only arrived at by taking the narrow, hard path that leads to eternal life, yet few find it (Matt. 7:13-14).

Alongside those mentioned above, yet another reference to Jesus standing at the door should be added, from the letter to the lukewarm church of Laodicea (Rev. 3:20). There, Jesus warned, if the church does not stop buying from the world (being like the world), it will be vomited out (Rev. 3:16). Being vomited out refers to being judged and vomited out of the kingdom (cf. Lev. 18:25, 28). So the answer to the gate question is simply this; a gate is a place of judgement, where the Judge (Jesus) determines who and who does not enter His city. Only those traveling on the narrow and hard path will be judged righteous and given access.

Question five: Who are the other trees? The other trees refer to Gentile nations. As already established, the fig tree symbolises the nation of Israel as a sign for (Gentile) nations (Isa. 11:12). When Israel starts to put forward its leaf, Gentile nations will also (Lu. 21:30). Again, Israel was reborn in a day, in 1948. That sign commenced the visible prophetic countdown for the return of Jesus. Since then, other nations have also been formed and have produced signs, fulfilling prophecy in preparation for Jesus' return. Since Israel became a nation again, Gentile nations collectively have allied with her or become her enemy.

Those blessing Israel will be blessed, and those cursing her, will become a curse (Gen. 12:3). The blessing is extended to those coming to faith in Christ (cf. Jn. 4:22), being the spiritual children of Abraham (Acts 3:25, Gal 3:8). Western nations are/were predominantly Christian, and consequently, the same countries traditionally stood by Israel. Arguably, they have been blessed by God as a result. However, that is changing due to replacement theology and apostasy.

Question number six: Which kingdom of God, being nearby, is referred to? The kingdom (king's domain) referred to in Luke's account is not here and now, as taught by kingdom now 'theology' subscribers. Contrary to kingdom now teaching (nonsense), the kingdom Luke refers to (Lu. 21:31) is 'near', but not hear. Near, not here, refers to the coming kingdom, where God's will, will be done on earth as it is in heaven (Matt. 6:10). Jesus taught His disciples to pray in God's kingdom, signifying His literal future return. Before Jesus returns, the god of this world rules and reigns on the earth, which is why he could tempt Jesus with its wealth (Matt. 4:9). Satan is the god (2 Cor. 4:4), ruler (Jn. 13:31), and the prince of this world (Jn. 14:30), and he will remain to be until Jesus' return. When Jesus returns, He will cast Satan into the pit (Rev. 20:1-3). Then, Jesus will begin His rule and reign on the earth, and the saints will rule with Him (Rev. 1:7, 2:22, 5:10, 11:15, 20:4-5). Until that time, followers of Christ can expect persecution (Matt. 10:16-25) and tribulation (Jn. 16:33).

In conclusion, the fig tree represents the nation of Israel as a significant sign of the times. When Israel was rebirthed in 1948, the prophetic clock was visible to the wise and the awake, having eyes to see. Jews who witnessed Israel's rebirth will also see all the signs fulfilled, including the return of Jesus Christ. The youngest is 73 years old today.

Before Jesus returns, 'summer' will come first, being the great tribulation. The season of summer reveals Jesus is at the gate, ready to judge, at His literal return. Again, those witnessing the rebirth of Israel will see all the signs fulfilled, ending with Jesus' return and His judgement of the nations.

Those who witnessed Israel's rebirth will witness the Gentile nations responding to Israel's rebirth, being either friends or foes. They will also see the nations responding to Jesus during the tribulation, and they will witness the establishment of the coming kingdom under the Messiah's earthly rule and reign.

Led Astray / Falling Away
'Stay Awake'
(Matt. 24:4-5)

Just this week, I saw a post where a Jewish rabbi calculated the arrival of their messiah (Mashiach), and according to his calculation, he was due to arrive in the year 2021. He did this by considering the year of the Hebrew calendar (5782) from the time of Adam, whose name is also an acronym in Hebrew for Adam, David, and Mashiach. David was at the midway point of the year 5782, being then 2891 - 2891, twice timed is 5782. According to the calculation, the conclusion is, in 2021, the Jewish messiah will appear—5782 in the Hebrew year, which starts on March 14th, 2021 (1st of Nisan).

The Jews have long awaited the arrival of the Mashiach, believing he was even at the gates of the gas chambers; there, many Jews sang 'Ani Maamin' – (I believe in the coming of Mashiach). The above-mentioned proposes a date set for the Mashiach's arrival, in agreement with the Talmud, stating there is a predestined time when he will come. Devout Jews, however, believe if they are worthy, he may arrive even before that predestined time.

Orthodox Jews, like many Christians, have been date-setting for centuries. And, up until today, every date-setting 'prophecy' has failed. If scripture alone forbidding this practice is not enough to discourage people from doing it, the 100% failure rate should be. However, connected to the above-mentioned calculated number of 5782, the same number (5782) in the Strong's Concordance is attention-grabbing, translated as 'Awake' or to WAKE UP, to be aroused and restored from sleep. It also can be applied to being stirred up in the spirit. In other words, to wake up and be awake to the trouble ahead applying to the birth pains pointing to the beginning of 'Jacob's trouble' (Jer. 30:7). Jacob's trouble applies to the seven-year tribulation.

An equivalent of the Hebrew word *Ur* (Strong's number 5782) is the Greek word *gregoreo,* which is in the book of Revelation (3:2). The verse is a warning to the members of the sleepy, soiled (with the world) church of Sardis, telling them to 'Wake up,' and repent, or else be left behind and fought against (Rev. 3:3). Prophetically speaking, if they fail to wake up and repent, Jesus will come against them in the tribulation.

Again, seen with the parable of the Ten Virgins (Matt. 25:1-13), another similar Greek word *egeiro,* is seen, translated, 'Rise!' When the drowsy and sleeping ten virgins (Matt. 25:5) heard the announcement, "Here is the Bridegroom, come out and meet Him" (Matt. 25:6), they all 'rose' and trimmed their lamps. Five, however, did not have oil, therefore were not ready, and were subsequently locked out of the marriage feast (Matt.

25:11). The purpose of the parable is to remind believers to 'Watch' (Matt. 25:13) and to 'Stay awake' (Matt. 24:42), and to 'Be ready' (Matt. 24:44).

When considering the references mentioned above, alongside the context of Matthew, chapter twenty-four, the warning to be on guard against the increase of false teachers and false teaching is reinforced - always pointing towards the nearness of the return of Jesus Christ. However, before Jesus Christ returns, the antichrist must be revealed first. Unfortunately, many overlook this simple fact when claiming, 'Today will be good and tomorrow will be better' (Isa. 56:12). Like the false prophets in Isaiah's days, irresponsible leaders (Isa. 56:10) today proclaim the same kind of foolishness (e.g., Your Best Life Now), deceiving the naive into a false sense of confidence. Instead of warning of the danger to come, they distract with empty words.

Dominionism/Reconstructionism (Seven Mountain / Kingdom Now 'Theology') falls into the same category, foolishly proposing believers will re-establish everything lost through the Fall in preparation for Christ's return. That is, everything will get better and better. Nonsense!

False hope is what Jesus warned against in Matthew, chapter twenty-four, stating, "Do not be led astray" (Matt. 24:4, 5, 11, 24) by empty promises, for "The worst kind of trouble must come first" (Matt. 24:6, 21). For the original Jewish audience, the warning of false teachers and teaching points directly at the coming of the antichrist, who will say, "I am he, the Christ, leading many astray" (Matt. 24:5). For professing Christians, the warning points to the spirit of antichrist (1 Jn. 4:3) now operating within the church (2 Thess. 2:7), conditioning believers for the antichrist to come (2 Thess. 2:8).

Those failing to wake up this side of the tribulation, ensuring they have oil in their lamps by maintaining an intermit relationship with God through His Holy Spirit and by holding fast to sound biblical doctrine, will wake up in the tribulation left behind. For the Jews, this is unavoidable (Rom. 11:25). For the church, this would be tragic and is precisely the warning to the church of Sardis (Rev. 3:2-3). Instead of being removed from the hour of trial (Rev. 3:10), the sleepy church will wake up in it.

As seen above, the topic of deception, as a significant end-times sign, should be addressed in two parts: 1). In consideration of the Jews, and 2). In respect of professing believers in Christ.

1). Jesus' audience from Matthew, chapter twenty-four, are Jews who are in danger of being deceived by the false messiah. The warning from the Olivet discord of the coming antichrist (Matt. 24) should also be considered alongside the book of Daniel, chapters eight and eleven. Antiochus and the coming antichrist should be compared because Antiochus is a type of antichrist, foreshadowing the antichrist to come. In the same way, Antiochus deceived the Jews; the coming antichrist will do again shortly. When he appears, most will accept him with open arms; they are looking and longing for him now, ready to receive him.

When the antichrist appears, the wise will recognise him as the one signing (sign off on) the (false) peace treaty between Israel and their Middle Eastern neighbours (Isa. 28:15, 18, Dan. 9:27). The peace treaty will not just impact the Middle East but the whole world. For decades, scholars of international relations have said that if war breaks out in the Middle East, the world will be at war; World War III would be the result. In the same way, Antiochus turned back an invading army, approaching the Holy Land, and then deceived the Jews through flattery into entering a covenant with him; the coming antichrist will do the same.

According to Daniel, the future king is from the line of David; the Mashiach, therefore, clearly has Jewish roots, yet he will rise out of the newly revived Roman Empire, a Gentile nation (chapter 7). He will be anointed to rule the Jewish people and the world. He will establish worldwide peace and begin a one-world religion where the world worships one God, which will be 'him' (Dan. 7, 2 Thess. 2, Rev. 13).

The awaited Mashiach will set himself up and proclaim to be God through the rebuilt temple. The one Jews are awaiting is also said to end wars and famine and sickness (cf. Isa. 35:5-6), 65:17-25), and in general, he will offer a higher standard of living. When the Mashiach appears, he will do so in (false) humility, inspiring all people to strive for man's version of good. He is also said to demonstrate the leadership qualities of Moses.

During the tribulation, everything the false messiah will claim to do, Jesus will counter. The first four seals of the tribulation are deception, war, famine, and sickness (Rev. 6:1-8), the very things the antichrist will promise to stop. The reference of Moses is interesting, considering in the tribulation there will be two witnesses standing at the temple, operating in signs and wonders, proclaiming Christ, and calling for repentance (Rev. 11). While we know one is Elijah (Mal. 4:5), the other is argued to be either Enoch or Moses. Moses is more likely to be the other one due to Elijah and Moses appearing together at the Mount of Transfiguration (Matt. 17:1-8). Reinforcement for the case of support is the tribulation reference to the song of Moses (Rev. 15:3). Why Moses, why not David? Perhaps, because Moses is present in the tribulation?

Lastly, during the plagues of Egypt, where Moses was present, God poured out nine judgements against nine false gods. During the tribulation, God will do the same. As the expected Jewish (false) messiah is said to do away with wars, famine, and sickness, Jesus will open the seals, unleashing the same plagues to judge the rebellious. Among other judgements designed to turn the disobedient around, God will even plunge the throne of the antichrist into darkness (Rev. 16:10), demonstrating He is God, and the antichrist is not. As mentioned above, the Jews are looking for a man who will display Moses' leadership qualities. God will counteract every-

thing the antichrist does with His own signs, possibly, being the real resurrected Moses. If Moses is one of the two witnesses, it will help to answer
why Satan fought Michael and lost, over his dead body (Jude 9).

Despite God countering the antichrist at every turn, when he does
appear, he will still be incredibly convincing. He will operate with false
signs and wonders (2 Thess. 2:9, Rev. 13:13), including being resurrected
from the dead (Rev. 13:3, 12 14, 17:11), which is why Jesus said, even the
elect would be deceived, by him, if possible (Matt. 24:24).

Much more will be said about the coming antichrist in the following
chapters. This section deals with the signs leading up to the tribulation.
Again, the antichrist will not appear until the tribulation has commenced (2
Thess. 2:8), following the removal of the church (2 Thess. 2:7). Although,
some Jews are claiming they have already identified their Mashiach, and
they are having conversations with him.

2). Although Jesus' original audience was Jewish when answering the
question of the signs of the times, the warning of the things to come is
also given to the Gentiles. For example, the seven churches in the book
of Revelation also received similar notices, and they were Gentiles. The
churches not only received their letter (report card from Jesus) as individually addressed but the whole book of Revelation (Rev. 22:16). Matthew,
chapter twenty-four provides the same pattern and order of events as the
book of Revelation. The warning Jesus gave the churches was to repent, or
else. Prophetically speaking, or else go through what follows!

To avoid what would come, repentance was required from practicing
false worship driven by a watered-down, compromised, corrupted gospel.
The gospel was departed from due to self-serving deception. When considering that the most significant end-time sign is deception and that deception is a significant birth pain leading into the tribulation, conditioning

people for the greatest deceiver of them all, the antichrist, then a study of the antichrist spirit operating within the church today, is needed.

Jesus' letters to the seven churches (Rev. 2-3) should also be compared with Paul's warnings to the collective, universal church members. Several times Paul warned the church about false teachers within (1 Tim. 1:6, 10, 5:15, 6:3, 5, 2 Tim. 3:6, Tit. 1:13, 14, 19) and warned of increasing deception through false teaching in the last days (1 Tim. 4:1, 2 Tim. 3:1, 4:3-4). False teachers have always been around (cf. Jer. 14:14, 29:8), deceiving and conditioning the naïve; however, in the church age, they prepare biblically illiterate 'believers' to receive the coming antichrist. While the spirit of the antichrist has always been active within the church, it is evident more so today (1 Jn. 2:18, 4:3). Blessing abortion clinics and conducting same-sex weddings are obvious enough.

Today, the antichrist spirit is deceiving and disqualifying (1 Cor. 9:24-27, Col. 2:18) many with empty words (Eph. 5:6, cf. Col. 2:8), preparing those, who failed to love the truth, for the coming strong delusion (2 Thess. 2:9-12). The strong delusion is the antichrist, sent by God, that those desiring pleasure over purity would be condemned. Those failing to follow the teaching of the Apostles (1 Jn. 4:6) have already accepted the spirit of error (the antichrist spirit).

Those deceived by the spirit of error are already in danger of apostasy. Deception is married with the great end-time sign of apostasy (2 Thess. 2:3). Much more will be said about apostasy under its header in the following chapters. Therefore, little is said here, other than apostasy refers to rebellion resulting in falling away from a position once held.

The English word apostasy comes from the Greek word *apostasia*. The biblical definition of apostasy is, 'A public denial of a previously held religious belief and a distancing from the community that holds to it.' The term is almost always applied pejoratively, carrying connotations of rebellion, betrayal, treachery, or faithlessness. The Hebrew equivalent for the English word rebel/rebelled has the same meaning (e.g., Num. 14:9; Isa. 36:5), implying, God is no longer with those who are no longer with Him (2 Chron. 15:2, Matt. 10:33, 2 Tim. 2:11-13). In other words, the one now lost was once with God, and He was also once with them (cf. Lu. 15:24).

Here lies the danger of false teaching - it will lead people astray and lead them away from the truth. Because of vast amounts of false teaching within the church today, Christianity had gone astray from its biblical roots. Peace and prosperity are promoted instead of holiness and holding fast to sound biblical doctrine, promoting a gospel of sacrifice and suffering. Sacrifice and suffering are a significant part of the salvation story. Instead of looking to, and living for Jesus, a majority are looking to the world, living for themselves. A vast majority are so in love with the world, and themselves, that you cannot tell them apart (like the churches of Sardis and Laodicea). Those guilty often say things like; "I want Jesus to delay - to enjoy my day." In their ignorance, they fulfill prophecy (2 Tim. 3:2).

Within the seven churches addressed (Rev. 2-3), the church of Laodicea is the worst of the failing five, defined by everything mentioned above. Jesus rebuked this church by saying, "You say, 'I am rich; I have grown wealthy and need nothing.' But you do not realize that you are wretched, pitiful, poor, blind, and naked." (Rev. 3:17). Jesus warned the church of Laodicea, if they did not repent (stop buying from the world, stop being like the world), they would be vomited out (of the kingdom, cf. Lev. 18:25, 28). The church of Laodicea was a literal church and is also a prophetic reflection of the 21st-century lukewarm church, the last church before Jesus returns for His bride, the faithful church.

In conclusion, Jesus warned that deception would be a significant sign of the end times, leading to tribulation (Matt. 24:4-5). During the tribulation, deception will increase (Matt. 24: 11-12, 23-26). Now, due to the level of deception rising among those who confess to know God, whether Jew or Gentile, the stage is already set for the coming antichrist.

While the Jews are looking for their messiah, professing 'Christians' are seeking their best life now, led by blind fools, repeating the sins of Israel. Isaiah summed it up this way, "Israel's watchmen are blind, they are all oblivious; they are all mute dogs, they cannot bark; they are dreamers lying around, loving to slumber." (Isa. 56:10). Isaiah's statement was in the context of Israel's spiritual leaders failing to warn of the dangers ahead. Instead, they deceived the congregation with lies of peace and security. A good life today, and a better one tomorrow (Isa. 56:12).

For us, alongside Paul, Peter, John, and Jude's warnings (to name a few), Charles Spurgeon (among many) also warned of the coming, (now current) condition of the church. He said, "A time will come when instead of shepherds feeding the sheep, the church will have clowns entertaining the goats." Indeed, the time HAS come. The apostate church is now ripe and ready for the coming antichrist.

In closing: Remember the warning to the members of the church of Sardis, telling them to 'Wake up', and repent, or else be left behind and be fought against (Rev. 3:3). When considering the context of Matthew, chapter twenty-four, the warning to be on guard (Mk. 13:22-23) against the increase of false teachers and false teaching is paramount, pointing towards the conditioning for, and the appearing of the antichrist, and the imminent return of Jesus Christ (Mk. 13:33).

Like the church of Sardis, the 21st-century church is spiritually asleep, while having a reputation of being alive, it is (spiritually) dead. The current church is so drunk with worldliness, deceived by prosperity preachers that it also shares the same condition as the lukewarm church of Laodicea. Unless the sleepy, lukewarm church wakes up and repents this side of the tribulation, its members will be left behind (Rev. 3:3), vomited into (Rev. 3:16), and waking up on the other side of the tribulation.

Wars (Sword), Famine, and Sickness

'Does Disaster Come Unless God Sends it?'

(Matt 24:6-7)

Following deception, Jesus warned of four more signs leading to the tribulation, 'wars, famine, sickness, and earthquakes'. We will cover the first three, for this section, leaving earthquakes for the next.

As mentioned previously, Matthew, chapter twenty-four is somewhat of a blueprint for the book of Revelation. The signs leading into the tribulation are also the same signs commencing the seven-year ordeal. Revelation, chapter six begins the tribulation with the opening of the seals. The first four seals refer to the antichrist (deception), war, famine, and sickness. The first four signs are in the exact order of Revelation, chapter six as foretold by Jesus when telling the disciples what would indicate that He is near or about to return.

To understand the combined signs of war, famine, and sickness and how they might apply today, the same combination should be considered from the Old Testament. First Chronicles (21), Jeremiah (14), and Ezekiel (5-7) are critical to interpreting the signs and seals of Revelation, chapter six, as foretold in Matthew, chapter twenty-four. Like with Revelation, chapter six, in First Chronicles (21), we see that God sends the judgement, giving David a choice over the sword (war), famine, or pestilence. The same combination was repeated with Jeremiah and Ezekiel's account. During the tribulation, Jesus opens the seals (Rev. 5:5), and God sends the antichrist (2 Thess. 2:11). Amos confirms the same, God sends disaster. God sent disaster to deal with David (1 Chron. 21), and Judah (Jer. 14, and Ezek. 7), and will again, when dealing with this generation (Rev. 6-19).

As mentioned above, the starting point with understanding the signs (war, famine, and pestilence) is First Chronicles (chapter 21), where God gave David a choice of one of three plagues for his rebellion. David's sin was putting his trust in himself and Israel's ability to defend herself rather than in God. David, incited by Satan (1 Chron. 21:1), went against the word of God, spoken through the prophet Joab (1 Chron. 21:6-7). God quickly responded due to the danger of David leading the whole nation astray and away from God. First, God judged David, and Israel, to bring correction, resulting in repentance. Every account of judgement from God is purposed to do the same, to save. Next, struck Israel (1 Chron. 21:7) and threatened even greater punishment for the sin of apostasy (1 Chron. 21:13).

Even before the distribution of unavoidable judgement, God's mercy is still seen where He gave David a choice of famine for three years, the sword for three months, or pestilence for three days (1 Chron. 21:13). Again, although David recognised his foolishness and repented before the wave of judgement came, the things to come were irreversible. No amount of pleading for mercy would turn back the hand of God; the penalty for sin could not be satisfied short of sacrifice. Human blood was required.

Although David knew the punishment would be severe, he also knew God was merciful, so he put the choice of famine, sword, or pestilence back on Him. You choose, he had said, and God did. Three days of pestilence followed, killing 70,000 Israelites. Behind pestilence, God sent an angel to destroy Jerusalem. The angel stood at the threshing floor between heaven and earth with sword drawn. Previously, David said, "Let me fall into the hand of God and not into the hands of men" (1 Chron. 21:13) when considering judgement by the sword. David sought to avoid the sword of man yet came face-to-face with the sword of God. Those dismissing the severity of Jesus' warning to the church of Pergamum (Rev. 2:12, 16) should consider David's experience.

Before the sword-drawn angel struck Jerusalem, God stopped the judgement, saying, "It is enough" (1 Chron. 21:15). Here, a comparison should be made with the seventh tribulation bowl, where a voice came out of the temple, from the throne (probably Jesus), saying, "It is done!" (Rev. 16:17).

When God stopped the angel of death, David saw it. He fell on his face, repenting (1 Chon. 21:16-17). Real repentance this time, David 'now' knew the seriousness of his sin (1 Chron. 21:8). The punishment fit the offence. David repented, and God relented, but not before 70,000 Israelites died. David's experience of God's judgement is just a glimpse of the things to come through the coming tribulation. The result of judgement produced a healthy fear of God in David (1 Chron. 21:30), previously lacking.

Here, compare the warning to the church of Thyatira (Rev. 2:22-23) alongside the judgement of Ananias and Sapphira (Acts 5:5, 11). God will strike His foolish people when lacking fear, specifically where there is a danger of leading others astray and away, which is why David, Ananias and Sapphira were dealt with so harshly, albeit justly.

Alongside David's experience of God's judgement, we should also consider Jeremiah's account. In Jeremiah, chapter fourteen, seen again is the combination of the sword, famine, and pestilence, which played a significant role in disciplining Judah. After many years of warning (Jer. 25:2-3), God judged Judah for their apostasy (Jer. 14:7, 10). Like David, Judah trusted in themselves, going even further than David, trusting other gods. Like David, Judah repented (Jer. 14:7-9), but God would not hear them (Jer. 14:10, 12). Too little too late! God even instructed Jeremiah not to pray for them (Jer. 14:11). Judgement was unavoidable (Jer. 14:12, 15b, 16, 16:11-12), despite the false prophets saying God would not judge the backslidden nation (Jer. 14:13-15a, cf. 6:14, 23:16-17).

The coming plagues sent by God are referred to as 'A time of trouble' (Jer. 14:8). Jeremiah uses this phrase six times, referring to God's judgement against Judah (Jer. 2:27, 28, 11:12, 14, 14:8, 15:11). The prophesied judgements (a time of trouble) have been partly fulfilled through Judah's captivity, with the worst still yet to come. The worst of the prophesied judgements will be fulfilled during the tribulation (Jer. 30:7, Ezek. 7:7, Dan. 9:25, 12:1, Joel 2:2b, Matt. 24:21, cf. Rev. 3:10). Again, like David, Judah's judgement came because they put their trust in themselves, resulting in their hearts being turned away from God (Jer. 17:5). Because of this, they were considered 'bad figs' (Jer. 24:1-10), causing God to send the sword, famine, and pestilence (Je. 24:10). Due to trusting in themselves, instead of God, Judah/Israel was cursed (Jer. 17:5).

On the contrary, only those trusting in God alone are blessed (Jer. 17:7). Many who trusted in themselves then and now thought/think they were trusting God, all the while were deceived (Jer. 17:9-10, cf. Matt. 7:21-23). Like modern Israel, many deceived churchgoers will wake up in the tribulation believing they were saved when they were not.

Ezekiel should also be compared to Jeremiah's account (chapters 5-7). Again, the problem is trusting in self, and a key contributor causing the difficulty for Judah was wealth, which God did/will remove (Ezek. 7:11, 19). Here, the church of Laodicea should come to mind (Rev. 3:14-22). The warning to the church of Laodicea, and us, was also given to Israel. How God treated Israel in their apostasy is how God will treat the lukewarm church for the same (Rom. 11:22), again using the sword (war), famine, and pestilence (Rev. 6:1-8).

Judah's day of judgement will be the coming tribulation described as an inevitable disaster after disaster (Ezek. 7:5, 26) and doom (Ezek. 7:7, 10). God pronounced irreversible judgement with the , "Your end has come" (Ezek. 7:2, 6), "Your doom has come" (Ezek. 7:7, 10), paralysing Judah with terror (Ezek. 7:27). The purpose of the judgement is to produce a healthy fear of God, reminding Israel (and us) that God is the Lord their God (Ezek. 7:4, 9, 27). The words, "That you will know I am God," are found twenty-seven times in the book of Ezekiel. The point is to remind Israel (and us) that He is God and that there is no other (cf. Isa. 44:6-8, 45:5, 46:9). He is God, and we are not (we are not even little gods)!

Due to forgetting God, forsaking, and replacing Him, God warned Judah the unavoidable and inescapable day of doom and tumult is near (Ezek. 7:7). Like Jeremiah's account, Ezekiel's prophesied event is fulfilled in the coming tribulation (Ezek. 14:12-23). While the judgement of the sword, famine, and pestilence (Ezek. 5:12, 17, 6:11, 12, 7:15) are seen throughout history, they will be seen again. They will dwarf anything of the past (Matt. 24:21). The collective judgements are seen several times through prophetic literature as signs of the end times, leading up to and into the tribulation, where God will destroy the bulk of Israel's population and the secular.

During the tribulation, a third of Israel will perish by fire (Ezek. 5:2a), and a third by the sword (Ezek. 5:2b), with another third scattered and pursued again by the sword (Ezek. 5:2c). The reference to 'a third' should be compared to the tribulation trumpet judgements where a third of the earth will be burned up (Rev. 8:7), and a third of the sea becomes blood (Rev. 8:8), and a third of the living creatures die, and a third of the ships are destroyed (Rev. 8:9). A third of the earth's freshwater is positioned, killing many people (Rev. 8:10-11). Next, a third of natural light is darkened (Rev. 8:12). Following are the demonic locusts (Rev. 9:1-11), assuming a third is stung by them, then another third perishes by the fire-breathing, sword-wielding mounted troops. two-hundred million of them (Rev. 9:18, cf. Joel 2). As with the previous trumpets, it is safe to assume another third will die with the seventh trumpet judgement (Rev. 11:15-19).

Ezekiel's prophecy of a third perishing by fire and another third by the sword, etc., alongside the tribulation trumpets, supports the inescapable judgements, coming wave after wave. So the application is, if you escape one plague, you will be met by another and another. Amos confirms the same (5:18-12).

Amos also addressed Israel in a time of stability and prosperity. Trusting in themselves, having everything, and no need for anything (cf. Rev 3:17), the people of God slipped into idolatry, extravagance, and corruption. As a result, Amos warned the people in their apostasy, who were deceived by 'their' good works regarding social injustice. Amos warned that God would soon bring judgment against them for their apostasy. The required response was to leave the hypocrisy of their 'solemn assemblies' (5:21) and seek God. In doing so, God would remember His covenant with them and restore a faithful remnant. The saved remnant is prophetic of those being saved through the tribulation (Rom. 9:27). Unfortunately, most will die in their sin.

Israel's problem of apostasy is also our shared problem today. As Israel did, we forget God and what He did for us, how He saved us and made a way for us (Amos 2:9-11; 3:1b). Due to forgetting God, Israel (and the church) have committed a great sin (Amos 5:12c), wandering far from the truth, thus far from God, trusting in their/ourselves (Amos 6:13). In replacement of God, apostates trust in wealth (Amos 5:11-12; 6:4-6), and worst of all, in other 'gods,' including self (Amos 5:5), to the point, they (we too) no longer want to hear the voice of God (Amos 2:12, 5:10b; 7:10b, 12-13, 16). We no longer hear God's voice due to having itching ears, only desiring to listen to what suits (2 Tim. 4:3). In other words, they/ we are so distracted and so consumed by the world we forget God when He should consume us, alone.

Due to distraction, Israel (the lukewarm church also) rendered themselves deaf and blind to what God was doing and saying (Amos 3:6-8), to the point of no longer knowing right from wrong (Amos 3:10, cf. Rev. 3:17-18). Furthermore, God said, "Because you do not want to hear My voice, a famine will come upon you - a famine where My voice will not be heard among you, no matter how badly you want to hear it" (Amos 8:11-12).

The prophet announces, "Prepare to meet your God" (Amos 4:12). This was a result of not returning to God (Amos 4:6b, 8b, 9b, 10b, 11b) after many warnings to do so, through separate events (Amos 4:6-11), including famine, drought. plant disease, locust, and pestilence/plague, The former plagues (birth pains) served the purpose that Israel (and the lukewarm church) would return to the Lord (Amos 4:6, 11). By doing so, they (and the lukewarm church) would be saved, 'as a brand, plucked out of the burning fire' (Amos 4:11). A direct New Testament reference to this (Amos 4:11) is found in Jude, where Jude says, "Save others by snatching them out of the fire" (Jude 23a). Save them from what? Apostate false teachers (Jude 4) and scoffers (Jude 18).

The testing God inflicted (Amos 4:6-8) and struck (Amos 4:9-10) Israel with, and will again, was/is purposed to overthrow them (Amos 4:11) while blinded by sin. It came, and will again, when Israel was deceived into thinking they were secure (Amos 6:1) and in right standing with God, even desiring the 'Day of the Lord'. The Day of the Lord refers to the event following the coming tribulation, where God warned the people. "Woe to you... There will be no escaping the things to come. When you 'think' you have avoided one crisis, another will be added, and then another again, and again and again" (Amos 5:18-20; 9:1-4). Amos' prophesied 'woe' should also be compared with John's tribulation woes (Rev. 8:13, 12:12). The last sorrow refers to the return of Jesus (Rev. 11:15-19, cf. 6:12-17, 19:11-21), woe to any not ready on that day.

As mentioned above, the 'Day of the Lord' refers to the concluding event of the coming tribulation, where faithless Israel, the unrepentant lukewarm, and the rest of the remaining rebellious world will be judged by Jesus. Still, and despite the spiritual condition of Israel and the lukewarm church, God continues to call out to the remnant, even now, "Seek Me and live" (Amos 5:4b, 6a, cf. Rev. 3:20). "Seek good, and not evil that you may live" (Amos 5:14).

Through the partial fulfilment of Amos' prophecy, God shook ancient Israel, and He will again (Heb. 12:26-27, Rev. 6-19) that a remnant would be tested, separated, and saved. Remember, God did and does the shaking. He did it then, and He is about to do it again! Amos makes the point clear, stating, "Does disaster come to a city unless the Lord has done it?" (Amos 3:6b). The question is rhetorical, and followed with a resounding, NO! Despite false teachers saying judgement will not come and does/will not come from God (Jer. 14:13), disaster does not come unless God sends it, as seen with all the examples mentioned above.

Throughout this section, Amos joins David, Jeremiah, Ezekiel, and Jesus, making it clear, God sends disaster to a city (world, cf. Rev. 3:10) to test, separate, and save. Even now, Jesus' predicted birth pains of war (sword), famine, and pestilence are serving this purpose. None more so than pestilence, evident through COVID.

Specifically, the 'vaccination' has set the stage for the coming mark of the beast (666), where without it, none can buy or sell (Rev. 13:17). Even now, the 'vaccination' is separating one from another, the vaxxed from the un-vaxxed, in the same way the mark of the beast will do.

The signs of the times serve to test and separate one from the other, uniting those of like mind and strengthening them as they fix their eyes on Jesus, trusting Him alone, thereby avoiding the things to come (Rev. 3:10). As for those failing to see and heed the warning, they will have another opportunity during the tribulation (unless they take the mark, Rev. 14:9-11) to break away from their sins and come to their senses. Sadly, however, most will not (Rev. 9:20-21, 16:8-11).

Earthquakes
'All these are But the Beginning of Birth Pains'
(24:7b-8)

Earthquakes are another birth pain that will add to the previously mentioned signs of the times of the tribulation. Like deception, apostasy, wars, famine, and pestilence, earthquakes will play a significant role in the days leading up to Christ's return.

Earthquakes have always been evidence around Jesus, signifying something meaningful. For example, His death on the cross, causing the awe-filled centurion to say, "Truly this was the Son of God!" (Matt. 27:54). Again, when Jesus was resurrected, another earthquake occurred (Matt. 28:2), and another will signify He return. (Rev. 6:12, 11:15-19, 16:18). The prophets Ezekiel and Zechariah prophesy the same (Ezek. 38:19, Zech. 14:5), concluding the event of the tribulation at the battle of Armageddon. John narrows in further (Rev. 16:18), following his description of the judgement administered through the sixth bowl (Rev. 18:12-15).

While there are earthquakes now, and always have been, during the tribulation, there will be a great earthquake (Rev. 11:13), following the resurrection and ascension of the two witnesses (Rev. 11:11, 12). Like with Jesus, when the two witnesses are resurrected, the earth will shake. It could be argued the same will occur again with the rapture of the church.

As mentioned previously, when Jesus died, there was an earthquake, signifying the close of one covenant, and dispensation, commencing another

(Matt. 27:51-54). At the same time, graves opened, releasing the dead saints from prison, where Jesus spent three days preaching. Peter records the event in his first letter, "For Christ also suffered for sins once for all, the righteous for the unrighteous, to bring you to God. He was put to death in the body but made alive in the Spirit, in whom He also went and preached to the spirits in prison who disobeyed long ago when God waited patiently in the days of Noah while the ark was being built. In the ark, a few people, only eight souls, were saved through water" (1 Pet. 3:18-20).

While some say Jesus was preaching to the lost in hell, Luke confirms Jesus was in paradise (Lu. 23:43), not hades. Luke describes and distinguishes paradise from hades in chapter sixteen (Lu. 16:19-31). When Jesus preached to the spirits in prison, it was not a message of salvation due to the imprisoned playing a part in corrupting God's creative design of mankind (Gen. 6), resulting in the Flood (Gen. 7). The message preached was not one of salvation, it was instead of victory over sin and Satan (Col. 2:15). While in the grave, Jesus was not offering salvation to the departed due to their rejection of salvation while having the opportunity through Noah's preaching (cf. Heb. 9:27).

Noah preached righteousness (2 Pet. 2:5), for one-hundred and twenty years (Gen. 6:3), and none listened; therefore, they perished in and for their sin. Through Noah's preaching, that generation heard Christ and 'formally' did not obey (1 Per. 3:20). For this reason, it is doubtful Jesus spent three days preaching to those who disobeyed but rather spent the bulk of that time in paradise.

As mentioned above, following Jesus' death on the cross, He went to paradise, and after three days, He led the captives out, where they ascended with Him to heaven (Eph. 4:8-10, cf. Ps. 68:18). The captives are the saints in paradise, as described by Luke (Lu. 16:19-31). These released saints are the same seen wandering the earth after their tombs broke open, following

Christ's death resulting in an earthquake (Matt. 27:51). Matthew records the event in chapter twenty-four, saying, "At that moment the veil of the temple was torn in two from top to bottom. The earth quaked, and the rocks were split. The tombs broke open, and the bodies of many saints who had fallen asleep were raised. After Jesus' resurrection, when they had come out of the tombs, they entered the holy city and appeared to many people" (Matt. 27:51-54). No doubt they were preaching Christ's victory for three days, sandwiched between two earthquakes (Matt. 27:51-54, 28:2).

After a short time on the earth, the released saints ascended to heaven with Jesus, and from there, now witness the remaining saints on the earth who continue the race they ran (Heb. 12:1). Soon, those released saints will receive their glorified bodies, following another possible occurrence of tombs breaking open (1 Thess. 4:15-17). Like with the first occurrence of tombs breaking open following an earthquake, the same may reoccur with the next, when the dead in Christ are raised, and the church is removed from the earth. Arguably, with the rapture, there will likely be a great earthquake as the final birth pain sign commencing the tribulation. At that point, the church age ends, beginning another, being the time of trouble.

The importance of understanding the significance of an earthquake commencing the tribulation runs with the proclamation of the Roman soldiers at the foot of the cross. Following an earthquake, they said, "Truly this was the Son of God!" (Matt. 27:54). The same will be declared the moment the left behind wake up in the tribulation. Jews, among many lukewarm 'Christians,' will confirm the rapture was God's doing. In contrast, the world will make all sorts of false statements, attempting to explain away why millions have now disappeared, claiming, 'An alien invasion/obduction.' Nevertheless, the removal of the church will be evidence enough for many, waking up millions of Jews and left behind professing believers. At that time, Jews will call on the name of the Lord Jesus and be saved (Rom.

11:25-32). Following the departure of the church (Rom. 11:25), THEN the Jews will say. "Blessed is He who comes in the name of the Lord.'" Until they do, Jesus will not return (Matt. 23:39).

As noted, earthquakes signify judgement, for good and for bad. Earthquakes are also a sign that God is nearby. The book of Revelation, three times, records that an earthquake will coincide with Jesus' return (Rev. 6:12, 11:15-19, 16:18), foretold by both Ezekiel and Zechariah (Ezek. 38:19, Zech. 14:5). When Jesus returns, He will judge the rebellious (Rev. 19:11-21). However, quakes also serve as a warning from God, a sign of His displeasure and anger (Ps. 18:7). Psalm eighteen should be compared to the cry of persecuted Christians today, calling out to God for help. God hears their plea and will respond accordingly by casting their persecutors into the tribulation. Psalms sixty should also be considered, addressing God's people in rebellion.

Today many will wake up in the tribulation for this same reason, which is likely to commence with a quake (Ps. 60:2). During the tribulation, God will set up a banner (Jesus) for those who come to fear Him. They will flee to Him, bow before Him (Ps. 60:4), and then be saved (Ps. 60:5). Those who turn to God during the tribulation, enduring until the end will see His Salvation and His rule (cf. Ps. 68 (v. 8), 99 (v. 1)).

Joining in, Isaiah also references quakes as a judgement against God's people (Isa. 5:25), with a pronounced, "Woe to those who call evil good and good evil" (Isa. 5:20). Isaiah, chapter five should be considered against today's corrupt practice, alongside chapter six, where the prophet encountered God (Isa. 6:1-4), resulting in repentance (Isa. 6:5), and cleansing forgiveness (Isa. 6:6-7).

Jeremiah is yet another prophet addressing corrupt practices and false prophets, saying, "Peace, peace" (Jer. 8:11, 15), when there was no peace. Instead, only terror awaits (Jer. 8:15b). For Judah's rebellion, the whole land will quake (Jer. 8:16). Joel warned of the same - God will judge the earth through earthquakes. Joel's prophecy will be fulfilled in the great tribulation (Joel 2:10, 3:16).

There are nineteen references to earthquakes in the Bible and seventeen more to quakes, which generally speak of judgement. In the same way, God sends the sword, famine, and pestilence; God also shakes the earth. He did it before, and He is going to do it again. Soon, everything will be shaken and only the things that cannot be shaken will remain (Heb. 12:27).

The book of Hebrews (12:18-29) should be considered and compared against the passages mentioned above, confirming God does the shaking and what He did to Israel then; He is about to do again to the lukewarm church. What God did to Israel; He did through tribulation. The coming tribulation will catch many claiming to know God by surprise (Lu. 21:34), dwarfing anything of the past (Matt. 24:21).

Again, the above-mentioned has established God shakes the earth to wake His people up and to turn them around. In doing so, great moves of God have resulted, such as the Azusa Street revival.

On April 14, 1906, four days before the San Francisco earthquake killing more than three thousand people, a religious revival, led by the Rev. William J. Seymour, started in a rundown building on Azusa Street in Los Angeles, lasting until 1915. Through this revival, thousands came to Christ through repentance. Throughout this great move of the Holy Spirit, many committing their lives to Christ took up their cross and died through missionary service. Thousands gave up their comfortable lives relocating to developing countries such as Africa and India to endure hardship and even death. Great urgency drove the otherwise complacent church to spread the gospel, with a message mainly consisting of eschatology. Soon after the revival ended, the world was plagued by the Spanish flu (1918-1920), infecting one-third of the global population, amounting to around five hundred million. Some fifty million died.

In 1918 the world population was just short of two billion. Around the same time, another remarkable event occurred in (1917), where Israel was recognised, calling for support to provide Jews with a homeland in what was then known as Palestine. This is known as the Belfour Declaration. Also, in 1914, WWI began, lasting until 1918, killing twenty million people. As a result, famine reportedly claimed another two million lives.

God shook the planet using the sword (war), famine, pestilence, and earthquakes throughout this time. In just fourteen years, more than seventy million died. Another seventy-five million died through WWII (1939-1945). You could also say the previous fourteen years of war, famine, pestilence, and earthquakes were birth pains, setting the stage for the antichrist type, revealed through WWII, being Hitler. The same will be repeated in our time, only with fewer years between the two world-shaking seasons. A season of birth pains seamlessly leads into the next. Right now, the season of summer (judgement) is near, indicating it is time to harvest (Matt. 24:32).

At present, we are at the close of spring (prophetically speaking). Globally, we are now dealing with the great falling away from sound biblical doctrine (2 Thess. 2:3) and a worldwide plan-demic (deception), disguised as a pandemic. Deception is now at an all-time high, evident with those professing to be wise no longer being able to distinguish between male and female (i.e., gender fluidity, nonsense). Deception has conditioned humanity and set the stage for the antichrist. Further evidence of the stage being set is seen with the announcement of a tower being built in the Middle East, promoting a 'One World Religion.' The tower will be built in 2022. Pope Francis and Muslim leaders join endorsing the OWR headquarters. Yet another indicator that the stage is set is with Israel being in the news daily. This is significant due to Israel being directly linked to the prophetic time clock.

As mentioned earlier, there is also increased earthquake activity with predictions of 'the big one' still to come. This week, (at the time of my writing), Australia experienced the biggest earthquake in recorded history (M6.0). The quake erupted in Melbourne, sending shockwaves to Canberra. The question asked - is God sending a message to the Australian federal government from the world's number one lockdown state and the leading state in the nation for abortion? Remember, God, shakes the earth signalling His anger (Ps. 18:7).

Reports say in the last three days (third week of September 2021), the world has seen high seismic activity across the earth. with a total of twenty-one earthquakes at or above M5.0. These events included a M6.5 quake off the coast of Nicaragua, a M6.0 quake off the coast of central Chile, a M6.0 quake near the Kuril Islands and a M6.0 northeast of Melbourne, Australia. Four M6.0+ earthquakes within three days are well above average. The most significant quake the world has seen is M9.5. A quake of M10 would be likened to something out of Hollywood, where the ground would shake for an hour or more and tsunamis would result, potentially killing millions. Revelation, chapter eleven (v. 13) predicts such an event.

*Important to note: not every earthquake is from God, but every earthquake is a result of sin. Paul makes it clear; the earth groans due to corruption (Rom. 8:20-23). Because of sin, the world is in bondage to decay yet will be set free (restored) when Jesus returns (Rom. 8:21). However, as mentioned above, current decaying conditions are set to get worse, a whole lot worse, before they get better. Each sign of the end times, indicating Jesus is nearby, is purposed to wake people up, starting with the sleepy church, having the reputation of being alive, but is dead (cf. Rev. 3:1-3). Remember, judgement begins in the household of God (1 Pet. 4:17).

Peter's reference (1 Pet. 4:17) should be compared with Malachi (chapters 3 and 4), where one person is tested and separated from the other. Through suffering (1 Pet. 4:12-16, 19, Rev. 2:10, 3:10), the faithful follower of God is judged and saved (1 Pet. 4:18). Persecution is another birth pain (sign) of the end times and will be addressed in chapter two.

In conclusion, as previously addressed, it has been established that God sends the plagues (signs) to produce repentance, confirmed by the Roman soldiers who said, "Truly this was the Son of God!" (Matt. 27:54). The signs were designed to wake humanity up and save them from the things to come. Although the coming tribulation is unavoidable (Matt. 24:6b), no one must go through it. Those who repent and hold fast to God will escape (Lu. 21:36) by being removed before the tribulation commences (Rev. 3:10). The removal of the church is otherwise known as the rapture. The rapture will occur in the 'nick of time,' snatching God's people out of the way. In other words, when all hope looks lost, the church will THEN be saved from the coming tribulation. The current signs witnessed are but the beginning of birth pains (Matt. 24:8), followed by much, much worse to come (Matt. 24:21) in the very near future.

As were the Days of Noah, so will be the Coming of the Son of Man
'The Corruption of God's Creative Design'
(Matt. 24:37-39)

Alongside deception, wars, famine, pestilence, and earthquakes, another end-time sign will be a repeat of the days of Noah. For centuries many have speculated what a repeat of 'the days of Noah' means. Many in modern times have concluded that homosexuality was the main issue. To arrive at this conclusion, they interpreted 'marrying' (Matt. 24:38) to apply to same-sex marriage because only traditional marriage between and man and a woman is lawful in God's eyes and therefore not sinful. Supporters of same-sex marriage as the problem have also connected 'the days of Noah' to 'the days of Lot' (Lu. 17:28). While the reference to the days of Lot does refer to homosexuality, it is not directly connected to the days of Noah. Again, while the two repeated conditions signify the end times, they apply to different things. The days of Lot will be addressed in the following section.

As for the days of Noah, Jesus' words regarding that end-time sign are broken up into three verses, as follows: "For as were the days of Noah, so will be the coming of the Son of Man. For as in those days before the Flood they were eating and drinking, marrying, and giving in marriage, until the day when Noah entered the ark, and they were unaware until the Flood came and swept them all away, so will be the coming of the Son of Man" (Matt. 24:37-39).

Luke says it this way, "Just as it was in the days of Noah, so will it be in the days of the Son of Man. They were eating and drinking and marrying and given in marriage, until the day when Noah entered the ark, and the Flood came and destroyed them all" (Lu. 21:26-27).

To understand the prophecy, the reader needs to consider the origin found in the book of Genesis. Chapter six, verses five to twelve are helpful, recorded as follows: "The LORD saw that the wickedness of man was great in the earth and that every intention of the thoughts of his heart was only evil continually. And the LORD regretted that he had made man on the earth, and it grieved him to his heart. So, the LORD said, 'I will blot out man whom I have created from the face of the land, man and animals and creeping things and birds of the heavens, for I am sorry that I have made them. But Noah found favor in the eyes of the LORD. These are the generations of Noah. Noah was a righteous man, blameless in his generation. Noah walked with God. And Noah had three sons, Shem, Ham, and Japheth. Now the earth was corrupt in God's sight, and the earth was filled with violence. And God saw the earth, and behold, it was corrupt, for all flesh had corrupted their way on the earth'" (Gen. 6:5-12).

The word 'blameless' translated from Hebrew also translates 'complete, intact, without fault, impeccable,' meaning Noah was as God created him. His DNA had not been corrupted. The word 'corrupt' was used three times in the verses referenced above (Gen. 6:11, 12), referring to being 'ruined.' God's creative design was ruined due to no longer being what God intended and created it to be; it had been changed; therefore, corrupted and spoiled. The specific problem in the days of Noah was the corruption of God's creative design through the sons (angels) of God who came to the daughters of men, producing the Nephilim (meaning fallen).

The sons of God are fallen angels who had intercourse with humans, creating a hybrid demigod offspring, called Nephilim (Gen. 6:1-4), also translated, giants. The Nephilim became the heroes (mighty men) and famous warriors of ancient times, with many myths and even modern-day fictional superhero characters resembling them. Any hybrid mythological creature is likened to the Nephilim, such as a faun, centaur, minotaur, mermaid, echidna, harpy, the gorgons (medusa), mandrake, and sphinx. In modern times, Aqua Man, the Hulk, Spiderman, Batman, the X-men, even Superman, and Wonder Woman, etc., are well-known demigods, albeit their origin is overlooked and or downplayed as innocent entertainment.

Interestingly, Wonder Woman, is also known as Diana. Intriguingly in Roman religion, Diana, goddess of wild animals and the hunt, is identified with the Greek goddess Artemis, mentioned five times in the book of Acts (19:24, 27, 28, 34, 35). Although often presented as 'heroes' (cf. Gen. 6:4), demigods are not good. Medusa is a classic and obvious example of an evil demigod. Modern demigods, superheroes, and supervillains are inspired by Greek mythology, which was stirred by the biblical account of the Nephilim, the 'heroes of the ancient world' (Ge. 6:4).

In the same way, the Bible refers to the Nephilim as "The heroes and famous warriors of the ancient times" (Gen. 6:4); Hollywood does the same by creating modern-day heroes and saviours of the world. As mentioned above, Hollywood's superheroes are nothing new, originating from the biblical account (Gen. 6:4). Solomon said it this way, "What has been, is what will be, and what has been done is what will be done, and there is nothing new under the sun" (Ecc. 1:9).

As mentioned earlier, the Nephilim are the offspring of fallen angels who had intercourse with women. Jude referenced these fallen angles that overstepped the mark (Jude, v. 6-7), as does Peter (2 Pet. 2:4), connecting the act with Enoch, who prophesied of Jesus' return (Jude, v. 14). Interestingly, although the book of Enock is considered Apocrypha (biblical writing not forming part of the canon of scripture), Jude gives Enock credibility by referencing him while under the inspiration of the Holy Spirit (2 Tim 3:16, 2 Pet. 1:21).

The first part of the book of Enoch describes the fall of the 'watchers,' who are the fallen angels who fathered the angel-human hybrids called Nephilim. Enoch provides a great deal of information about the watchers and the circumstances that surround the creation of Nephilim. Enoch states the Nephilim were destructive and incompatible with humans (Enoch 7:12-14), likened to beasts. The book of Enoch also gives insight into the destruction of the watchman's offspring (Enoch 10:13), where the messenger angel Gabriel caused them to turn on each other, slaughtering one another until none remained. Satan and his demons do the same, forcing humanity to turn on one another.

Both Peter and Jude, supported by Enoch, state the angels involved in the corruption of humanity have been imprisoned and will be again released during the tribulation (Rev. 9:11, 14). During the tribulation, the bound angels will be freed to lead an army of unstoppable superhuman warriors (Rev. 9:13-19, 16:12-16, Joel 2), meaning this world will be, once again, filled with violence and corrupted by the Nephilim (Gen. 6:11, 13, Matt. 24:37-39).

The Genesis account (Gen. 6) states God destroyed the Nephilim with the Flood (Gen. 7), yet Moses mentioned them again in the book of Numbers (13:33), linked to Deuteronomy (9:2). Giants were again in existence after the Flood. Goliath (cf. 1 Sam. 17, 2 Sam. 21:19) was also a giant who loved to fight, likened to the Nephilim, having six fingers and toes (2 Sam. 20:21). The name Goliath means a huge and powerful person or organization. How Nephilim continued to exist after the Flood remains a mystery yet is not void of speculation. While it is unclear how the giants survived the Flood, we know they did (through scripture), and we also know they will exist again during the tribulation.

Jesus confirms the giants will be seen again during the tribulation, "As were the days of Noah, so will be the coming of the Son of Man" (Matt. 24:37). As mentioned earlier, the phrase refers to hybrid superhuman beings roaming the earth. Like the Nephilim of old, the new breed of hybrids will be warriors, super-soldiers, unlike anything we have ever seen before, or will again (Joel 2:2). These super-soldiers are the 200 million mounted troops, who kill a third of the earth's population during the tribulation (Rev. 9:15). The 200 million are led by the bound angles that overstepped the mark, as recorded in Genesis (chapter 6), and are spoken of in greater detail by Enoch. Again, both Peter and Jude also mentioned them, with Jude confirming Enoch.

The 200 million mounted troops are most likely to be China and company, supported by Revelation, chapter sixteen, referring to them as the "kings of the East" (Rev. 16:12). Daniel, chapter eleven strengthens the argument, again stating (towards the end of the tribulation) the kings from the east and the north will alarm the antichrist (Dan. 11:43). The antichrist will go out with great fury to destroy and devote many to destruction, yet he will not prevail (Dan. 11:43-44). The reference to the antichrist attempting to destroy the invading kings will be fulfilled at the battle of Armageddon, where the armies of the whole world will gather for battle (Rev. 16:14-16). The battle will end before it starts, with Jesus returning in the 'nick of time' (Matt. 24:22). Revelation, chapter nineteen (vv. 11-21) describes the event in greater detail.

When comparing Ezekiel's famous prophecy (chapters 38 & 39) with Revelation, chapter nineteen, the events are the same (Ezek. 39:4-6, Rev. 19:17-18). Ezekiel's prophecy refers to Russia and the nations further north. Daniel confirms that both the north (Russia) and the west (China) will attack the antichrist in Jerusalem. Russia and China have been good friends since the 1950s, also having a mutual dislike for the United States. The United States is Israel's closest and strongest ally, yet scripture remains silent concerning this current hegemonic nation. Some speculate the USA can't be found because they are no longer around or no longer have the same capacity they do now, towards the end of the tribulation. A possible explanation for that is - either China or Russia or both attack the USA, crippling their capacity.

China has been threatening to attack the USA for some time, boasting of its ability to wipe out the Unites States' satellites, sending them into the dark ages. China's population and capacity have increased enormously over the past few decades. When writing the book of Revelation, the world's population was estimated to be around 200 million. Yet, John predicts an end-time eastern army of 200 million. Only in the last few decades has this been possible. China now can field an army of 200 million and has boasted of being able to, claiming to have 200 million men and women fit for military service. China boasted this in the year 2000. This number rises at the rate of about 10 million per year.

As never seen before, this massive army will be released, and unleashed by God (Rev. 9:13-14) during the tribulation, killing upwards of 1.7 billion of the world's remaining population. The army of 200 million is the second woe of the tribulation (Rev. 8:13). The third woe is the return of Jesus Christ, resulting in what is described in Revelation, chapter nineteen (vv. 11-21). The prophecy of the 200 million mounted troops is unparallel to anything seen before (Joel 2:20), taking place in the second half of the tribulation. This unfulfilled prophecy thoroughly debunks the preterist argument.

As were the days of Noah: China's desire to create genetically modified super soldiers can be traced back to biblical prophecy. Getting back to the issue at hand, where human DNA was, and will be corrupted again (as were the days of Noah), being genetically modified, the evidence of this is seen in modern times with super soldiers. China is currently developing soldiers with 'biologically enhanced capabilities.' According to US intelligence officials, China has been conducting tests on its soldiers in the People's Liberation Army (PLA) to create a biologically enhanced soldier. China is using advanced techniques for gene editing, which can assist soldiers in performing in certain conditions and can even be used to grow human-like organs for use in transplants. A genetically modified soldier might be capable of running faster, jumping higher, hitting harder, thinking more quickly, or withstanding certain diseases. A genetically modified soldier might also have dramatically increased height or muscle growth or have bio-implants that allow them to control electronics with their body.

Another fascinating parallel between biblical prophecy and China concerns the dragon. The national symbol for the kings of the east (China) is the dragon. The dragon's (Satan) released angels lead China (Rev. 9:14), who may also have, once again, played a part in their genetic modification. John describes these super-solders, likened to fire-breathing dragons (Rev. 9:17-18), as Joel also does (2:2-3).

Additionally, corresponding with China and biblical prophecy is where Napoleon once said, "China is a sleeping giant. Let her sleep, for when she wakes, she will shake the world." Joel makes the same connection, predicting the earth will quake before the coming super-soldiers (Joel 2:10).

Concurrent with today's primary problem, COVID-19, the warfare focus does not stop with the idea of genetically modified soldiers but includes genetically modified diseases that can attack enemy soldiers. According to PLA Gen. Zhang Shibo, former president of the PLA's National Defense University, today's biotech advances unlock the possibility to create new synthetic pathogens that are "more toxic, more contagious, and more resistant." China's elite Medical Military Medical Sciences argued in November 2017, "Obviously, genetic weapons possess many advantages over traditional biological weapons." Again, the augmented soldiers can be traced back to biblical prophecy, seen with the kings of the west (China) and the North (Russia).

However, Zechariah reveals more from Ezekiel's prophecy (Ezek. 38-39). "When these prophets (Ezekiel and Zechariah) described the pre-Messiah War of Gog and Magog, they explained it in terms that were entirely unlike wars in biblical times," writes Israel 365 News. "Rather than wounds from arrows, spears, or swords, Zechariah described a scene similar to the aftermath of germ warfare." The prophet Zechariah writes, "And this shall be the plague with which the LORD will strike all the peoples that wage war against Jerusalem: their flesh will rot while they are still standing on their feet; their eyes will rot in their sockets, and their tongues will rot in their mouths." (Zech. 14:12).

Ezekiel's prophecy connects the warriors of the Gog and Magog War with the Bashan region. King Og of Bashan was Rephaim, which can be said to have been somewhat biologically modified humans. According to Deuteronomy (3:11), the king was 13 ½ feet tall. In sum, Joel's prophecy and John's revelation are likely to be fulfilled through the genetically modified Chinese soldiers, modern-day 'giants,' who will attack Israel in the last days (Dan. 11:44).

Alongside the genetic modification of soldiers, producing super-soldiers, another genetic modification of humanity is said to be seen with the COVID-19' vaccination, often referred to as the 'jab.' The jab contains tiny fragments of the genetic material known as 'messenger ribonucleic acid', which affects the recipient's genome genetic codes. That is, the jab is said to genetically modify human beings; rewriting, or overwriting their coded DNA; thereby, corrupting God's creative design, 'As were the days of Noah.' Some claim once a person has taken the jab, due to the modification that has taken place, they are no longer defined as human; instead, they are transhuman. While it is too early to know the full extent of what the jab will do to the human body, biblical prophecy connects the dots.

Revelation, chapters thirteen (v. 16-18), fourteen (vv. 9-11), and twenty (v. 4) reference the Mark of the Beast (666), where, once taken, the effects cannot be reversed. Any who receive the Mark of the Beast will be eternally dammed (Rev. 14:9-11). There is no means of salvation once the Mark has been taken, which confirms it cannot be reversed or removed. While some have said they would go as far as to cut off their hand to rid themselves of the Mark, once taken, the Bible says it cannot be untaken, once taken.

The connection between the suggested gene-altering COVID jab and the Mark of the Beast is interesting, supporting the idea that it cannot be untaken once taken. Once the jab (mRNA) properties have been injected into the human body, many creditable experts say the body is turned into a spike protein-producing factory, breeding more of the same and cannot be stopped or reversed. Effectively, the person's DNA, which contains the 'God Code,' has been rewritten or overwritten. Likewise, the inoculated person who receives the Mark of the Beast will become tainted, corrupted, defective, no longer intact, as God designed them to be. Essentially, they will no longer be categorized as human but rather transhuman, thus void of salvation.

*Important note, the COVID-19 jab is not the Mark of the Beast, but rather leads towards the Mark. The greatest evidence for the lead-up is with the threat of not being able to buy or sell unless inoculated. Those who have taken the COVID jab are not disqualified from salvation. The jab has set the stage for the Mark (666). A simple rule of thumb is this, no Beast, no Mark. The Mark will not be offered until the antichrist appears. It will be forced halfway through the tribulation. Therefore, you cannot accidentally take it (Rev. 13:16-17, 14:9-11).

In sum, until recent times, the term "As were the days of Noah" was initially connected to violence (Gen. 6:11, 13), followed by the changing of the law, were marrying the same sex was legalized, homosexuality became a popular interpretation. While both positions are still correct, they are only partly right. The Genesis account provides references to the whole world filled with violence, which will be repeated, and Jude makes the connection of angels and men pursuing unnatural desires (Jude 1:6-7). The Genesis account, alongside the book of Enoch, reveals that fallen angels had intercourse with women (strange flesh), producing the offspring of Nephilim.

A similar term to "As were the days of Noah" (Matt. 24:34) is "As it was in the days of Lot" (Lu. 17:28), quoted by Jude (Jude 1:7), referring to homosexuality. Homosexuality will be addressed in the following section. As for the reference to the days of Noah, that seems to fit most closely with the modification, and corruption of God's creative design, being humankind. That is the changing or altering of a person's DNA, overwriting and or removing the God code, which is precisely what the Mark of the Beast will do. For this reason, it is impossible to reverse a person's condition once they have received the Mark (666). Essentially, they are no longer considered to be human. Salvation is reserved for humankind alone.

As a final note, the reference to eating and drinking and marriage and giving in marriage (Matt. 24:38) should be compared with Luke's concluding account of the Olivet Discourse (Lu. 21:34-36). There, Jesus says, "Watch yourselves, do not get weighed down with dissipations (overindulgence), and drunkenness, and the cares of this life" (Lu. 21:34a). Those who do, "That day will come upon them suddenly like a trap" (Lu. 21:34b, Matt. 24:39). "It will come upon all who dwell on the face of the whole earth" (Lu. 21:35). Only those 'awake will escape' (Lu. 21:36, Rev. 3:10). Jesus said, in those days, most will be living life as normal, either unaware of the signs of the times or are dismissive altogether. Scoffers, in other words (2 Pet. 3:3, Jude 1:18), will reject prophecy signifying Jesus' return.

Today, like in Noah's day, few listen, continuing as if nothing is wrong. For Noah, after 120 years of preaching (Gen. 6:3), God warned He would bring the Flood and blot out every living creature on the face of the earth (Gen. 7:4). Once Noah and his family were inside the ark, God shut the door (Gen. 7:16), and then He destroyed every living thing, except for Noah, his family, and the animals on the ark (Gen. 7:21-24). God shutting the door should be compared with the parable of the ten virgins in Matthew, chapter twenty-five (v. 10). The story of the ark and the parable are related and will be addressed later under the parable of the ten virgins.

As seen through the verses referenced, eating, drinking, and marrying refers to living life as normal (Your Best Life Now) while ignorant and or dismissing biblical prophecy and the signs of the time. In Noah's day, only a remnant survived the Flood. During the tribulation, only a remnant will survive the Fire - most will be corrupted beyond saving. "As were the Days of Noah, so will be the coming of the Son of Man."

As Were the Days of Lot

'Because they Refused to Love the Truth'
(Luke 17:20-37)

As mentioned in the previous section, this section will cover the quote, "Just as it was in the days of Lot" (Lu. 17:28). The quote is addressed here because it is directly linked to the previous quote, "Just as it was in the days of Noah" (Lu. 17:26-28, cf. Matt. 24:37-39), also addressing another sign of the end times. Like Matthew, Luke refers to a repeat of the behaviour of Noah's day before the return of Christ, such as eating, drinking, marrying, and giving in marriage (Lu. 17:27). The same was seen in the days of Lot, with eating and drinking. However, Lot adds, buying and selling, building, and planting. Another difference between Noah and Lot is that with Noah, God used the flood to destroy the earth's population, whereas, with Lot, He used fire. As a result, fire rained down from heaven and destroyed every living creature in Sodom (Lu. 17:29).

Another difference is that when God destroyed every living creature in Noah's day, except for those on the ark, He promised never to repeat the flood again. As a sign of that promise, God gave the rainbow as an eternal reminder (Gen. 9:11-16). However, with Lot's account, where God used fire to judge the rebellious, unlike the flood, Jesus said that fire will be repeated, saying, "So will it be on the day when the Son of Man is revealed" (Lu. 21:30). During the tribulation, leading up to the return of Jesus Christ, God will pour down fire on the earth as in the days of Lot (Rev. 8:5-8, 16:8, 17:16, 18:8).

During the tribulation, fire will rain down from heaven, and it will also proceed out from the mouths of the 200 million mounted troops, killing a third of the earth's population (Rev. 9:17-18), and again fire will proceed out from the mouths of the two witnesses (Rev. 11:5). The two witnesses will be preaching repentance, unstoppable and untouchable for three and a half years, which is the first half of the tribulation (42 months, Rev. 11:2). If anyone tries to harm them, they will be destroyed by the fire coming out of the witnesses' mouths.

Through the 200 million mounted troops, God judges the nations between Asia and the Middle East as the unstoppable super-soldiers (Joel 2:2) march toward Jerusalem. Through the two witnesses, God judges any who oppose the gospel of repentance from the rebuilt (third) temple in Jerusalem.

Interestingly, to counterfeit God during the tribulation, the antichrist will also call down fire from heaven (Rev. 13:13). Calling down fire from heaven is nothing new, for the prophets of Baal attempted it, albeit failed. Elijah, on the other hand, did see fire come down from heaven by the power of God (1 Kgs. 18). Elijah repeated that miracle in II Kings, killing the king's soldiers (chapter 1). James and John also desired to call fire down from heaven, only to be rebuked by Jesus (Lu. 9:54-45) due to it not being the right time.

However, in the tribulation, it will be the right time where the antichrist successfully calls down fire from heaven. "With the activity of Satan, with all power and false signs and wonders, and with all wicked deception for those who are perishing because they refused to love the truth and be saved" (2 Thess. 2:9-10). Because the majority refused to love the truth, God sends the 'Strong delusion' (2 Thess. 2:11), who is the antichrist. The antichrist will be incredibly deceptive, "Performing great signs and wonders, to lead astray, if possible, even the elect" (Matt. 24:24). As discussed under the first and leading sign of the end times, deception is the number one, catching most off guard. Even now, there is 'false fire' flowing from many pulpits, deceiving countless clueless confessing Christians.

God sends the antichrist to those who refused to love the truth. Therefore, those who perish through the beast's activity do so as a judgment from God. As a result of fire raining down from heaven, most of the remaining earth's population during the tribulation will be destroyed, as it was in the days of Lot, as were the days of Noah. Few survive. Alongside eating and drinking, the other similarity with the things to come is, none survive outside of the remnant elect.

To get an idea of the known numbers perishing by fire during the tribulation, John reveals one-third of the population will be killed by the fire breathing 200 million mounted troops. That number amounts to around 1.7 billion if we generously consider some two billion have been raptured before the tribulation, leaving five billion behind (using round numbers). Others will perish due to opposing the fire breathing two witnesses, among other judgements.

Consider three billion are now remaining when God rains fire on the earth, killing another third of the population, being one billion, leaving two billion. Many more die because of hail and fire mixed with blood thrown on the earth, burning up a third of the world (Rev. 8:7). Many more again perish due to the waters being poisoned by a blazing star falling to the earth (Rev. 8:10-11). Assume at least another third of the population will die through these plagues, killing some 666 million, then leaving a little over 1.3 billion. Others will lose their lives through the sword, famine, sickness, and earthquakes, among other judgements, leaving just a fraction of the original population to face Jesus. He judges the remaining nations with fire on His return (Rev. 17:16, 18:8).

While many will perish through a range of judgements during the tribulation, fire will kill the majority, confirmed by Jesus who said, "But on the day when Lot went out from Sodom, fire and sulphur rained from heaven and destroyed them all— so will it be on the day when the Son of Man is revealed" (Lu. 17:29-30). When that day comes, everyone will know it (Lu. 17:34, cf. Matt. 24:27, 30, Rev. 1:7), although the faithful followers of Christ will long for it before then and not see it (Lu. 17:22). When Jesus foretold of His return, He said, before then, He first must suffer many things (Lu. 17:25), which is also true of His faithful followers (1 Pet. 2:21, 4:1).

As mentioned earlier, leading up to Jesus returning to the earth, literal fire will rain down from heaven (Rev. 8:5-8, 16:8), as it was in the days of Lot (Lu. 17:28). While the above-mentioned describes the 'What,' as in what will happen during the tribulation, the 'Why' now needs to be addressed. That is, why God rained down fire on Sodom, and why He will do it again. Luke's account provides some clues, like with the days of Noah, the population was eating and drinking. Again, Luke also provides, 'buying and selling, planting, and building' (Lu. 17:28). During the tribulation, only those with the Mark of the Beast (666) will be able to buy and sell (Rev. 13:16), meaning, only those committed to and consumed by the coming beast system or New World Order will be able to trade.

Luke adds more in chapter twelve (vv. 35-48), with the 'big idea' that "You must be awake when Jesus comes knocking" (vv. 36-39); and therefore, "You must be ready" (v. 40). Again, the issue was becoming distracted and overcome with worldly matters, 'eating and drinking, and getting drunk' (v. 45). These additional verses added by Luke are essential, indicating in the last days, as were the people of Sodom, materialism will be a big problem, as it was for the church of Laodicea (Rev. 3:17). The lukewarm church of Laodicea was prosperity-driven and arguably the earliest example of kingdom now 'theology,' in practice. Remember, the church of Laodicea is prophetically fulfilled by us, being on the biblical timeclock the last church before Jesus returns.

The difference between what the members of the church of Laodicea (and this generation) pursued and what Jesus taught are miles apart. Kingdom now theology teaches that the church is to have dominion over the seven key mountains of worldly influence, otherwise known as seven mountains, 'theology,' or dominionism, or reconstructionism. Reconstructionism focuses on everything lost in the garden of Eden, with the belief everything lost can be regained in preparation for Jesus' return. Before Jesus returns, this world is going to get better and better. A good day today and a better one tomorrow. Isaiah had something to say about that, yet nothing good (Isa. 56:9-12).

Reconstructionism or dominionism is absolute nonsense, running in the opposite direction to what the Bible teaches. Instead of having dominion over this world (kingdom now), our dominion will come later, following Jesus' return (Rev. 2:25-26, 5:10, 11:15, 20:4). When Jesus returns, He will rule and reign, and so will we because He is. Before Jesus returns, this world is heading for trouble like never seen since from the beginning or will be seen again (Matt. 24:21). Luke's record confirms that everything will worsen before improving, comparing the end of this dispensation with Noah and Lot's experience (Lu. 17:26-30).

Noah and Lot's generation were consumed with wordiness; therefore, they were not ready for God's judgement (cf. Gen. 19). Their overabundance and overindulgence caused them to be oblivious to God, blinded by the world (cf. 2 Cor. 4:4, Rev. 3:17). That will change when Jesus returns. In the tribulation. whether the worldly left behind are relaxing on their rooftops or working in their field (Lu. 17:31), whether it be night or day

(Lu. 17:34-35), judgement will come swiftly like a thief, when they least expect it (1 Thess. 5:2, Pet. 3:10, Rev. 3:3, 16:15).

Luke ends his record of the Olivet Discord with precisely this same warning, only addressed to the followers of Christ (cf. Rev. 3:3), confirming, those who are caught up in the world will not be caught up by Jesus, escaping (raptured) the things that are going to take place (Lu. 21:34-36, cf. Rev 3:10). When Jesus returns to set up His kingdom, He will judge the nations to determine who can and cannot enter His kingdom (Lu. 17:26-35). While many have mistaken this passage (Lu. 17:26-35) for the rapture, it refers to the return of Jesus after the tribulation.

Regarding those judged worthy, or not, Lot's wife is an essential reference, where Jesus says, "Remember Lot's wife" (Lu. 17:32). Any trying to save their life (i.e., possessions, Lu. 17:31) will lose it, and everything else (Lu. 17:33).

The doctrine of the rapture is that the church will be 'caught up' (harpazo) in the clouds to meet the Lord (1 Thess. 4:17). This event will take place before a seven-year tribulation commences. Luke's account (Lu. 17:26-37) does not refer to the rapture confirmed by the context. Verses thirty-four to thirty-six fall within the context of verses twenty to thirty-seven and should be interpreted first and foremost within that setting, and secondary, using applied, systematic theology.

Regarding verses thirty-four to thirty-six, when the disciples asked where the 'One taken' would go (v. 37a), Jesus answered by saying, "Wherever the body is there, eagles will be gathered" (v. 37b). Another way to translate the word 'eagles' is 'vultures,' which is how the English Standard Version and the New American Standard Version present it. The inferred meaning is that the dead body will attract scavengers (cf. Job 39:30; Matt. 24:28; Rev. 19:17-19). The 'one taken' clearly does not refer to a faithful follower of Christ being raptured, but rather the unbeliever being taken into judgment.

To understand the passage correctly, one needs first to consider verses twenty to twenty-one. Here, the Pharisees ask about the coming kingdom of God. Jesus told them that it is already here, in part. The translation 'Within you' would be better said, 'Within your midst', otherwise, Jesus would have been saying the kingdom of God was within the Pharisees, which was not the case.

On the contrary, Jesus told them, "For all your study; you'll never see the kingdom" (v. 20b; Jn. 5:39). The reason is, they refused to accept Jesus as the Messiah (v. 25; Jn. 5:40). Instead of surrendering all to Jesus, the religious leaders were lovers of themselves and this world (vs. 27a, 28, 32). Verse thirty-three, in response, comes as a stern warning, "Whoever seeks to save his life (refuse to give it up) will lose it." The warning highlights the danger of loving worldly possessions (vv. 28, 31), the very thing that caused the Pharisees to stumble (Lk. 16:14). Again, the same caused Lot's wife to 'look back' (v. 32). The message in context (vv. 20-37) is clear; you can't serve two masters! (Lu. 16:13). Those who love the things of this world (materialism) will not be a part of the coming kingdom (Jn. 2:15-17). Sadly, like those in the days of Noah (vv. 26-27), and Sodom (v. 28), and the Pharisees; right up to the current day and last moment (v. 24), many will be consumed by the love of this world, and then judged (Lu. 12:20), as the 'One taken' (Lu. 17:34-36).

Jesus reminded His disciples that people in Noah's day were not prepared for the flood, and therefore they were destroyed (Gen. 6 & 7). The same was true for the people in Lot's day (Gen. 19). Again, the same problem will exist when the kingdom comes—people will not be ready, and will perish, which is why Jesus said, "You must be ready!" (Matt. 24:44).

The love of self, and the love of this world, being materialism, as with the days of Noah and Lot, is another end times sign (Matt. 24:12, 2 Tim. 3:1-5), further addressed in chapter two. However, alongside materialism, there was yet another problem for the people of Sodom. It was to uncover, the original record that needs to be examined found in Genesis, chapters eighteen and nineteen. When Abraham was ninety-nine years old (Gen. 17:24), the Lord appeared to him (Gen. 18:1), and then two more angels appeared (Gen. 18:2). Abraham immediately recognised the Lord, asking whether he had found favour in His sight (Gen. 18:3). He had! The Lord came to inform Abraham he would have a child one year from now (Gen. 18:10). While the odds seemed impossible, the Lord and the angelic beings reassured Abraham; nothing is too hard for God, and it will happen at the appointed time (Gen. 18:14).

However, the purpose of the visit was not only to inform Abraham and Sarah they would have a child but to reveal what God was about to do to Sodom. After some deliberation, the Lord told Abraham what they were about to do (Gen. 18:17), following an investigation of Sodom (Gen. 18:20-21). Regarding the first prophecy concerning Abraham's future son, Isaac, Abraham, unlike Sarah, had no trouble believing in God. The same was true for the next, regarding Sodom. Finally, the evidence is seen with Abraham pleading and interceding for the lives of those about to perish (Gen. 18:22-33).

Abraham knew God came down to destroy Sodom because of the great sin and outcry reaching as high as heaven (Gen. 18:21, 19:13). Following an investigation, God brought judgement against Sodom, which will be repeated in the days before Jesus returns (Lu. 17:28). The latter will even dwarf the former (Matt. 10:15). The specific sin for Sodom was homosexuality (Gen. 19:4-7, Jude 1:7). Sodom is the root of the word sodomite, which defines a person who engages in anal sexual intercourse, referring to homosexuals. The people of Sodom were so corrupted and driven by their sin, even after the angels struck them with blindness, they still groped for the door to have sex with 'the visiting strangers' (Gen. 19:11). Following the men of Sodom being struck with blindness, the angels told Lot to hurry up, to gather his family, and leave Sodom before they destroy it (Gen. 19:12-15). Lot told his family, yet his sons-in-law thought he was joking (Gen. 19:14b) like Sarah did (Gen. 18:12).

Many today do the same when hearing of the things to come. They scoff at Bible prophecy and by doing so, they fulfill it negatively (2 Pet., 3:3, Jude 1:18). Scoffers are yet another end times sign, likened to the days of Noah and Lot. As a result of scoffing, the sons-in-law did not escape the coming judgement. They were not in the company of Lot and his family when fleeing from Sodom (Gen. 19:15-22, 28). Sadly, the sons-in-law had their opportunity and lost it. That same was true of Lot's wife, who was departing Sodom and then perished from looking back (Gen, 19:26, Lu. 17:32).

Again, another similarity between the days of Noah and the days of Lot is, until they were safely out of the way, judgement would not fall (Gen. 6:1, 19:22). The same will be true for the church (cf. Rev. 3:10); the tribulation will not commence until the faithful followers of God have been removed (2 Thess. 2:6-8). Following the removal of Lot and his family, God rained down fire on Sodom and Gomorrah, destroying every living thing (Gen. 19:23-25), including Lot's wife, who looked back (Gen. 19:26).

In the days of Noah and Lot, both preached righteousness (2 Pet. 2:5, 7), warning of the coming judgement, yet none listened, and consequently, all perished. As mentioned earlier, as were the days of Noah and Lot, so will it be leading up to Jesus' return; none listened then, and few will listen now. On this, both Ezekiel (14:14) and Jeremiah (15:1) confirm that even if Noah, Daniel, and Job were around, none would listen to them either, neither would God grant them their request if they interceded for those not having ears to hear.

Ezekiel confirms the above-mentioned in chapter fourteen (vv. 12-23), listing Noah, Daniel, and Job (vv. 14, 16 18, 20), stating that not even these three righteous men could prevent God's judgment. Through Ezekiel, God informed His rebellious people their judgement would be even worse than that of the days of Noah, Daniel, and Job, firstly, due to not having these three righteous giants interceding for them (v. 21). And secondly, if these three righteous men could not save their own families and land, how would any save Judah! Even if they stood together and prayed collectively for Judah regarding the coming judgement, they would still not be able to save them, not even their own sons and daughters (Ezek. 14:18, 20). Only their own lives would be saved (Ezek. 14:16, 18, 20.The same was true for Noah, and Lot, and the same applies today and will during the tribulation.

The primary issue for the people in the days of Lot, which was homosexuality (Gen. 19, Jude, 1:7), is also seen today, and escalating, leading to every other sin (cf. Rom 1:24-32). Paul states those involved exchanged the truth for a lie (Rom. 1:25). Sexual sin led to every other sin (Rom. 1:28-31). Otherwise said, sin is never satisfied - it is all-consuming and self-pleasing. Included in the mix of self-serving sin is the love of self and money (2 Tim. 3:1-5), taking its follower further and further away from God. Just as it was in the days of Lot (Lu. 17:28), so it is evident today. Sin binds and blinds, as seen with the blinded men still groping for the door in Lot's day (Gen. 19:11).

Today, churches affirm and even welcome homosexuals, but Jesus never mentioned it, therefore never condemned it. As seen above, Jesus warned that when He returns, those days will be like the days of Lot. Homosexuality was the great sin for Sodom, and the outcry of that sin reached as high as heaven. Being materialistic (a lover of money) was also added (Lu. 17:28). Paul also has plenty to say about the sin of homosexuality (Rom 1:24-32, 1 Cor. 6:19, 1 Tim. 1:10); Jude also mentioned it (1:7), prophesying a repeat of the days of Lot as a consequence. Paul also has plenty to say about materialism, which will be further addressed in chapter two.

In sum, as in the days of Lot, so shall be the days of the Son of Man. On THAT day, when Jesus returns, fire will fall, suddenly and unexpectedly, on the lovers of self and pleasure, who refused to love the truth, exchanging the truth for a lie. Although the coming judgement will be a repeat of the days of Lot, it will again exceed anything ever seen before or again afterward.

Drunkenness
'Be Sober-Minded'
(Matt. 24:38, 49)

In common with the last two sections is eating and drinking (Matt. 24:38, Lu. 12:45, 17:27), implying, when Jesus returns, the remaining population of the earth will be unaware of the times, distracted, and intoxicated by the things of this world. As addressed in the previous section, the primary issue discussed in Matthew and Luke's account was materialism. However, much more is discovered when diving into the original text (Matt. 24 – Gen. 6, Lu. 17 – Gen. 19). Nevertheless, materialism is an incredibly significant end-time sign. So much that even confessing followers of Christ are consumed and blinded by the things of this world. They will be entirely ignorant of the time they now live in (like the church of Laodicea).

Unsurprisingly, the Bible has a lot to say about money, which has not gone unnoticed by many charismatic Christians. However, verses quoted by the charismatic Word of Faith camp to support their 'theology' of divine wealth, generally, if not always, are taken out of context. Like materialism, the Bible also has much to say about drunkenness. Like money, drinking has been misunderstood. While both money and alcohol are acceptable when controlled, however, the love of either is very dangerous.

The danger of alcohol is that it is very addictive and unless the casual drinker exercises self-control over it, they will be controlled by it. The definition of being drunk is to lose control by being intoxicated. The biblical definition of an alcoholic refers to someone who is habitually drunk—drunkenness results from an excessive amount of alcohol which slows the brain, causing overall numbness. Numbness affects the body, mind, and spirit. In the same way, the drinker is numb to the things (problems) of this world; they are also numb to the things of God. They are earthly minded, not heavenly minded (Col. 3:2), which is why Paul said, "Do not be drunk with wine but be filled with the Spirit" (Eph. 5:8). Due to a lack of being filled with the Spirit, but rather filled by the things of this world, most cannot discern the signs of the times. Those filled by the things of this world are drunk on the cares of this world, often, materialism.

John warned of the same condition in the closing chapter of the tribulation, stating, just before Jesus' return, an angel will say, "Fallen, fallen is Babylon the great! She has become a lair for demons and a haunt for every unclean spirit, every unclean bird, and every detestable beast. All the nations have drunk the wine of the passion of her immorality. The kings of the earth were immoral with her, and the merchants of the earth have grown wealthy from the extravagance of her luxury. Then I heard another voice from heaven say: 'Come out of her, My people, so that you will not share in her sins or contract any of her plagues'" (Rev. 18:1-4).

John's revelation further warns, those intoxicated by (in love with) the world, when Jesus returns, will be "Paid back…, and repaid… double for their deeds" (Rev. 18:6), in a single day (Rev. 18:8), in a single hour (Rev. 18:10, 17, 19), everything they (love) put their trust in will be no more (x6, "No more," Rev. 18:21-23).

Due to not remaining sober, therefore ready for Jesus, those who are asleep and intoxicated will not be taken out of the way before the tribulation commences (cf. 1 Thess. 5:6-8). However, the left behind will have another opportunity to wake up, sober up, and get ready before Jesus returns, or else be repaid by Jesus after the tribulation for their rejection of Him.

Following Paul's section addressing the 'Coming of the Lord,' or the rapture (1 Thess. 4:13-18), he talks about the 'Day of the Lord' (1 Thess. 5:1-11). The day of the Lord refers to the tribulation. Each section (1 Thess. 4 & 5) ends with the words, "Encourage one another" (1 Thess. 4:18, 5:11). The term, encourage one another, relates to giving hope in a time of difficulty, supported by Paul's second letter to the church of Thessalonians (2 Thess. 2:1-12), where some had said they were already in the tribulation (2 Thess. 2:2). The other purpose is to encourage the believers to continue living a life pleasing to God (1 Thess. 4:1), warning them to keep control of their bodies (1 Thess. 4:4-7), contrary to those who are drunk and out of control (2 Thess. 5:7).

While the first passage (chapter 4) explicitly discusses sexual sin, it is often fuelled by drunkenness. The second passage (chapter 5) focuses on intoxication, connecting the two passages. In the second section, Paul uses the words 'Sober' (1 Thess. 5:6, 8) and 'Drunk' (1 Thess. 5:5, 7), joined with awake/asleep (1 Thess. 5:6-7). The reference to being either awake or asleep is spiritual. In other words, those who are not awake, therefore alert to spiritual, heavenly things, have no way of discerning the signs of the times. Like a drunk person, those spiritually drunk (on the world) are oblivious, and unable to comprehend or respond appropriately to surrounding events. They are in darkness (1 Thess. 4:4, 5, 7), blinded by the world and the god of this world (2 Cor. 4:4). Alongside the word 'sober,' four times Paul uses the term 'sober-minded" (1 Tim. 3:2, 11, 2 Tim. 4:5,

Tit. 2:2). Peter uses the same words three more times (1 Pet. 1:13, 4:7, 5:8), instructing Christians to be spiritually alert/awake.

Contrary to the one who lives in darkness, being blinded by sin, Paul exhorts the believers, telling them they are children of the light; therefore, they should continue to walk in that light (1 Thess. 5:5). Those walking in darkness will be caught out by the thief in the night (1 Thess. 5:2); they will not escape the things to come (1 Thess. 5:3). However, the one walking in the light will escape, not being destined for the wrath (1 Thess. 5:9, Rev. 3:10).

Whether walking in the light or night, soon, a 'Sudden' (1 Thess. 5:3) shift will occur, leaving one behind to suffer the wrath while removing the other, escaping it altogether. On that day, there will be sudden destruction for those left behind, and for the one removed, there will be a sudden transformation (1 Thess. 4:16-17, 1 Cor. 15:51-52).

The forthcoming event will be as the days of Noah and Lot were (Matt. 24:37-39, Lu. 17:26-30). The elect was removed, and the rest perished. Interestingly, following both judgements consisting of the flood and the fire, Noah and Lot got drunk (Gen. 9:21-22, 19:32--36), resulting in perversion. As mentioned earlier, alcohol fuels sexual sin, and from sexual immorality, every other sin follows (cf. Rom. 1:26, 29-31).

The purpose for Paul writing the mentioned passages (1 Thess. 4 & 5) is to encourage the believer, who is walking in the light, pleasing God (1 Thess. 4:1), standing fast in the Lord (1 Thess. 3:8), in preparation of the rapture. Alongside Paul's encouragement to the church of Thessalonians, a similar reference is seen in the letter to Titus (Tit. 2:13). As mentioned earlier, both chapters encourage the believer in a time of difficulty.

In the letter to the church of Thessalonians, Paul was concerned the believers might be tempted by Satan (1 Thess. 3:5a) to fall away (1 Thess. 3:5b) due to news of his suffering (1 Thess. 3:3-4, 7). So Paul reminds the Thessalonians; he was destined for this (1 Thess. 3:3), and so is every true believer who will have their faith tested (Matt. 5:10-12, 10:16-25, Lu. 14:27, Rom. 5:3, 2 Cor, 4:17, 2 Tim. 3:12, 1 Pet. 1:6-7, 4:1, 12-13, 5:10, 2 Pet. 2:19-21, Ja. 1:12).

Paul's concern was over the doctrine of suffering, which had caused some to be tempted and led astray due to replacing the doctrine of suffering with the doctrine of prosperity. Now, those living for their best life were easily disheartened and derailed when trials came. You can hear them saying, "We did not sign up for this." They depart as quickly as they come in. Essentially, those who have come in through a message that 'God will make your life better, giving you whatever your heart desires,' have responded to another gospel, promoting another Jesus (2 Cor. 11:4).

Like the first concern, where Satan may have tempted the followers of Christ (1 Thess. 3:3:5), as Jesus was (Matt. 4:1-11) the second concern is where the believers were in fear they were already in the tribulation (2 Thess. 2:2). The third reference is like the first, recorded in the letter to Titus (Tit. 2:13), where Paul appealed to Titus to teach sound doctrine (Tit. 2:1), countering false teachers.

Paul's instruction was also that older men are to be sober-minded, and older women are not slaves to much wine, being self-controlled (Tit. 2:2-4). Here, there is both a figurative and literal application of drunkenness in reference to older men and women, emphasising self-control. Younger men are likewise instructed to have self-control (Tit. 2:6), and slaves also (Tit. 2:9). Implying, all are to "Renounce ungodliness and worldly passions to live self-controlled, upright and godly lives in this present age, waiting for our blessed hope and appearing of the glory of our great God and Saviour Jesus Christ" (Tit. 2:12-13). The blessed hope is the rapture, reserved alone for the sober-minded, self-controlled, watchful follower of Christ (cf. Lu. 21:34-36).

Getting back to the text (Matt. 24), alongside Jesus' first reference to drunkenness (Matt. 24:38) as a sign of the end times, He gave another (Matt. 24:49) in the parable of the faithful, wise servant (Matt. 24:45-51). The connection between the Olivet Discord and this parable is that they both refer to the sudden and unexpected coming of Jesus Christ, catching many off-guard (Matt. 24:50). While some will be found faithful (Matt. 24:45-47), others will fail and be severely judged. Jesus states that the one caught out and judged thought the Master (Jesus) was not returning for a long while therefore lived wickedly, without exercising self-control, like those in the days of Noah did (24:37-39). In the same way, God's judgement came unexpectedly for the generation of Noah and Lot; it will again for this generation (Matt. 24:50). When the judgement comes, it will separate one from another (Matt. 24:51). The separation will occur first with the rapture and then when Jesus returns, after seven years of tribulation.

While the above-mentioned considers both the literal and figurative application of drunkenness, there still remains the question dividing many within the church today regarding whether a Christian can drink alcohol. The answer to that depends on your ability to stay self-controlled and maintain a clear conscience (Rom. 14:23) while protecting another's conscience also (1 Cor. 8:12). Therefore, it is not a sin to drink alcohol, but it is a sin to lose control, to go against your conscience or another's, by causing them to stumble.

Two common biblical words for wine are 'yah-yin' (fermented wine) and 'oy-nos' (literal wine). Both words refer to alcohol of the fermented type, and to drunkenness. Interestingly, the word 'oy-nos' is the same word found in John's gospel (Jn. 2:1-12), referring to the story of the wedding in Cana where Jesus turned water into wine, which is also the same word used by Paul (Eph. 5:18), when saying, "Do not get drunk with wine." The same word is used again by Paul in his letter to Timothy (1 Tim.

3:18) when telling deacons not to be addicted to much wine. Also, where Paul tells Timothy: "No longer drink only water but use a little wine for the sake of your stomach and your frequent ailments" (1 Tim. 3:18). Paul instructs Titus similarly (Tit. 2:3), saying that older women are reverent in behaviour, not slanderers or slaves to much wine. Paul addresses the same issue when giving instructions to the church of Colossians (Col. 2:16), stating, "Therefore let no one pass judgment on you in questions of food and drink." Alcoholic wine is evidently what Paul was referring to, as there would not have been a problem worth addressing for one who drank apple or grape juice over another who only drank water.

The implied message with the references mentioned above is 'do not get drunk,' rather than 'do not drink at all.' Further support is perceived where Jesus made the comparison between Himself and John the Baptist (Matt. 11:18-19). John came neither eating nor drinking (Lu. 1:15) and was not received, yet Jesus came eating and drinking and was called a glutton and a drunkard. The KJV says: winebibber again found in Luke (Lu. 7:24) compared with Matthew's record (Matt 11:18-19). This word 'oy-nop-ot'-ace' for winebibber is also found in Proverbs (Prov. 23:20), stating. "Be not among drunkards or among gluttonous eaters of meat."

Clearly, the Bible does not state Christians are not to abstain from alcohol any more than they are to abstain from meat or sleep. Instead, followers of Christ are to practice self-control and soberness; not being drunkards. Again, a drunkard refers to someone who is habitually drunk. Jesus said drunkards would not enter the Kingdom of God (cf. 1 Cor. 6:9-11, Gal. 5:19-21), neither will gluttons and sloughs or sluggards.

Jesus warned of those failing to qualify, He was not referring to one who has an occasional alcoholic drink any more than the one who ate meat or who sleeps. On the contrary, it is the abuse and dependency on alcohol that lead to the problem just as the abuse of eating and/or the laziness of the sluggard.

Drunkenness as a sign of the end times refers to both physical and spiritual drunkenness; the latter relates to being figuratively drunk (overcome and conquered) by the world. Here, and noteworthy is the closing statement to each of the seven churches (Rev. 2-3), Jesus said, "To the one that conquers…". Jesus promised, to one that conquers, they would inherit the reward, which is connected to salvation. The one that does not conquer, or who does not overcome this world, will not inherit the reward. Here is a sobering warning and reminder to remain sober-minded and self-controlled. The watchful, sober-minded believer is in the running to reap the reward because they are looking for the Rewarder. Therefore, they are mindful and discerning of the signs of the times, while living, and longing for the return of Jesus.

Faithfulness Vs. Faithlessness
'Blessed is the Servant Who his Master Finds Doing When He Comes'
(Matt. 24:45-51)

As mentioned in the previous sections, the love of materialism is a significant end-time sign, leading right up until Jesus returns. Also mentioned in the last section is the parable of the faithful and wise servant versus the faithless and wicked servant. The same parable is again found in Mark and Luke's gospel (Mk. 13:34-37, Lu. 12:41-48). The parables of the faithful and wise should be compared with two more, seen in Matthew, chapter twenty-five. The common theme with each is division and separation. The faithful ones who do well and are blessed with rewards, including entering into the joy of the Master (Matt. 25:21, 23), compared to the faithless failing one who is cut down and cast out (Matt. 24:30).

A major difference between the faithful and faithless is that the faithful does not treat what they have as their own. The similarity of the parable of the wicked servant and the parable of the talents is that both parties are entrusted with God's possessions (Matt. 24:47, 25:14). The same is seen again in the parable of the minas, found in Luke (Lu. 19:11-27), commonly teaching whatever we have, belongs to the Master (Jesus). The application of the parables is faithfulness and preparedness, meaning we must be living for Jesus to be ready for His return -we must be about the Master's business, not our own. All the parables point to Jesus and His return; with the parable of the minas, the words, "Occupy until I come" (Lu. 19:13b) confirm.

Ludicrously, some today use this term, "Occupy until I come" to dismiss end-times teaching, responding to biblical prophecy by saying something along the lines of, "Oh, I am not worried about all that; I am just going to occupy until Jesus comes." By doing so, they misquote and misunderstand the verse, and they ignore the context. The half verse they misquote in the ESV says, "Engage in business until I come" (Lu. 19:13b). In preparation for the King's return, the business they/we were/are to engage in was/is kingdom business (Lu. 19:13, 15). Kingdom business does not refer to kingdom now 'theology' but rather living for and serving Jesus by proclaiming and bringing glory to His name.

At the time Jesus taught, the disciples thought He was going to set up His kingdom there and then (Lu. 19:11). They, like many today, misunderstood Him. He would first return to His Father, receive the kingdom, and on His return set it up (Lu. 19:15, 23). While Jesus was/is away (in heaven), many religious leaders did/do not want Him to return and reign over them (Lu. 19:14). They were/are too busy enjoying life, their 'Best Life Now.'

Like the church of Laodicea, meaning: People Ruling. The lukewarm congregation of Laodicea prophetically represents us as the last church before Jesus returns. The last of the seven churches addressed by Jesus in the book of Revelation, the lukewarm Laodicean church thought they were rich and had no need for anything, including Jesus, but Jesus said they were poor because they did not have Him (Rev. 3:17). While they were 'worshipping' inside the institutional church building (organised religion), Jesus was on the outside, shut out, and knocking on the door (Rev. 3:20). The image of Jesus standing on the outside, knocking, accurately reflects and represents today's expression of 'doing church,' and doing it without Jesus. In sum, it is a religion void of a relationship with God. True salvation results from an intermit relationship with God, with works confirming and following (Matt. 5:16, Jn. 15:4-5, Eph. 2:10, Ja. 2:17, 18, 26, 1 Jn. 3:17-18).

When Jesus returns, those He entrusted with gifts to 'occupy until He comes' (to do good works, live for Jesus and proclaim His name) will have to give an account for what they had done (Lu. 19:15). They will give an account for what they have gained by doing business for the King, using the King's gifts. In the parable of the minas, the first servant did well and was given authority over ten cities (Lu. 19:16-17). The cities that the faithful servant would have authority over are in the millennial kingdom; the kingdom Jesus sets up when He returns, WHEN HE RETURNS (kingdom then, not kingdom now, Lu. 19:11b). The second servant was called forward and received a similar reward for doing well; he was given the authority of five cities (Lu. 19:18-19). And then came the third servant who, unlike the first two, failed to occupy or engage in (kingdom) business (Lu. 19:20-21). Due to his failure, Jesus condemned him, calling him a wicked servant (Lu. 19:22). This wicked servant failed to do what the others had because he did not expect Jesus to return, at least not when He did (Lu. 19:23). In other words, he was living for himself and not for God.

When someone is truly saved, they no longer live for themselves, therefore they are no longer consumed by this life (Col. 3:1-6).

A similar story to the minas is in Matthew, chapter twenty-five (Matt. 25:14-30), where the failed servant who mishandles the talent was cast into hell (Matt. 25:30). His excuse for doing nothing was that he was afraid (Matt. 25:25). However, Jesus called him out, not accepting that he was afraid but rather wicked and slothful (Matt. 25:26). Being wicked indicates the failed servant belonged to the group who did not want Jesus to return and reign over them (Matt. 25:14), like the Laodicean (people ruling) group, who were overcome by the world, living for themselves; that is, enjoying 'their' best life now. *If this is your 'best life now' then your worst life is yet to come. Meaning, you are going to hell, or at least, you are going through the tribulation unless repentance comes first and fast.

In contrast to the rewarded two servants who were expecting Jesus to return and therefore were 'engaged in kingdom business,' including proclaiming His name and His return, preaching repentance in preparation, the third failed servant was put to death (Lu. 19:27). No doubt he had been deceived by a different (kingdom now, best life now) sugar-coated 'gospel.'

Again, the parables, as mentioned above, present the analogy that Jesus is going away to receive His kingdom; then, after some time away, He will return to establish His kingdom on the earth. On His return, those waiting and working for Him will be rewarded, while those who were too busy doing their own thing, living for themselves, will be rejected. Those rejected by Jesus will be the same who rejected Jesus. Thus, the context of each parable is eschatological, focused on living for Jesus in preparation for His return.

Circling back to the original text; the message taught through Matthew, chapter twenty-four (vv. 45-51) is repeated times over, with the emphasis on being ready (Matt. 24:44), by being awake (Matt. 24:42), and therefore watching (Matt. 25:13) for the return of Jesus Christ. Those who are alert are prepared for that day by living for Jesus, and knowing and connecting the signs of the times with scripture.

As previously mentioned, the most significant distraction and danger in this life is this world, with its worldly teaching of 'Your Best Life Now'. Luke's concluding Olivet Discord account confirms the same by inferring, "Those caught up by the cares of this life will be left behind" (Lu. 21:34-36). Again you could say it this way, "If you are not living for, therefore looking for Jesus, He is not coming back for you."

The application is seen with the wicked servant who was caught up with the cares of this/his life. Loving his life and this world was precisely the problem for him, and for many more today. This lead them to think, "My Master is delayed (Matt. 24:48), therefore I will do whatever I like." Like in the days of Noah and Lot, the wicked servant was self-consumed, eating and drinking (loving materialism). The same was seen in Luke's account of chapter twelve (vv. 35-48), and by no coincidence, it follows the parable of the rich fool (Lu. 12:13-21).

Another thing in common with the above-mentioned parables is the faithless and wicked servant or fool, who confesses to know God, and yet is cut off and cast out (Matt. 24:51, 25:12, cf. Lu. 12:20, 47, 19:27). Other parables worth considering are:

- Parable of the Weeds - Matthew 13:24-30
- Parable of the Fishing Net - Matthew 13:47-50
- Parable of the Unmerciful Servant - Matthew 18:23-35
- Parable of the Two Sons - Matthew 21:28-32
- Parable of the Tenants - Matthew 21:33-46
- Parable of the Wedding Banquet - Matthew 22:1-14
- Parable of the Talents - Matthew 25:14-30

- Traveling Owner of the House - Mark 13:34-37
- Wise and Foolish Builders - Luke 6:46-49
- Unfruitful Fig Tree - Luke 13:6-9
- Parable of the Great Banquet - Luke 14:16-24
- Parable of the Lost Son - Luke 15:11-32
- Parable of the Shrewd Manager - Luke 16:1-12
- Parable of the Good Shepherd - John 10: 1-5 and 11-18

In common with each of the listed parables is two types, the faithful and faithless, the wise and the foolish, the true and the false, the sheep and the goats, blended and compared, judged, and destined for two opposing outcomes. On each occasion, the one lacking thought they were right with God, deceived into a false sense of security. Here, hyper-grace teaching and the doctrine of 'once saved always saved' comes into question and are under fire. Each of the seven churches addressed in John's revelation (Rev. 2-3) is also comparable. All represent the people of God, yet some, most, are destined for destruction unless repentance comes first, like with the wicked servant (Matt. 24:51).

Another similarity with the parable of the wicked servant (Matt. 24:45-51), like with the wicked people of Noah's day (Matt. 24:37–39), is that he was unaware of the sudden coming judgment (Matt. 24:50). But the judgement will come, and he will be dealt with as Jesus will deal with all hypocrites (Matt. 24:51). A hypocrite is precisely what an unfaithful servant is. While claiming to be a servant of God, the pretender seeks only his/her own interests. For his/her self-serving wickedness, and departure from the true gospel, it will result in eternal judgement (weeping and gnashing of teeth (cf. Matt. 13:42); eternally separated from 'their' Master.

When considering the warnings given through each of the listed parables and the threats to the failing five churches of the book of Revelation, the biblical Jesus who is warning and making threats is nothing close to resembling what many proclaim and present Him to be today. Today, many live for themselves (and not for Christ) due to having departed from the gospel - they are deceived into accepting another Jesus, declared through a different gospel (2 Cor. 11:4, Gal. 1:6). The 'other Jesus' is one better suited to their self-serving interests (cf. Ex. 32). The different gospel distorts the true gospel of Christ (Gal. 1:8), replacing it with 'man's version of the gospel' (Gal. 1:11), crafting something entirely different from what is intended.

An example of creating a self-serving version of the gospel, and Jesus is where, some time ago, I briefly worked with a ministry that used Matthew, chapter twenty-five (vv. 33-40). This was to encourage people to give, blended with other verses taken out of context (i.e., Matt. 13:8). In doing so, that ministry deliberately avoided the introductory verses of Matthew, chapter twenty-five (vv. 31-33), and the concluding verses (vv. 41-46). In fact, in the prepared script there were the words, STOP READING, after verse forty. This approach to handling scripture is called, 'editing the Bible;' the proclaimer manipulates and mishandles God's Word by cutting and pasting, chopping, and changing parts whenever and wherever it suits. By doing this, the context is then ignored - therefore the meaning or application is changed and lost.

Like the parables above, Matthew, chapter twenty-five (vv. 31-45) speaks of the final judgement, with a strong warning to those not living and looking for Jesus, the biblical Jesus, in preparation for His return (v. 46). Again, as mentioned earlier, the saddest and most frightening common theme of all the parables mentioned is where the wicked, or fool, thought they were right with God. However, Matthew, chapter twenty-five, among other passages, confirms in verse forty-four that many thinking they belong to God do not (cf. Matt. 7:21-23).

Throughout the parables and the letters to the seven churches, the warnings and threats of Christ serve to keep the confessing follower of Jesus Christ focused and faithful. That is living, looking, and longing for Jesus and not living for themselves. Here, the reader should be reminded of the words of Jesus, "When the Son of Man comes, will He find faith on earth?" (Lu. 18:8b). The words are designed to motivate faithfulness. Therefore preparedness, to be awake, to be watching, and thus to be ready. Through the parables, and every other eschatological passage and book, we have been forewarned of what must happen soon (Rev. 1:1, cf. Amos 3:7). Yet few have ears to hear what they need to hear, only desiring to listen to what they want to hear (2 Tim. 4:3). By doing so, they fulfill biblical prophecy, having been distracted and derailed by the things of this world (cf. 2 Thess. 2:3). The distraction comes through the love of self and materialism - a significant end-time sign, leading into the tribulation. As the days of Noah and Lot were, so will it be for this generation, just as predicted.

*Remember Lot's wife... (Lu. 17:32). Come out of the world, and worldly religion (Rev. 18:4) and do not look back!

The Love of Many Will Grow Cold
'Endure Until the End'
(Matt. 24:12)

Following on from the last section, addressing faithfulness versus faithlessness, another prominent end time sign is lawlessness. Leading into, and during the time of trouble, the love of many will grow cold because of lawlessness. While verse twelve contextually applies to the tribulation, confirmed by the words "Then" (Matt. 24:9), representing a shift, after this time, the reason many find themselves in the tribulation is a result of lawlessness.

At the end of the tribulation, the lawless will be dealt with by Jesus, who sends His angels out to gather them up (Mk. 13:41). The lawless will stand before Jesus on judgement day, believing to be saved, only to realise, to their shock and horror, the Jesus they accepted and followed was not the biblical one (cf. 2 Cor. 11:4); for the biblical Christ, "Never knew them" (Matt. 7:21-23). Lawlessness was the reason Jesus 'did not know them' (Lu. 6:46).

According to Jesus, most confessing to follow Him never knew Him, and He, them (Matt. 7:21-23). However, plenty more did know Jesus and did not remain due to worldly distractions and or persecution. Contextually, lawlessness and persecution are a repetitive theme throughout the tribulation (Matt. 24:9-10, 12, Mk. 13:9-13, Lu. 21:12-19, Jn. 16:2). Through persecution, the love of many will grow cold, repeating what happened in the days of Antiochus (Dan. 8, 11). When Antiochus set himself up as the ruling king in Jerusalem, he changed the law, forbidding Jews from practicing Judaism instead, instructed them to erect and worship Greek gods and bring a pig to the temple to be sacrificed. Those refusing either fled or lost their lives. Many, failing to endure and remain faithful, submitted to lawlessness through the lawless one, Antiochus (type of antichrist), to save their lives and lifestyles.

Subsequently, as the faithless defector turned away from God, they then turned on the faithful. As their lawlessness increased their love for God decreased, having grown cold (lit. snuffed out). The lesson learned from the days of Antiochus is when persecution comes, unless the persecuted are prepared, even the once most radical proclaimer of God can quickly fade away, culturally falling into line and swept up along with the worldly flow (narrative).

For the reason stated above, Jesus warned, in the last days, the love of many will grow cold. The original language of Matthew's recorded words of Jesus state, "The love of many will grow cool and go cold," relating to the image of a fire losing its heat and going out. In literal terms, the fire is 'extinguished' or 'snuffed out.' The once red-hot fire loses its heat due to a lack of fuel. **The loss of fire causes even the professor of Christ to persecute their believing brothers, all the while thinking they are doing God's work (cf. Jn. 16:2)**

As mentioned above, persecution is a factor that leads to the love of many growing cold; it is evident now, and it will increase until Jesus returns (Matt. 24:14).

However, on the flip side, through the coming intensified persecution, the gospel will spread like wildfire throughout the world (Matt. 24:14a). Persecution will test and separate one from the other. While the fire of many will go out, the flame of others will be fanned up (2 Tim. 1:6). The same occurred during the first century, as recorded in the book of Acts. The believers then were persecuted and scattered, spreading the gospel wherever they went (Acts 8:1, 4). Without persecution, the gospel would not have expanded the way it did. Persecution was also accompanied by the Holy Spirit's power seen throughout the book of Acts. While many today say, "I want to be a book of Acts church," persecution best defines and describes what it was and is to be a book of Acts church.

In the first century, how the church started will be how it ends in the twenty-first century, prophesied by Jesus (Matt. 24:9-10, 12, Mk. 13:9-13, Lu. 21:12-19, Jn. 16:2). Many today have said, "We are the twenty-ninth chapter of the book of Acts." That being the case, persecution will return, accompanied by Holy Spirit power. As prophesied by Peter (Acts 2:17-18), revival will result in the tribulation (Acts 2:19-21).

Again, as mentioned above, due to increasing persecution, many will fall away, which is why Jesus said, "But the one who endures to the end will be saved" (Matt. 14:14b). While the quoted verse relates to the tribulation, it repeats the same, referring to the days before and leading into the tribulation (Matt. 10:22). Like with the second quote (Matt. 24:14b), the first (Matt. 10:22) falls within the context of persecution (Matt. 10:16-23). Note verse twenty-three, where Jesus states persecution will continue for His faithful followers until He comes. Verse twenty-four states the followers of Jesus will receive the same treatment He did, confirming they are indeed His disciples.

All true disciples of Christ can expect to suffer persecution (cf. Jn. 17:20), not prosperity, as some falsely claim. Jesus reveals those persecutors will be family members (Matt. 10:21) and they will be from the synagogues (Matt. 10:17), dragging the persecuted before the courts, governors, and kings (Matt. 10:18). The household of God will be maligned by those claiming to know God (Matt. 10:25), which spreads the gospel further and faster.

*Note that the persecutors are aligned with the world, contrary to the persecuted who resist wordiness and rebuke false worldly teachers in the church. Through first-century persecution, the gospel spread like wildfire. As recorded in the book of Acts (8:1, 4), Jesus said, persecution will spread the gospel in the same manner until He comes (Matt. 10:18, 23b, 24:14b).

Contrary to the popular prosperity message proclaimed today, persecution for the faithful follower of Christ is promised (cf. Jn. 16:33). Those living for 'Their Best Life Now' will go to great lengths to maintain it, and they will quickly fall away when persecution comes. Again, this is why Jesus said, "Those who endure (not enjoy) until the end, shall be saved" (Matt. 10:22, 24:13). You could say it this way, "ONLY those, and those ALONE who endure until the end, will be saved," which is why Jesus addressed five of the seven churches in the book of Revelation with a commendation or command to endure (Rev. 2:2, 2:10, 2:13, 2:19, 25, 3:10). The common problem within the seven churches was false worship. While the remnant resisted it, which resulted in persecution, the majority incorporated it.

Persecution follows faithfulness to God and His Word. John introduced the revelation (revealing or unveiling) of Jesus Christ (Rev. 1:1) to the churches by addressing the same shared experience of enduring persecution (Rev. 1:9). As mentioned above, persecution for the faithful follower of Jesus Christ is the promise and should be the expectation; it is the reality of both sides of the tribulation. Those who do not endure this side (Matt. 10:22) will have another opportunity to endure on that side (Matt. 24:14, Rev. 13:10, 14:12).

Again, all the seven churches were commanded to endure, (Rev. 2-3). However, a remnant was commended because of their endurance and was explicitly encouraged to do so (Rev. 2:2, 10, 13, 2:24-25, 3:4, 10) until the end. The general message to all seven churches, and us, therefore, is to endure by conquering or overcoming the world and by remaining in an overcoming state until Jesus returns (Rev. 2:7, 11, 17, 26, 3:5, 12, 21).

Interestingly, the only churches doing well, being commended without rebuke, were persecuted churches, suffering persecution from those claiming to be Jews (Rev. 2:9, 3:9). The seven churches represent the CHURCH throughout the age, sharing the same collective conditions, both good and bad. Both then and now, Jesus' warning to the church is to repent (overcome) and or remain faithful by holding fast until He comes (rapture), or else!

The threat of 'Or else' contains tribulation language and is always significant for salvation. For the best part, the threat or warning for the five failing churches (70%) results from false worship linked to worldliness. The most obvious churches imitating this world are Sardis (Rev. 3:1-6) and Laodicea (Rev. 3:14-22). Sardis had a reputation of being alive but was (spiritually) dead (Rev. 3:1), while Laodicea was a prosperity-driven church, consumed with and by worldliness, yet void of Christ. (Rev. 3:16-17). Both churches imitated this world, being so full of it they could not be distinguished apart from it.

For this reason, Sardis was in danger of being left behind (Rev. 3:3), and Laodicea was in danger of being vomited out (Rev. 3:16). The reference to being vomited out is linked to another, found in the book of Leviticus (Lev. 18:25, 28), where God warned Israel, if they did what the surrounding nations did, then He would vomit them out of the Promised Land. The same application applies to the church of Laodicea, meaning God would vomit them out before reaching the Promised Land (heaven), thereby vomiting them into the great tribulation. Laodicea would be vomited into the tribulation because of missing the rapture. That exact threat was made to the church of Thyatira (Rev. 2:22). Compare the threat with the promise made to the church of Philadelphia (Rev. 3:10).

Contrary to the churches of Sardis and Laodicea, a lesser example of worldliness is seen with the church of Ephesus, who received what started, and ended with a glowing report for patiently enduring against and testing false teachers (Rev. 2:2-3, 6). However, their love had grown cold. The order of words in Greek is forceful; translated, "Your first love you have left." Jesus used the word agapēn, applying the unconditional, unwavering kind of love that God has for His people. Unless the members of the church of Ephesus repent, Jesus threatened to remove their candlestick.

As mentioned earlier, love growing cold is like a fire being snuffed out or extinguished. Around thirty years earlier, Paul praised the church of Ephesus for their agapēn (love) for the saints (Eph. 1:15-16). Yet Jesus warned them, "Remember therefore from where you have fallen, repent, repent and do the works you did at first" (Rev. 2:5). Jesus warned the church if they did not repent, the light of their witness (testimony) would be extinguished (Rev. 2:5). If Jesus removed or extinguished their lampstand, the church of Ephesus would no longer be counted among the seven (Rev. 1:4, 11, 12, 20).

The lampstand refers to their witness and testimony of Christ (cf. Rev. 11:3-7, 10, cf. Zech. 4). No testimony results in no salvation (cf. Rev. 12:11). Remember, Israel was also called to be a light-bearer (Isa. 42:6–7; 49:6), yet their fire for God went out; that is, their love grew cold, they lost their first love, and were temporarily put aside (Rom. 11). Israel is temporarily put aside until they repent (Matt. 23:39), which a remnant will do through the tribulation (Rom. 11:25b-27). Here, the church should not be deceived, if she does what Israel did, God will treat her the same way (Rom. 11:22). Like Israel, any from the church left behind, caught like a trap (Lu. 21:34) in the tribulation will have another opportunity to respond during that time, or else perish eternally, that is, be snuffed out (cf. Prov. 13:9, 24:20), or blotted out (Ps. 9:5 cf. Rev. 3:5).

An important note: The lampstand carries oil, which fuels the fire. No fuel, no fire. The oil is representative of the Holy Spirit (Rev. 1:4). While the church of Ephesus was doing well in works (Rev. 2:1-3), their lamp had run dry, lacking oil, therefore fire, symbolic of the Spirit and relationship - thus they were in danger of judgement. Remember the Ten Virgins (Matt. 25:1-13), where five did not have oil, and therefore were shut out when the Groom (Jesus) returned (Matt. 25:10b). Those who were ready went with Jesus (Matt. 25:10a).

The above statement is made clear when comparing the words of Jesus to the church of Ephesus, "I will come" (Rev. 2:5), against the repeated threat to the church of Sardis (Rev. 3:3). Jesus' warning to Sardis refers to His coming, 'by way of the rapture' (like a thief in the night, Matt. 24:43,

1 Thess. 5:2, 2 Pet. 3:10, Rev. 3:3), leaving those not ready behind, contrary to those ready who will escape (Rev. 3:10). The same is seen with the church of Pergamum, threatening tribulation judgement (Rev. 2:16). For those prepared, John's record confirms they will go with Christ when He comes, "And if I go and prepare a place for you, I will come again and will take you to myself, that where I am you may be also" (Jn. 14:3, cf. Acts 1:11).

On the condition that the church of Ephesus does repent by returning to their first love, their lampstand will remain; it will not be removed (cf. Matt. 13:12, 25:29). Due to being faithful, they will be given more, which is the right to eat from the tree of life in the paradise of God (Rev. 2:7). The tree of life is first mentioned in Genesis (3:22), in the Garden of Eden. Later it reappears in the New Jerusalem, where it bears abundant fruit (Rev. 22:2). Those who eat of it will never die (Gen. 3:22). Those who do not have access to it will die. Those who perish in their sin die physically and spiritually, for all eternity. Eternal death refers to everlasting, never-ending suffering (Mk. 9:42-50, Rev. 14:11, 20:10).

Again, the reason most will not have access to the paradise of God is due to lawlessness. The Greek word for lawlessness is ánomos, which means 'without the law,' or 'against the rules,' seen through hyper and perverted grace teachings (cf. Jude). Jezebel, the harlot leader in the church Thyatira (Rev. 2:20), was an antinomian. Antinomian groups always object to following any rules. Jezebel taught her followers that it did not matter what they ate or who they slept with, or even if they denied Christ when arrested by the Romans and faced execution, thereby failing to endure until the end. Antinomian groups also include the Nicolaitans, whom the church of Ephesus rejected (Rev. 2:6). The Nicolaitans were also rejected by the faithful remnant within the church of Pergamum (Rev. 2:15). Famous within the church of Pergamum, was Antipas, whose name means, 'against all.'

While the Nicolaitan's were against the law of God, Antipas was against their false teaching, which cost him his life (Rev. 2:13).

Lawlessness is a cause of love growing cold, leading to more lawlessness (Rom. 6:19b), which conditions the heart and prepares the way for the lawless one (2 Thess. 2:3b). Lawlessness also refers to rejecting God by trading His truth for lies (cf. 2 Thess. 3-11). Like Antiochus, the antichrist will do the same, changing the Laws of God (Dan. 7:25). Even now, the mystery of lawlessness is at work (2 Thess. 2:7), in the church, changing the laws (e.g., blessing abortion clinics, and same-sex relationships, and universalism. All roads lead to the same place, you can do whatever you like, it will be alright) leading multitudes into apostasy (2 Thess. 2:3a).

John states that those who practice (perfect) sinning make a practice of lawlessness (1 Jn. 3:4). As lawlessness increases, love (of and for God) decreases. One gives way to the other. Those practicing lawlessness are called hypocrites by Jesus (Matt. 23:28, cf. 2 Cor. 6:14); they will not enter His eternal rest (Matt. 7:23). However, in the case of the church of Ephesus, they were not lawless; instead, they lacked love. The lack of love for God and others resulted in their fire being in danger of going out (being snuffed out) connected with their candlestick being removed. The requirement was to repent and be restored regarding their relationship with God. They were to put Jesus first, above everything else, that everything else would flow from being in the right relationship with God.

Prayer, producing (Holy Spirit) oil, is the remedy. Prayer maintains a relationship with God through Christ, guarding the prayerful saint against worldliness and dead religious works. Jesus' concluding statement in Luke's record of the Olivet Discord confirms that prayer is the key to staying awake and escaping the tribulation (Lu. 21:36). Prayer, mixed with keeping God's uncompromised Word (Law), is essential to be saved from the hour of trial that is coming on the whole world to try those who dwell on the earth (Rev. 3:10). Remember, only those who endure until the end (not part of the way, or even most of the way) shall be saved. The rest will be tested through the tribulation fire. Those failing to repent will perish eternally, just like in the days of Noah and Lot.

False Peace
'Spoken of by the Prophet Daniel'
(Matt. 24:15)

As a reminder, following Jesus' prediction of the destruction of the temple (Matt. 24:2), He was privately asked, "When will the signs be, and what will be the sign of your coming" (Matt. 24:3). 'When,' and 'what' were the questions asked. Before answering the 'what' question, Jesus first answered the 'when' by listing the signs of the time. However, we have responded to the 'when' question first due to the 'when' sign being fulfilled already.

The 'when' question relates to the reformation or rebirth of Israel in 1948. The sign of Israel's rebirth commenced, or at least made visible, the prophetic biblical timeclock (cf. Isa. 66:8, Ezek. 37:21-22, Matt. 24:32-35). From the day Israel became a nation again, the biblical time clock commenced its visible countdown, for Jesus said the generation that sees the rebirth of Israel would also see the return of Jesus Christ (Mat. 24:32-35). Israel was reborn seventy-three years ago; therefore, the youngest living person today witnessing the nation's rebirth is seventy-three years old. The average person lives between seventy and eighty years (Ps. 90:10). Whichever way you interpret the word 'generation,' time is very, very short.

Following the 'When' question, the 'What' question has been covered, so far addressing the following signs as topics, including the rebirth of Israel:

1. Rebirth of Israel (Matt. 24:32-34)
2. Led astray / falling away (Matt. 24:4-5, 23-26)
3. Wars, Famine, and Pestilences (Matt. 24:7 (KJV) (cf. Lu. 21:11)
4. Earthquakes (Matt. 24:7)
5. Days of Noah (Matt. 24:37)
6. Days of Lot - Homosexuality (Matt. 24:38, Lu. 17:20-37)
7. Drunkenness (Matt. 24:38, 49)
8. Faithfulness Vs. Faithlessness (Matt. 24:45-51)
9. Love growing cold (Matt. 24:12)

As mentioned at the beginning of this series and seen throughout all the above-listed topics, deception is the number one sign of the end times. It is closely followed by, or connected to, the love of money and or materialism. The love of money (1 Tim. 6:9-10) and the love of this world (2 Jn. 2:15-16) is another reason why the prosperity 'gospel' is so dangerous. The Prosperity' gospel' claims to offer everything you ever wanted, which is essentially everything lost at the Fall (Gen. 3), that can only be regained after Jesus Christ returns, not and never as some suggest.

The prosperity 'gospel' majors on three things; 1). Health, 2). Wealth, and 3). Happiness. In other words, Peace. Perfect peace where nothing is missing and nothing is broken. The charismatic camp misuses the Greek word 'Sozo,' promoted as the 'complete package of salvation to support this false teaching,' The term 'sozo' is used in verses relating to being saved, healed, and delivered. Yet in no way does any of the passages where used, contextually promise what the charismatics claim; that being, everything lost through the Fall has been regained, resulting in 'Your Best Life Now.'

In confirmation that the word 'Sozo' does not imply salvation, believers in Christ, this side of His return, are to expect divine health, wealth, and happiness, the same word (Sozo) is used by Jesus when warning those who try to save (Sozo) their lives, that in doing so, they will lose it (Matt. 16:25).

The theme of that passage (Matt. 16:24-28), and many more, run in the opposite direction to what charismatics teach. For example, the referenced verse (Matt. 16:25), in the context of the passage, commands the believer to take up their cross (die to self and this world) to follow Jesus. The image of taking up the cross to follow Jesus should be compared with Jesus carrying His cross to Calvary. When Jesus carried that cross, He was bruised, bloodied, battered, and broken. He was essentially a 'dead man', walking on a narrow and difficult path (Matt. 7:13-14). Jesus was dead to self and dead to this world, yet He was fully alive unto God. Death to self and death to this world is required of every believer to gain life in the next. Count the cost!

As mentioned above, the charismatic camp claims Sozo salvation,' implying, even demanding, absolute health, wealth, and happiness, that is, nothing missing, and broken. However, as mentioned above, the Bible provides no such promise and no such guarantee.

Again, the Bible teaches the opposite of what the Word of Faith camp does. For instance, perfect health, this side of the Messianic Kingdom, is never absolute. God heals but does not necessarily heal absolutely. If He did, all in Christ would be physically restored. Scripture confirms that Epaphroditus nearly died (Phil. 2:30), Paul had a problem with his eyes (Gal. 4:13), and Timothy had a problem with his stomach (1 Tim. 5:23). Paul's co-worker, Trophimus, was left sick (2 Tim 4:20), and although Old Testament, Elisha, was the great miracle worker, he died from illness (2 Kings 13:14, 20).

The same is true regarding wealth. The prosperity gospel claims God will give you an abundance of whatever you ask (a better job, a bigger house, a faster car, etc.). However, the Bible promises prosperity for purpose. God will supply your 'need' in accordance with His calling (Phil. 4:19; Matt. 6:25-34), not your self-centred greed or fleshly desire. Not even if, and no matter how much, you 'command and demand it or declare and decree it.' Those taking this approach treat the Bible as a book of spells, and treat God like an ATM or a genie in a bottle. In sum, they command God to serve them rather than serve Him.

Effectively, the root of the prosperity 'gospel' is an idol of the heart (Ezek. 14:1-11). Modern-day idols are fleshly desires which can quickly lead us astray (Mk. 4:19; 2 Pet. 1:4b). Unsurprisingly, Scripture has plenty to say about those who preach and chase after prosperity (for example, 2 Cor. 2:17; 1 Tim. 6:3-10, 3:3b; Jude 11b). Scripture clearly states not to toil to acquire wealth (Prov. 23:4; 28:20), neither desire it, love it or put your trust in it (Matt. 6:19; 1 Tim. 6:9-10; Heb. 13:5).

As with false promises of health and wealth, the fabricated promise of happiness also goes against the teaching of the Bible. Ecclesiastes (9:2-3a), Luke (13:1-5), and Matthew (5:45) reveal that all are subject to good and evil while living in a world compromised by sin (Rom. 8:19-22). Peter has plenty to say on the matter of the suffering believer (1 Peter), confirmed by James (1:2), John (16:33), and Luke in the book of Acts (14:22), to list but a few.

The Bible tells us that sinful man yearns for money, pleasure, security, significance, health, food, self-righteousness, worth, power, knowledge, and happiness - every sort of blessing squandered at the Fall. Yet, God's children should look to, long for, and thirst after Him alone (Ps. 42, Lu. 11:9-13).

The importance of reiterating the above-mentioned notes at this point is that leading into the tribulation and during the tribulation, many false teachers and even false Christs will lead multitudes astray (Matt. 25:5, 11, 15, 23-26). False teachers and false Christs always come promoting self-help, packaged with a promise of peace and prosperity, in the same way Satan did with Jesus (Matt. 4:8-9), at a cost, of course. The price for exchanging the truth for a lie is your eternal soul (Rom. 1:18-32, 2 Thess. 2:11-12, cf. Rev. 14:9-11).

On this side of the tribulation, false teachers actively condition and prepare the deceived for the ultimate false teacher of them all, the antichrist. God sends the antichrist (the strong delusion) to those failing and refusing to love the truth (cf. 1 Tim. 4:1, 2 Tim. 4:3), who believe what was false and take pleasure in unrighteousness (2 Thess. 2:11-12).

Again, the top end time sign is deception, wrapped in the empty promise of peace and prosperity. The spirit of the antichrist promoting peace and prosperity is active within the church today, leading many astray. Those led astray by being caught up in the things of this world will remain in it after the church has been removed (Lu. 21:34-36). When the antichrist arrives on the scene, it will only be after the world rejecting church is first removed (2 Thess. 6-8, cf. Lu. 21:36, Rom. 5:9, 1 Cor. 15:51-52, 1 Thess. 4:16-17, 1:10, 5:9, Rev. 3:10, 4:1). Once the church has been removed, only then will the antichrist be revealed (2 Thess. 6-8) and only revealed to those with eyes to see and ears to hear; however, that revelation will come at a high cost (Dan. 11:33-35, Matt. 24:9-10). Having failed to count the cost and endure (Matt. 10:22) this side of the tribulation (Lu. 14:25-33), by taking up the cross and following Jesus (Matt. 16:24-25), the left behind will have another opportunity to endure (Matt. 24:13) in the tribulation (Rev. 12:11, 13:10, 14:12).

When the church has been removed, the antichrist will be exposed. He will be revealed in the tribulation through the signing of the false peace treaty (Dan. 9:27, Isa. 28:15, 18), repeating the deeds of Antiochus (Dan. 11). Antiochus was a deceitful man speaking words of peace while secretly planning evil. Those deceived will be so as a result of their own pride, as it was for Edom (Obed. 1:3-7), which is not dissimilar to the church of Laodicea (Rev. 3:17). Edom was deceived first by pride and then delivered to those claiming to be their allies. Those destroyed by the antichrist during the tribulation will be first deceived by the deceptive antichrist, and then delivered and destroyed by those not claiming to be foes but friends.

In sum, during the tribulation, the 'awake' will be turned on first by the antichrist (Dan. 11:32) and then by those following the antichrist (Dan. 11:34). Those following the antichrist may even think that they are doing God's work by killing the true and faithful followers of Christ (Jn. 16:2).

Again, the most significant end-time sign is the deception, wrapped in a false proclamation of peace while in a time of judgment, which is a case of history repeating itself (cf. Ezek. 13:10). Like Ezekiel, Jeremiah suffered the same false teachers, religious leaders, and false prophets declaring everything was well between God and Israel. "Peace, peace," they said, when there was no peace, instead the people of God were in great danger at the hand of God (Jer. 6:14, 8:11, 14:13, 23:17).

The same condition of deception is repetitive today and is the fulfilment of prophecy. Paul said, "For you, yourselves are fully aware that the day of the Lord will come like a thief in the night. While people are saying, 'There is peace and security,' then sudden destruction will come upon them as labour pains come upon a pregnant woman, and they will not escape" (1 Thess. 5:2-3, cf. Jer. 4:31, 6:24, Lam. 1:17, 2:21, Matt. 24:43, Lu. 21:34, Rev. 3:3). The book of Lamentations (3:1-18, 37-54, and 5:16-22) provides insight into how the warned, yet judged, responded, and will respond again.

Through the book of Lamentations, Jeremiah addressed Judah, who failed to hear God's many warnings over some forty years. Due to not having ears to hear (like many within the church today), the very thing their false prophets said would not happen, did happen, and will again soon to this generation. The same warning was given to the church of Sardis (Rev. 3:1-6) and is seen at the close of Luke's account of the Olivet Discord (Lu. 21:34-36). Paul's summary of Christ's return should also be considered over chapters four and five of his letter to the church of Thessalonica (1 Thess. 4 & 5). Chapter four refers to the rapture, and chapter five refers to the tribulation and return of Christ after the seven-year event.

Again, the church is removed before the tribulation (1 Thess. 4:16-17, 5:9), leaving the rest behind. Therefore, those asleep and left behind (Matt. 24:43-44) will be subject to further and increasing deception in the tribulation by the coming antichrist, proclaiming, "Peace and security" (prosperity). However, multitudes will wake up in the tribulation due to missing the rapture and then recognising the antichrist through signing the peace treaty. On the realisation of being left behind, "Men will faint from fear and anxiety over what is coming upon the earth" (Lu. 21:26), while others fully embrace the deception of peace, peace, and prosperity.

Those rejecting the antichrist will be targeted, persecuted, and even put to death (Rev. 13:10). Countless millions will lose their lives in the tribulation, having failed to take up their cross on this side. Persecution, not prosperity, of the saints is the identifying mark of the faithful follower of Christ, and it will be a continual, increasing theme throughout the tribulation. During the tribulation, the chief persecutor of the saints will be easily identified as the antichrist (Rev. 11:7, 13:7).

During the tribulation, the false promise of prosperity, or 'kingdom now' teaching, will be fully realised by those killed, slain by the biggest promotor of that lie, the antichrist. The tribulation slain saints then rejecting prosperity were once among those embracing and chasing after it this side of the tribulation. In the same way, Satan deceived Eve in the Garden (Gen. 3) and attempted to deceive Jesus with the false promise of prosperity, his son of perdition, the antichrist (2 Thess. 2:3), is doing and will continue to do likewise.

Like father, like son, the antichrist spirit has been actively deceiving millions within the church with the false prosperity gospel until this today (2 Thess. 2:9, cf. 1 Jn. 4:3). He will continue to deceive, even escalating in deception through lying signs and wonders (2 Thess. 2:7-10), until the church is removed, leaving the deceived, behind.

Those deceived by the spirit of the antichrist will be left behind, waking up in the tribulation to face the antichrist. This is the reason Jesus warned the churches to repent or else (Rev. 2-3). The forthcoming event will be as Daniel proclaimed (Matt. 24:15). But before the antichrist announces himself to be God from the rebuilt tribulation temple (2 Thess. 2:4), he will deceive most through a false covenant of peace and prosperity, just like Antiochus did. (Dan. 11:32).

Remember, the antichrist is the rider of the white horse having a bow, with invisible arrows of deception, to conquer (Rev. 6:2). To inherit the reward (salvation), the seven churches were told they must first conquer this world (Rev. 2-3). The issue with each of the five failing churches was that the world was conquering them. We either conquer this world by coming out of it and rejecting it, or the world conquers us by imitating it, through the false promise and deception of worldly peace and prosperity.

Consider this: The peace Jesus gives His followers is not the peace the world gives (Jn. 14:27). The context of Jesus' words relates to being left in a world of trouble yet knowing He will return for His own. Maranatha!

'Commencement of the Tribulation'

(Matt. 24:9-14)

Once the tribulation has commenced, persecution of the left behind saints and the Jews will be a significant sign, hated by nations for Jesus' name (Matt 24:9, cf. Mk. 13:13), even betrayed by family members (cf. Mk. 13:12). During that time, many will fall away (Matt. 24:10). False prophets will increase, leading many more astray. Lawlessness will also increase and the love of many will grow cold (Matt. 24:12). Nevertheless, through these hardships the gospel will be preached throughout the whole world, continuing until the end (Matt. 24:14).

Great Oppression
'A Scandalous Satanic Strategy'
(Matt. 24:21)

For at that time, there will be a great tribulation (pressure, distress, oppression), such as has not occurred since the beginning of the world until now, nor ever will [again] (Matt. 24:21, AMP)

Many (most) will be deceived by a false proclamation of peace, peace, and prosperity. They will be tricked into believing the worldly narrative (If you just do this, then everything will return to normal, selling fear for freedom), but those resisting that lie will be targeted and subject to oppression. Oppression is a significant end times sign, leading to tribulation. While in the tribulation, oppression will increase significantly, causing many to fall away from the One (Jesus) they should be trusting (Matt. 24:10). Instead of trusting Jesus, most will submit, whether willingly or through coercion, to the rulers of this world, namely Satan, through the antichrist.

Even now, through forced 'vaccinations,' we see the evidence of the things to come. The current narrative will lead most into the tribulation and will even continue to deceive the majority when there. Most have already fallen under Satan's spell, consumed by fear, giving up what little freedoms they have left, including sovereignty over their own bodies. The deceived have been conditioned to receive the Mark of the Beast (666). From the time the Mark of the Beast is enforced, there will be 'great tribulation' (Matt. 24:21), also translating, 'great oppression.'

Once the tribulation commences, many will faint with fear from the expectation of what is coming on the earth (Lu. 21:26). Many left behind and caught like a trap (Lu. 21:34) in the tribulation will have some (albeit limited) understanding of what has happened. Many churchgoers will be counted among the left behind, having little knowledge of the tribulation due to attending weak churches, false doctrine, and where pastors refuse to preach repentance in preparation for the return of Christ. Although limited in their understanding, those left behind may still have some insight, perhaps gained from a fictional means, such as Tim Lahaye's Left Behind series. Those with some understanding may then also be motivated, if not forced to investigate Bible prophecy for themselves, leading to either salvation or falling away completely.

During the tribulation, many will fall away entirely after counting the actual cost of salvation (cf. Lu. 14:28), being the road of the cross (Matt. 16:24), on the narrow and difficult path (Matt. 7:13-14). The purpose of the tribulation is to wake the left behind up, to shake, test, and separate them, one from the other, separating the goats from the sheep (Matt. 25:31-46), resulting in conflict and division (cf. Matt. 10:34-36).

One of the increasing signs of the tribulation is division (Matt. 24:9). The divide will cause those siding with the world to turn on those now following Jesus (Matt. 24:9-10). As mentioned earlier, due to intense coercion and persecution, many, (the majority), realising they have been left behind, will fall away from God altogether (Matt. 24:10). Many, even at one point, confessing Christ, will fall away (cf. Matt. 13:1-9, 18-23), failing to endure unto the end (Matt. 24:13).

The Greek word translated to English 'fall away' is 'Skandalon,' also meaning 'to stumble, and or 'to cause to sin' and 'to take offense.' From the Greek word 'Skandalon' we get the English word 'scandal.' The definition of Skandalon is a stick-bait, or bait-stick (a trap), literally used as a snare, to cause to fall (through sin, or take offense, therefore, sin).

In sum, a scandal (Skandalon) is carefully designed and set to trap the unsuspecting victims. The biblical application of the scandal (Skandalon) is to lead many (most) away/astray by causing them to stumble and or causing them to take offense, resulting in sin (Matt. 24:10). An example of this is seen with the church of Pergamum, who Jesus addressed, and accused of being baited by false teachers. The church members had taken the bait, causing them to stumble into sin. The English word 'stumble' is also translated from the Greek word, 'Skandalon' (Rev. 2:14). The same word is used many times throughout the New Testament referring to all forms of offense, such as where a body part causes you to sin, cut it off (Mk. 5:29-30), or for the one who is not securely rooted in Christ, they fall away (Matt. 13:21). The word is used for those offended by the teaching of Jesus (Matt. 15:12) and for those who are not (Matt. 11:6). Also, the word is applied to those attempting to cause Jesus to stumble (Matt. 16:23) or cause others to sin (Matt. 18:6), providing a solid warning for those who do (Matt. 18:7) and the remedy for those who have taken the bait, and stumbled into sin (Matt. 18:8-9).

Using the same Greek word (Skandalon), through the gospel of Matthew, Jesus prewarns those not securely rooted in Him; that when tribulation or persecution comes, they immediately fall away (Matt. 13:21). The great falling away within the church (2 Thess. 2:3) will result mainly from false teachers proclaiming another gospel (do whatever you want), promising 'Your Best Life Now.' Those buying into this 'other gospel' expect something entirely different from what Jesus promised (Jn. 16:33), and therefore, quickly 'fall away' (skandalon) when trouble comes. Offenses can also swiftly come on the realisation of being sold a lie. Still, some will pursue the lie leading them, and others further away from sound biblical doctrine.

Such was the problem within the church of Pergamum. Instead of rejecting the false teaching of Balaam (hyper-grace and prosperity 'gospel'), the church members opened themselves up to all manner of sins, resulting in lawlessness (Rev. 14-15), like with the church of Thyatira (Rev. 2:20-21). Unless repentance came first, Jesus would fight against the members of Pergamum's church with the sword of His mouth (Rev. 2:16). To understand what Jesus fighting against you with the sword of His mouth looks like, refer to Revelation, chapter nineteen (v. 15). As for the church of Thyatira, unless repentance came first, its members would be thrown into the great tribulation (Rev. 2:22). Being thrown into the great tribulation needs no further explanation!

Like with the church members of Pergamum, leading into the tribulation, and throughout the tribulation, many have and will fall away due to lawlessness (Matt. 24:12), that is, failing to obey God's Law. Failing to obey God's Law results in falling away due to following false teachers (Matt. 24:11). As mentioned in the previous sections, false teachers will be, and are, known for promising the opposite for what God is saying. For example, 'Peace, peace, and prosperity instead of proclaiming judgement. During the tribulation, when judgement, not peace, is the reality, many will fall into despair, blinded by a spell of oppression.

Again, the afflicted will be the deceived who were expecting something other than what they will experience in the tribulation. As the verse in the header (Matt. 24:21) suggests, severe oppression, resulting in chronic depression, will be the experience for most during the tribulation. Many, in the tribulation, will be left behind due to being tricked and caused to stumble and sin; because of unconfessed, unrepented sin, they are left behind.

Contrary to the peace, as mentioned earlier and prosperity 'gospel', oppression is nothing new, and certainly not for the faithful follower of Jesus Christ - albeit the modern 'gospel' has replaced oppression with opulence (prosperity). Withing the New Testament (ESV), there are ten verses addressing oppression, nine speak of demonic oppression, and one refers to the oppression of Israel under the Egyptians. Other verses not necessary using the word 'oppression' still use the sentiment of oppression (1 Cor. 15:9, 2 Cor. 5:4, 7:5, Heb. 11:37), speaking of the church being oppressed by the religious or the world. Often the two (the religious and the world) are inseparable.

Remember again, how the church started is how it will end, with persecution being the hallmark of the faithful follower of Christ. Even before the church is removed from this world, via the rapture (Rev. 3:10), persecution will be the experience for the household of God (cf. Rev. 2:9-10). Within the church mentioned above of Pergamum, the faithful remnant were oppressed by the rest (Rev. 2:13). Antipas (meaning against all), the faithful witness, was oppressed and killed because he resisted the false teachings of Balaam (Rev. 2:13). Balaamism is very evident throughout the church today (hyper-grace and prosperity).

As mentioned above, persecution, not prosperity, is the hallmark of every faithful follower of Jesus Christ. In the book of Acts, when the gospel spread throughout the region like wildfire, it was spread through persecution (Acts 8:1-4, 11:19-24). Christian persecution is prophesied to be repeated, leading into the tribulation and to increase throughout the tribulation (Acts 2:17-19, Rev. 7:9-14), resulting in revival. Persecution is a birth pain serving to shake, test, and separate, even on this side of the tribulation, and will cause many to fall away (skandalon). Like now, persecution will test those claiming to follow Christ, separating the faithful from the faithless through trials (Matt. 24:9, Mk. 13:13, Lu. 21:17, cf. Matt 10:22, Jn. 15:18-25).

The now-and-coming persecution will result in great oppression and severe depression for most. Interestingly, oppression is defined in Merriam-Webster dictionary as: 'Unjust or cruel exercise of authority or power especially by the imposition of burdens; the condition of being weighed down; an act of pressing down; a sense of heaviness or obstruction in the body or mind'. This definition demonstrates the intensity of oppression, showing how difficult such a challenge is to resist and overcome. Further, the word oppression comes from the Latin root primere, which means 'pressed down'. Oppression is also the social act of placing severe restrictions on an individual, group, or institution.

Oppression is also used to relate to 'dehumanisation' and 'exploitation'. These are terms that describe unjustness and cruelty. Characteristically, a government that uses and abuses its power to place restrictions, formally or covertly, on groups are guilty of dehumanisation, resulting in oppression. Opposing groups victimised and oppressed through the misuse and abuse of governmental power are often political and religious, causing psychological and physical distress. The psychological impact comes through control through a loss of rights and privileges, discrimination, social exclusion, and alienation, leading to violence—the victim of oppression loses power to the oppressor.

Power can persuade, coerce, command, and control situations and people, against their will. When a government is empowered, it can control resources, using them to reward or punish. The government can also control boundaries and social barriers, restricting who goes where and who says what. In other words, the government controls information and communication. For this reason, power and oppression can mirror reflections of one another where power is misused to control, oppression results. Oppression emerges because of a misuse of power; its roots are founded in globalism and conquests.

Two thousand years ago, when Jesus walked the earth, He also suffered oppression at the hands of an authoritarian and suppressive government and at the hands of the religious (Isa 53:7-8a). Following in the footsteps of Jesus, the church also suffered oppression (Rom. 5:3, 8:17, 18, 36), as did Paul (2 Cor. 3:8b-9). Paul was so severely oppressed - he despaired of life itself.

Solomon experienced something similar, as recorded in Ecclesiastes (4:1-3), "I looked again and saw people being mistreated everywhere on earth. They were crying, but no one was there to offer comfort, and those who mistreated them were powerful. I said to myself, 'The dead are better off than the living. But those who have never been born are better off than anyone else because they have never seen the terrible things that happen on this earth.'"

Furthermore, Peter has plenty to say about oppression (1 Peter, x14), which should be the expectation of every faithful follower of Jesus Christ. As a result of tribulation, many, unprepared, fall away (Matt. 13:21). Although the church will be removed before the tribulation (Rev. 3:10), beforehand, the church will still endure some trouble (1 Pet. 4:17), serving to shake, test, and separate. Remember the words of Jesus, "But all these things are merely the beginning of birth pangs [of the intolerable anguish and the time of unprecedented trouble]" (Matt. 24:8, AMP).

In sum, in the end times, the Bible clearly predicts that many (most) will fall away (Skandalon), either before the tribulation (2 Thess. 2:3), or in it. Most will be tricked and then trapped (Lu. 21:35) and caused to stumble into sin. Many will fall due to great oppression (Matt. 24:21), where the ruling powers force the population into total submission. Some will blindly follow worldly leaders, while others will resist at the cost of their natural lives. However, some resisting will still be out of sorts with Jesus due to their offense (Skandalon) with those who have tricked them, (false teachers and world leaders), resulting in retaliation and violence.

Leading into and throughout the tribulation, governmental oppression is promised and is already a reality. Right now, the whole world is suffering at the hands of abusive governmental controls, coercing, and forcing the population to take an experiential 'vaccination'. World leaders are punishing and oppressing people with penalties who refuse while praising and rewarding those who blindly follow.

An excellent example of this is seen with COVID-19, which has set the stage, where the whole world has come under a demonic spell that has prepared them for the Mark of the Beast (666). Make no mistake about it, the 'plandemic' of COVID-19 and resulting passports is a satanic strategy that has been cleverly crafted, giving governments more powers at the cost of those empowering them, working towards a New World Order. Indeed, a New World Order is here and will soon fully emerge, led by ten kings (Dan. 7:7, 20, 24, Rev. 17:12) and the antichrist, (Dan. 7:7-8, 19-26, 11:36-45, Rev. 13:11-18, 17:7-8, 10-11) lasting just seven years (Rev. 17:10).

Albeit short, the coming tribulation will be the most oppressive time in the history of humankind (Matt. 24:21), where most fall away from God beyond return (Matt, 24:10). Then, following the antichrist's rule, Jesus Christ will return, ruling and reigning for one thousand years (Isa 9:6-7); but before then, believers must endure (Matt. 10:22, 24:13, Rev. 14:12-13). Remember, "The one (only that one) who endures and bears up [under suffering] to the end will be saved" (Matt. 24:13, AMP).

Persecution

'They (the fallen) will Deliver (betray) You Up.'
(Matt. 24:9)

So, you want to be a book of Acts church? To be witnesses for Jesus, operating in the power of the Holy Spirit? While that is a good desire (if it's the right motive), it is mainly misunderstood by those claiming it due to having wrong reasons. Many are motivated to pursue 'power' to promote and prosper themselves and 'their' ministries. Remember, Simon the sorcerer desired the same thing (Acts 8:9-25). However, what is conveniently overlooked is the very thing producing power was perseverance under persecution (Act. 8:1-8).

Therefore, to be a book of Acts church, you must first accept that persecution, not peace and prosperity, is part of the package. Usually, those making the statement mentioned above, who pursue Holy Spirit power through signs and wonders, do not have a theology of suffering. However, power and persecution are never separate in the Bible; one follows the other, which is why we have not seen much power of the Holy Spirit (manifestation of miracles) in the West. Not yet anyway! No persecution, no perseverance, no power!

The opening chapter of Acts makes it clear where Jesus said, "You will receive power (Gk. Dynamis, lit. dynamite) when the Holy Spirit has come upon you, and you will be My witnesses" (Acts 1:8). The Greek word translated into 'witnesses' is also translated 'martyrs,' meaning, in context, "You will be My martyrs."

As mentioned in the previous section, most have failed to understand the narrow and difficult road of the cross. Therefore they fail to count the cost of following the biblical Jesus. For this reason, when tribulation (of any kind) comes, they cannot and will not endure (Matt. 21:13), and thus, they fall away (Matt. 24:10). Again, as mentioned in the previous section, the Greek word for 'fall away' is 'Skandalon.'

On both this side of the tribulation and throughout, persecution is guaranteed. On this side of that seven-year event, persecution is like the beginning of birth pains (Matt. 24:8). During the tribulation, persecution will be a continuous and increasing experience for those resisting the antichrist, which will be a repeat of the days of Antiochus (Dan. 8, 11). Remember, In Matthew's record of the Olivet Discord (chapter 24), the tribulation, with increasing persecution, begins from verse nine. Verses nine to fourteen cover the first half of the tribulation. The second half commences from verse fifteen, where the antichrist announces himself to be God from the rebuilt tribulation temple. The tribulation temple is the third temple (Dan. 9:24-27, 11:31, 12:11, 2 Thess. 2:3-4, Matt. 24:15, Rev. 11:1-2) that will be rebuilt from the signing of the Middle East Peace Treaty (Isa. 28:15, 18., Dan. 7:24-27), causing many to violate their covenant with God (Dan. 11:31-32a).

Once the antichrist claims to be God from the rebuilt temple, all hell will break loose (Dan. 11:32b-45, 12:1). Then, the persecution of the saints will go to a whole new level, like never seen before (Matt. 24:21), and if Jesus does not cut the days short, for the sake of the elect, none would be saved (Matt. 24:16-23). The Greek word for 'saved' is 'Sozo.' Meaning none of God's chosen would be delivered if Jesus had not have returned to set up His rule and reign on the earth.

As mentioned in previous sections, the Greek word 'Sozo' (physical healing and deliverance) does not apply to this side of Jesus' return in the way charismatics claim. Therefore, believers in Christ cannot expect to be absolutely physically healed and delivered from sickness, demonic oppression, and depression, and poverty. Complete salvation, relating to the physical body and even the mind, is not guaranteed this side of the millennium. In fact, during the tribulation, salvation will come at the cost of sacrificing the body and mind (Rev. 12:11). Moreover, on this of Jesus' return, the physical body and mind will deteriorate; it will be destroyed by aging, through sickness, and even through persecution, unto death. As the day draws nearer to Christ's return, persecution will increase, not decrease, contrary to what many claim today, namely subscribers to Kingdom Now' theology.'

As stated, subscribers of 'Kingdom Now' theology (it is not theology; it is poor scholarship at best) claim that life will get better and better (cf.

Isa. 56:10). This will happen as Christians take dominion over the earth by controlling the Seven Mountains (seven key areas of influence) in preparation of Jesus' return. Nonsense! Kingdom Now 'theology' (Dominionism, or Reconstructionism) runs opposite to what the Bible says. Those subscribing to Dominionism or Reconstructionism make such a mess of the Bible (mishandling it) because they have failed to recognise that Israel and the church are separated (cf. Rom. 11). By doing so, they claim for themselves Israel's promises, namely, those referring to the Promised Land (Deut. 11:24, 28:13, Josh. 1:3) and the millennial promises (Isa. 2:2, Mic. 4:1), applying them to themselves, here and now.

Due to Israel's faithlessness, instead of being the head and not the tail (Duet. 28:13), their head and their tail were cut off (Isa. 9:13-14) temporarily (Rom. 11:1-12, 14, 25b). Kingdom Now subscribers misunderstand that Israel has been cut off 'temporarily.' Therefore, the church has not replaced Israel, as they suggest (replacement theology). And, if lukewarm members of the church continue in Israel's footsteps, then they too will be cut off, joining the Jews in the tribulation (Rom. 11:22-24).

In sum, 'Kingdom Now' theology fails to understand Israel will be revived in the tribulation, and through that revival, the promises of God will be reinstated, starting with salvation (Rom. 11:29). Churchgoers left behind, due to false worship and or due to falling away, will likewise receive another opportunity to get right with God, alongside Israel, in the tribulation.

Due to adopting replacement theology, Kingdom Now subscribers cannot comprehend that Israel will be reinstated by God, starting with the nation's rebirth in 1948. Subsequently, endorsers fail to understand God's plans and purposes and His biblical timeclock (made visible through the nation of Israel). They misinterpret and even scoff at premillennial, dispensational eschatology, which is the original and biblical position.

Unless dispensational, pre-tribulation, pre-millennial theology is applied, there is no possible way of recognising and understanding the signs of the times, leaving many unprepared for the things to come. The things to come major around persecution. Persecution, not peace prosperity, is the expectation (Jn. 16:33); enduring not enjoying is the requirement of scripture (Matt. 24:13) this side of Christ's return.

Stemming from persecution, betrayal will be another sign of the end times, being 'Delivered up' (Matt. 24:9). 'Delivered up,' in Greek, also means to be 'betrayed.' The betrayal comes from being forced or compelled into a state or a condition, conceived as handing someone over to the authorities (Greek application). Even now, we are seeing this prophecy being fulfilled with the government urging citizens to notify them of any 'health' order breaches. The persecution leading to betrayal is specifically seen through COVID-19 passports, soon developing into social scoring methods. Soon, we will have two classes of citizens where one is vaxxed, and the other is not, turning one against the other, separated through social scoring. Through social scoring, the unvaxxed will be easily identified. Social scoring will also provide complete control, resulting in the New World Order.

The New World Order is far from a conspiracy theory; it is supported by scripture (Dan. 7:7, 20, 23, 24, Rev. 13:7-10, 16-18, 17:12-13, 18:10, 19) and other worldly sources. However, it will not officially arrive on the scene until the tribulation begins, albeit it is already here in theory. The evidence is where mainstream media networks are united in freely using the term 'New World Order' to condition their audience. "This is the New World Order," they say regarding COVID-19 regulations, claiming, "This is what we do now; this is just how it is from now on." In other words, accept and conform to it.

Yet, the concept is not new. On April 17th, 2020, Dr. Tedros Adhanom Ghebreyesus, CEO of the WHO, called for global partnership, saying, "This is a time for all of us to be united in our common struggle against a common threat, a dangerous enemy. When we are divided, the virus exploits the cracks between us." Ghebreyesus goes on to say, "The WHO welcomes the demonstration of global solidarity because solidarity is the rule of the game to defeat COVID-19" (Seetharaman, 2020). The WHO released this address due to the United States putting a stop to their financial contribution toward the WHO. Ghebreyesus reinforces the need to work together, even giving up some power to gain a win-win outcome. The United Nations Chief concurs with the WHO, warning, "COVID-19 threatens global 'peace and security' (UN.org, 2020), which calls for a new order."

Again, the call for a New World Order (NWO) is not new, and neither is it isolated to a few. Many have voiced the idea over the decades, including politicians and presidents, the Pope, activists, celebrities, billionaires, and bankers. The concept of a New Order or global hegemony has been partly achieved throughout different eras, generally following a crisis such as World War I and World War II, expressed by an international hegemonic organisation such as the United Leagues of Nations and the United Nations (Cox, 2016). Arguably, these and other international organizations have not achieved their intended goals fully; therefore, there is a growing need for something more.

Ex-UK Prime Minister Gordon Brown is just one of many calling for a new global order to deal with the economic crisis as he warned against the protectionist policies of the 1930s (Summers, 2009). The then UK Prime Minister went on to say, "Or we could view the threats and challenges we face today as the difficult birth-pangs of a new global order – and our task now as nothing less than making the transition through a new internationalism to the benefits of an expanding global society – not muddling through as pessimists but making the necessary adjustment to a better future and setting the new rules for this new global order." More recently, the former British prime minister called creating a global government - this time to cope with the coronavirus pandemic (McLean, 2020).

John Paul II said something similar, "More than ever, we need a new international order that draws on the experience and results achieved in these years by the United Nations" (Hooper, 2004). And again, John Paul said, "By the end of this decade, we will live under the first One World Government that has ever existed in the society of nations… a government with absolute authority to decide the basic issues of survival. One world government is inevitable" (Olsen, 2008). Likewise, Pope Benedict XVI proposed a new world political authority 'with real teeth', possibly in place of the United Nations, to enforce an ethical financial order and end the global financial crisis (Zwartz, 2009).

Similarly, dubbed the pope of climate change, Pope Francis echoed his predecessors favoring a one-world government (Palmer, 2015), making a similar statement to Gordon Brown and António Guterres (Pullella, 2019). Pope Francis's global goals are to be carried out by global citizens (unfccc. int, 2015). Furthermore, Pope Francis sees the Catholic Church playing a major role in the New World, enforcing worship on Sundays, if possible (Palmer, 2015).

From September 25th to September 27th, 2015, the United Nations launched a new universal agenda, which Pope Francis endorsed. Adding to the long list of NWO supporters are President Jimmy Carter (1977) and George Bush (1991), who said, "Until now, the world we have known has been a world divided – a world of barbed wire and concrete block, conflict and the cold war. Now, we can see a world coming into view. A world in which there is the very real prospect of a New World Order… A world in which freedom and respect for human rights find a home among all nations." In 2008, Henry Kissinger said something similar, "Now that the clay feet of the economic system have been exposed... this requires a new dialogue between America and the rest of the world... If progress is made on these enterprises, 2009 will mark the beginning of a New World Order" (economist.com, 2008). Joe Biden (2019) also recognised the benefits of the United League of Nations and the United Nations' benefits and said, "It is time actually to create a New World Order."

Many more names could be added to the list to support a new globalised government to better respond to economic concerns and pandemics. It is also expected that by creating a New World Order, state dictatorships would be quashed under the guise that a united front with a global constitution would see the end of independence, abuse of state powers, and misuse of emergency powers. An example of emergency abuse is Hungary's Prime Minister Viktor Orban, who has pounced on the crisis to complete his already near-dictatorial powers (Stelz, 2020). Australia has, however, since taken the lead, with Melbourne, Victoria being to number one lockdown city in the world under Premier (dictator) Daniel Andrews.

The dictatorship issue is not new or limited to a few. Wright and Campbell (2020) state, "Over the past decade, the world has grown more authoritarian, nationalistic, xenophobic, unilateralist, anti-establishment, and anti-expertise. The current state of politics and geopolitics has exacerbated, not stabilized, the crisis of COVID-19. Subsequently, there is a call and a growing need for a coordinated, united international response." Wright and Campbell (2020) looked to President Trump to lead the way, stating, "The government needs to recognize that this is already a global crisis with economic and security implications, as well as risks to health and human safety." Wright and Campbell (2020) go on to say, "National health organizations are working closely together, but the United States should be convening world leaders, whether in person or by conference and coming up with a global response." Instead of states seeking their own interests, now is the time to establish a World Order and a global economy, providing global security and accountability. Cox (2026) states, "Only a war of position can, in the long run, bring about structural changes, and a war of position involves building up the socio-political base for change through the creation of new historic blocs." In support of bringing about those structural changes, both the UN General Secretary and the WHO CEO, among many others, have said, "The world is at war against a global enemy, COVID-19." They have further said, "We need an immediate global ceasefire; we need to unite and fight together."

However, forming a New World Order will not come about without opposition - some states will resist, and others will be reluctant to hand over power. For example, Slaughter (2009) argues in favor of a global network's government over one ruling power. However, many would argue that networks such as the European Union and the United Nations have failed to achieve their goals. While these organisations have served some purpose, there is a need for more, achieving genuine peace in a world where states do not compete against each other for power, led by a global leader.

President Macron of France recently went on record, positioning himself for global leadership, and calling for a worldwide ceasefire (Andelman, 2020). Macron also has strong United Nations backing and has even been hailed 'Europe's Savior' with a picture of him walking on water (The Economist, 2017). Andelman (2020) also backs the idea, stating, "Indeed, it would appear that the world could use a new leader in this time of crisis, one who is prepared to put global interests above personal or political aggrandizement. And until the United States is prepared to offer such an individual, there may be no better to fill that void than France's young, fresh voice: Emmanuel Macron." Emmanuel (meaning: God is with us) has also received the blessing of Pope Francis as a proposed New World leader (O'Connell, 2020).

As the call for a New World Order emerges, the request of a one-world leader is nothing new. Henri Spaak, Secretary-General of NATA, said in 1957, "What we want is a man of sufficient stature to hold the alliances of all people and to lift us out of the economic morass into which we are sinking. Send us such a man, and be he god or devil, we will receive him" (Anderson, 2014). In addition to the Secretary-General of NATA, Spaak was a leader in the formation of the institutions that evolved into the European Union.

Make no mistake about it; the new world order is already here and will be fully established during the tribulation, where any resisting it will be punished. First, with further restrictions placed on them, followed by being removed from their homes and placed in 'quarantine' facilities (FEMA camps) for their own 'safety.' The same propaganda was used in Nazi Germany, resulting in the deaths of six million Jews. Yet, at the time, few believed what was happening, regardless of the evidence.

History is now repeating itself, and in the same way, Hitler, like Antiochus (being antichrist types), targeted the Jews; the antichrist will do the same, targeting anyone rejecting and resisting 'his' New World Order. Those opposing will be primarily made up of those claiming to follow the One True God: In other words, Orthodox Jews, and Christians. Evangelical Christians are among the greatest resisting the jab and, consequently, the COVID-19 passport, which is setting up the New World Order. Christians will be the greatest threat, and therefore will be among the greatest persecuted, even this side of the tribulation. Yet, due to the mounting pressure (oppression), many will subsequently fold and fall, even betraying their brothers and sisters in Christ (Matt. 24:9-10). Here Matthew, chapter twenty-five (vv. 31-46), has contextual, applied relevance.

Persecution is already a reality for Christians. Even now in the West, the prediction of persecution seen in the book of Matthew (24:9-10) is reserved for the first half of the tribulation, increasing into the second (Matt. 24:16-22). The second half of the tribulation will see great oppression (tribulation) resulting from persecution (Matt. 24:21). Few will be able to endure such oppression resulting in imprisonment and death (Rev. 12:11, 13:10, 15, 20:4). Yet only those (those alone) who do endure to the end will be saved (Matt. 24:13, Rev. 13:10, 14:12).

As you can see, 'this' gospel is very different from the health, wealth, and happiness version that charismatics are in love with. While one prepares you for the things to come, the other distracts and even derails you. One positions you to stand while the other conditions you to fall. Remember, most claiming and confessing Jesus this side of the tribulation will wake up in the tribulation, having been deceived by the 'god of this world' (2 Cor. 4:4) into following 'another Jesus' through a different gospel (2 Cor. 11:4).

The warnings to churches of Pergamum (Rev. 2:16), Thyatira (Rev. 2:22), Sardis (Rev. 3:3), and Laodicea (Rev. 3:16) make this point very clear. Each received a threat from Jesus to either repent or experience His judgement; the language of each threat is that of tribulation talk. Yet, the church doing well will avoid the tribulation (Rev. 3:10), although many still experience something of it this side (Rev. 2:10). Again, remaining faithful (Rev. 2:10) and holding fast (Rev. 3:11) is the requirement and the condition for salvation. But, again, most will fail to endure this side of the tribulation, and again fail in the tribulation (Matt. 24:10).

As previously mentioned, the most frightening reality for churchgoers left behind to endure the tribulation will be, albeit limited, the knowledge of what has happened and of the things to come (Lu. 21:26). The worst of the things to come will be persecution unto death. From the moment the bride of Christ, (the church) has been removed from the earth (raptured), those then confessing Jesus in the tribulation will perish (Matt. 24:10, Rev. 6:9-11, 7:9-14). Again, at the halfway point of the tribulation, persecution will severely increase (Rev. 7:9-14, 11:7, 12:4-17, (esp. 12:11), 13:10, 15, 14:12-13, 16:6, 17:6, 19:2, 20:4). Evident by the above number of verses and passages that reference persecution, persecution is an ongoing and increasing theme in the time of trouble. The persecution of the saints will not end before Jesus returns to rule and reign.

Again, the doctrine of suffering runs opposite to that of Kingdom Now' theology,' which falsely claims that Christians are to rule in this life as kings (cf. Rom. 5:17). The Bible offers nothing of the sort, but rather states this world will worsen (Jn. 16:33) before it gets better. The persecution of the saints will be directed by the antichrist and administered through his followers. Therefore, any persecution of Christians today stems from the spirit of the antichrist, operating even within the church. To support, compare the prediction of the book of Revelation:

"The beast that rises from the bottomless pit will make war on them and conquer them and kill them" (Rev. 11:7).

"It was allowed to make war on the saints and to conquer them" (Rev. 13:7).

The first verse references the two witnesses proclaiming Christ in the first half of the tribulation (Rev. 11:2). The antichrist will kill them when their testimony (Gk. martyr) is finished (Rev. 11:7). Until then, they are untouchable (Rev. 11:5-6). In the second half of the tribulation (Rev. 13:5), following the antichrist's resurrection from the grave (Rev. 13:3, 12, 17:8), he announces that he is God and is to be worshipped alone (Matt. 24:15, 2 Thess. 2:4, Rev. 13:15). He will, all the more, turn on the tribulation saints, driving them into the wilderness (Matt. 24:16-22, Rev. 12). Countless millions (Rev. 7:9-14) committing to Jesus in the tribulation will perish because of their testimony.

In the tribulation a popular means of execution will be by beheading (Rev. 20:4). Following their deaths, the saints will watch the remaining judgements poured out on the earth from heaven, even praising God for them. At the end of the tribulation, the martyred saints predict the world will worship God (Rev. 16:3-5). As seen through the verses mentioned above (Rev. 11:7, 13:7), the antichrist will be allowed to conquer (kill) the saints because of their word (message) and their witness (martyrdom), not loving (agapao) their lives (psyche/soul) unto death (Rev. 12:11). The antichrist will attempt to rid the planet of any following Jesus, especially the converted Jews (Rev. 7:4-8, 14:1-5), who are the key to Christ's return (Matt. 23:39). Before Jesus returns, the antichrist will even attempt to conquer Jesus Christ, yet fail, "They (the antichrist and his followers) will make war on the Lamb (Jesus), and the Lamb will conquer them, for He is Lord of lords and King of kings, and those with Him are called and chosen and faithful" (Rev. 17:14).

In sum, seen through the evidence of scripture, to be a 'book of Acts church' means you will suffer persecution rather than experience peace and prosperity. Persecution is predicted to be an ongoing and increasing experience for the faithful witnesses (martyrs) of Jesus Christ. The way the church started is the way it will end. The book of Acts (1:8) shows Christ's witnesses will also be His martyrs. This is seen again in the Book of Revelation (Rev. 6:9), commencing from the beginning of the tribulation, "When He opened the fifth seal, I saw under the altar the souls of those who had been slain for the word of God and for the witness (Gk. martyrdom/death) they had borne." As such, the call to endure (not enjoy) until Jesus returns is critical for salvation.

Leading into the tribulation and increasing within the tribulation, persecution will come from and through the antichrist to conquer the saints. It will even come from the spirit of the antichrist operating in the world and the church. Persecution will continue until Jesus Christ returns and conquers the beast and overrides the beast system (the New World Order). Those who conquer the antichrist do so at the cost of their natural lives (Rev. 12:11). The call to conquer the antichrist and the spirit of the antichrist (this world) was seen in all seven of the closing letters to the churches. It was connected with the words, "He who has an ear to hear, let him hear what the Spirit is saying to the churches" (Rev. 2-3). That is, to conquer and remain to conquer, or be conquered!

Increase of False Prophets

'Rise Up, Led Astray, Falling Away'
(Matt. 24:4, 11)

As mentioned, several times earlier, many who have failed to heed the warnings will wake up in the tribulation due to following false prophets and false teachers (Matt. 24:4-5). The false prophets will arise within and come out of the church (1 Jn. 2:19), deceiving many in these last days (Matt. 7:15, cf. Jer. 5:31, 27:15). The false prophets that are deceiving many today are still standing behind pulpits the world over; they are also seen on 'Christian' television, through online 'ministries,' and are heard on 'Christian' radio stations. It has been said before if you want to listen to a false prophet, turn on TBN, or God Channel, or the like. While these networks intend to do good, they are managed and operated by those lacking theological substance and spiritual discernment, evident by who they associate with and promote. Essentially, these platforms are conditioning the biblically illiterate and the naive for greater false prophets to come. Even within tribulation, many who have been deceived on this side will continue to be deceived on that side.

So many churchgoers will end up in the tribulation from the church because they failed to love the truth (2 Thess. 2:10, 12). Instead, they love to listen to and follow false prophets. In doing so, they repeat the sins of Judah and will likewise share their experiences (Lam. 2:14, Rom. 11:22, 25).

For decades leading into the tribulation (exile), Jeremiah warned the people of God about the coming judgement. Yet, Judah's false prophets said that tribulation would not come, instead of trouble, peace, and prosperity would be their experience (Jer. 6:13-14, 8:10b-11, Ezek. 13:10-11, 15-17). But, tribulation, not prosperity, did come, and it was severe. Jeremiah writes about the horrors and the hopelessness of Judah's exile in the book of Lamentations, which should be read with consideration of how it will be for those left behind in the coming tribulation.

The message of peace and prosperity is what distracted, deceived, and derailed Judah, and it is still leading many astray today by those peddling the gospel (2 Cor. 2:17) for greedy gain (2 Pet. 2:14-16). While majoring in prosperity, false teachers deliberately neglect to mention anything of sin and judgement, and unfortunately, these same 'preachers' draw the crowds (2 Tim. 4:2-4).

Like Israel, in the days of Isaiah (Isa. 30:9), many churchgoers today are unwilling to hear God's instructions, instead only wanting to listen to a self-serving message of peace and prosperity: "Give us no more visions of what is right! Tell us pleasant things, prophesy illusions... Stop confronting us with the Holy One of Israel!" (Isa. 30:10–11).

Again, like the people of Judah, many finding themselves left behind in the tribulation will be there because they did not listen or look for God's appointed preachers (Jer. 29:19), the watchman (cf. Jer. 6:17; Ezek. 3:17; 33:7–9, Hos 9:8). And while in the tribulation, they will continue to listen to the same false prophets who caused them to be there in the first place

(Jer. 29:21, cf. Jer. 23:16-22). In the tribulation, the same false prophets will be spruiking the exact message of peace and security (1 Thess. 5:3, cf. Rev. 18).

Like Israel, Judah loved to listen to the false prophets among them (Jer. 5:31), and so do many today within the church (2 Tim. 4:3). As a result of listening to false prophets, sleepy Judah woke up in the tribulation (Lam. 3:5), and while there, Jeremiah wrote to them (Jer. 29:1-4, 20, 31). Like before, Jeremiah again instructed exiled Judah not to listen to the false prophets among them (Jer. 29:8-9), continuing to deceive them (Jer. 29:15, 31). The same false prophets who caused Judah to be exiled were exiled with them. Again, the same will be repeated with the coming tribulation.

The same false teachers deceiving churchgoers today into the tribulation will continue to deceive them when in the tribulation (Matt. 24:11), with the same wrong message of peace and security (1 Thess. 5:3). For Judah, the false prophets who said tribulation would not come (Jer. 27:9, 14, cf. 14:14, 23:21, 25), were now saying it will not last long in the tribulation. However, Jeremiah states Judah would be exiled for seventy years (Jer. 25:11, 29:10).

Likewise, today many ridicule Bible prophecy within the church, saying the church will not be judged, yet God says otherwise (1 Pet. 4:17). Those scoffing fulfill prophecy negatively (2 Pet. 3:3, Jude 1:18) and will again during the seven-year event, leading many more away (Matt. 24:11).

Besides falsely preaching peace and prosperity, Judah's stupid shepherds (Jer. 10:21) also caused the people of God to become stupid (Jer. 4:22, 10:8, 10:14, 51:17) by preaching a false hyper-grace gospel. The hyper-grace gospel states you can do whatever you like, and it will be alright. Antinomianism is the Greek word meaning no law or no rules. In other words, there is no law. Due to believing there was no law, therefore, no consequence, Judah's false prophets did outrageous things in Israel, committing all manner of sins, including sexual immorality and falsely testifying in God's name (Jer. 29:23). Judah even sacrificed their children (Jer. 7:31) to Baal (Jer. 19:5) and Molech (Jer. 32:35), believing that God would not judge them. No matter how many times God warned His people through the prophet Jeremiah, over forty years, they would not listen (Jer. 7:27, 17:23, 29:19). God's people did not listen then, and they do not listen now. The consequence of being lawless is the eternal lake of fire (Matt. 7:23).

Jesus gave the church a similar warning to that of Jeremiah through the seven letters in the book of Revelation. Like Israel, the churches of Ephesus (Rev. 2:6) and Pergamum (Rev. 2:15) were also plagued by similar false teachers, known as the Nicolaitans. The name "Nicolaitans" is derived from the Greek word nikolaos, a compound of the words nikos and laos. The word nikos is the Greek word that means 'to conquer' or 'to subdue'. The word laos is the Greek word for the people. It is also where we get the word 'laity'. When these two words are compounded into one, they form the name Nicolas, which means conquering and subduing the people. The Greek could be summed as 'Clergy lording over the laity'.

The Nicolaitans were associated with the teachings of Balaam (Rev. 2:14), which was condemned by Jude (Jude 1:11-13). Jesus also condemned and hated their works and teaching (Rev. 2:6) and warned the church of Pergamum, if they did not repent from following them, He would war against them with the sword of His mouth (Rev. 2:16). In other words, the failing churchgoers would end up in the tribulation, facing Jesus' sharp sword, which will strike down the nations (Rev. 19:15).

The false hyper-grace message, accompanied by the prosperity gospel, is still deceiving millions today. Jesus addressed the problem in His letters to the churches of Pergamum (Rev. 2:14-15) and Thyatira (Rev. 2:20-21), who had corrupted and compromised God's word. Paul also addressed the issues of antinomianism in his letter to the church of Rome (6:1-2). John did likewise in his letter to the churches across Asia, now Turkey (1 Jn. 2:3-6, 5:3); the exact location of the seven churches from the book of Revelation (chapters 2 & 3). Joining Paul and John is the angel seen in the book of Revelation, chapter fourteen (v. 12), evangelising in the tribulation, who also mentions the commandments of God, calling for the left behind saints to endure (by keeping the commands). By keeping the commandments (Rev. 12:17), those who do endure will do so at the cost of their natural lives (Rev. 12:11). Still, most will not repent and obey; instead, they will be led further astray by the tribulation of false prophets (Matt. 24:11).

Like Jesus' address of the Nicolaitans, Paul addressed another group of false teachers known as the 'super-apostles (2 Cor. 11:5, 12:11), accusing them of preaching another gospel (2 Cor. 11:4). The other gospel being preached by these false teachers was popular, and, unlike Paul's gospel, it was not free (2 Cor. 11:7). Like the Nicolaitans, the slick 'super apostles' excreted their authority, taking the congregation's money and enslaving them (2 Cor. 11:21) to support their agenda and 'ministries.' Sound familiar…?

Which group of popular preachers today attract the crowds with slick speech, promising prosperity, if only you give to them, in faith, your best seed offering? These are the same boastful preachers who exercise great cult-like authority over their followers (lording over them) yet command that you do not touch them (do not touch God's anointed). They are the same preachers who make extraordinary claims with many (empty) words, prophesying falsely. By definition, they are false prophets because what they predict does not come to pass repeatably (Deut. 18:22).

On the other side of the ditch to the hyper-grace, prosperity preachers are the legalists, who also preach 'A different gospel' (Gal. 1:6), being a gospel of works. One group teaches no law and no rules, while the other teaches no grace, or that grace is not enough. Again, Paul addressed the issue of doctrinal apostasy where the church of Galatia had entertained these false teachers and was now in the process of 'turning away' from the truth. In exchange for a lie, the departure from the truth was a quick process (Gal. 1:6), needing a fast and firm rebuke (Gal. 3:1).

Again, the reason for the strong rebuke is that the Galatians' departure from the truth also led to their departure from God (Gal. 1:6, 4:11, 20, 5:1-4). The gospel of legalism adds works to faith, adding to the gospel of grace (Gal. 2:4, 15-16). Like the super-apostles, the false preachers, perverting grace, were very popular and influential (Gal. 2:6). So effective were these false preachers, even Peter and Barnabas were led astray (Gal. 2:11-14). Specifically, the works being added to the gospel of grace stemmed from the law of Judaism, being circumcision. Through works of the flesh, the members of the church of Galatians were now saved, according to the false preachers, which brought them back under a curse (Gal. 3:10, 4:9), from which they had been redeemed (Gal. 3:13).

Due to confronting the doctrine of the false teachers, Paul had become an enemy (Gal. 4:16) to those who once loved him (Gal. 4:13-15). Like the super-apostles, the legalisers had bewitched the Galatians (Gal. 3:1). They hindered them from the truth (Gal. 5:7) with flattery, shutting them out from Paul and his gospel (Gal. 4:17), and shutting the Galatians up with them, only being influenced by them.

Like with the super-apostles, the Judaizers were controlling, even cult-like, in their behaviour. The false teachers added and promoted circumcision, being works of the flesh, to the gospel of grace, to be popular (Gal. 1:10), and to avoid persecution (Gal. 6:12). That is, the persecution of the cross, thus failing to go down the narrow and difficult path (Matt. 7:13-14), failing to count the cost (Lu. 14:25-34) and take up their cross (Matt. 16:24-26, Gal. 6:14). In the same way, Paul condemned the super-apostles (2 Cor. 11:15b), He condemned the legalists who perverted the gospel of grace (Gal. 5:10b-12), even wishing they would go the whole way and castrate themselves.

Another example of a works-based gospel is seen with the Roman Catholic Church, where they pervert the gospel of grace by adding to it, even introducing and promoting idolatry. Interestingly, recently some well-known prosperity preachers stood in unity with the Pope declaring, "We are all, once again, one universal church." That is, no more protest (Protestant), instead, under the banner of ecumenicalism, we are all Catholic in an attempt to undo everything Martin Luther stood for, and millions have since died for.

Remarkably, these two false gospels (hyper-grace and works) have united, declaring, "We are one." The antichrist will do the same thing in the coming tribulation, and his false teachers are paving the way for this to occur by conditioning the naive ahead of time. They will continue to do so in the tribulation, up until the antichrist announces that he is God (Matt. 24:15).

To summarise, the Bible predicts an increase of false prophets in the last days, leading many astray, deceiving them into the tribulation (Matt. 24:4). The false prophets are the same as seen throughout the Bible, saying the same things. They are identified above as the hyper-grace, prosperity preachers, and legalists. Both are at opposite ends of the spectrum; however, both preach a perverted gospel to avoid persecution and suffering.

Both are self-serving, popular, cult-like, and incredibly influential. Both will attack any resisting and rebuking their teaching, and both will lead their followers away from sound biblical doctrine and Christ. Therefore, the followers of these perverted gospels will end up in the tribulation as those left behind unless repentance comes first. However, most will not repent. Even while in the tribulation, false prophets will continue to rise and deceive (Matt. 24:11).

Important to note, the false prophets Jesus warned about, as did Paul, Jude, and Peter, will come in His name (Matt. 24:5). The false prophets Jesus warned about are in the church, holding positions of pastor, and teacher, also assuming and claiming titles of apostle and prophet. These false teachers are conditioning their audience for the ultimate false teacher and false prophet of them all, the antichrist, and the false prophet. The greatest false teachers in the tribulation will be the false prophet and the antichrist (Rev. 13). These two individuals are among us today, even deceiving now in preparation for their appointed time. They are here now and will rise in the tribulation, as will many other false prophets occupying the pulpit across the globe (Matt. 24:11).

Pop Quiz

1. Q: Who are the false prophets and false teachers?
   a. The stupid shepherds and prosperity preachers within Israel
   b. The hyper-grace preachers and the legalist (Judaizers) within the church
2. Q: What were they saying?
   a. Peace and prosperity (security), do what you like, it will be alright
   b. Grace, faith, and works are required (converting back to Judaism)
3. Q: Why were they deceiving the people of God?
   a. Self-serving purposes, to control
   b. For their popularity and greedy gain
   c. To avoid persecution
4. Q: How did their prophecy of peace and prosperity go?
   a. Judgement, not prosperity came, and will again

5. Q: How did the perverted gospel of works go?
    a. Paul condemned those preaching it, and those following those who taught it
6. Q: What will be the result for those following false teachers?
    a. They will end up in the tribulation, as left behind (they will miss the rapture)

This Gospel will be Preached

'No Other Gospel, No Other Name'
(Matt. 24:14)

From the beginning of this series, it was said that false teachers and false teaching are the foremost end times signs, preparing the way for the false prophet and the antichrist. Jesus warned His disciples several times, false teachers would come, and they would increase, leading many astray and away (Matt. 24:4-5, 11, 23-26) before He returns (Matt. 24:29-31). During the tribulation, false teachers and false prophets will even operate with great signs and wonders (Matt. 24:24a), deceiving even the elect if possible (Matt. 24:24b). We are seeing false signs, or false, and strange 'fire' now (cf. Lev. 10:1) operating within the church. Leviticus (10:1) is where we develop our understanding of strange fire.

The word 'strange' in Hebrew means 'unauthorised,' or 'foreign.' In the account of those who brought strange fire to God's altar, being Aaron's sons, Nadab and Abihu, God was so offended, He responded by consuming them with His authorised fire. Following the deaths of Nadab and Abihu, Moses explains to Aaron why (Lev. 10:3). The reason is holiness or lack of it.

The lack of holiness results in a lack of fear. God made an example out of Nadab and Abihu, killing them, warning the rest, do not do what they did, or you too will die. The same warning is extended to us, and a similar story is seen in the book of Acts (5:1-11). In both instances, where God struck the fearless dead (OT: Nadab and Abihu, and NT: Ananias and Sapphira), He was introducing Himself. "This is who I am, worship Me reverentially!"

For Israel, the incident occurred the first time a sacrifice was offered to God at the altar. For the church, there was also a sacrifice of giving, and like Israel's commencement, the incident for the church occurred at its commencement. Through both examples, God revealed Himself and His position on reverential worship and holiness. What God did with Nadab and Abihu and Ananias and Sapphira will be repeated in the tribulation, and even before (1 Pet. 4:17), for the purpose of producing repentance and holiness through reverentially fear (Acts 5:5, 11, cf. Rev. 14:7).

Strange fire and false motives are counterfeit behaviours and signs to support a false gospel. In the last section, false gospels were addressed, known as "Another gospel" (2 Cor. 11:4) and a "Different gospel" (Gal. 1:6). In these last days, most will follow a false gospel (2 Tim. 4:3); they will be led astray and fall away (Matt. 24:11, 24, cf. 7:21-23). However, despite the majority going by the broad road that leads to destruction (Matt. 7:13), still, a remnant will find and follow the gospel of the kingdom. As mentioned previously, the gospel of the kingdom (kingdom means king's domain) is anything but what 'Kingdom Now' 'theology;' (Dominionism) teaches. Kingdom Now 'theology' serves man in his/her own interests and desire to rule and reign (cf. Rom. 5:17), whereas the gospel of the kingdom points to and serves Jesus alone.

An example of the above mentioned is with a well-known Kingdom Now gathering local to where I live, made up of dozens of businessmen and women. Most, if not all, identify as being Christian, yet few, if any, fellowships in a local church. Instead, they call that particular meeting their church. The problem with that is, within the forum, the gospel is not preached. Instead, motivational speakers spruik their self-help formulas, under the umbrella of Christianity, dressed in the ideology of 'preparing the planet for Jesus' return.' Furthermore, attendees even 'pay' the host to pray for their businesses. They either do not know how to pray, have no confidence in their prayers, or could not be bothered to pray, which reflects their lack of relationship with Jesus. If the attendees were genuinely seeking Jesus and not their individual successes, then they would be connected to a local church, where the gospel is preached; albeit finding a biblical church is challenging.

If Kingdom Now subscribers heard the gospel, they would no longer be concerned about preparing the planet for Jesus' return outside of evangelism. They would, however, be concerned about preparing themselves for His return through enduring repentance and obedience.

Following Jesus' lists of end times signs, majoring on false teachers and teachings, leading many to stray, who fall away, He states, "The one (only that one) who endures to the end will be saved" (Matt. 24:13). The enduring condition for salvation is absolute, followed by Jesus' following statement, "And this gospel of the kingdom will be proclaimed throughout the whole world…" (Matt. 24:14). The gospel being preached to all nations as a testimony (Gk. martyr) of Jesus (His death and resurrection) will be another end-time sign. 'This gospel' refers to salvation through Jesus, alone (Jn. 14:6, Acts 4:12), made known through scripture, alone. Scripture points to the biblical Jesus secured, alone, through faith and grace (Eph. 2:8-9). Sadly, due to a lack of sound biblical preaching, many are deceived into following another Jesus, introduced through a different gospel (2 Cor. 11:4), which is why they will find themselves waking up in the tribulation.

The phrase, "The gospel of the kingdom," is seen three times in the book of Matthew (Matt. 4:23, 9:35, 24:14), and only in the book of Matthew, with one similar reference in the book of Mark (Mk. 1:15). Through the listed references, we learn that the gospel of the kingdom is one of power (Matt. 4:23-24, 9:35) and compassion (Matt. 9:36), and repentance (Mk. 1:15). One leads to the other. The gospel is confirmed through signs that reveal Jesus, resulting in repentance and enduring obedience.

The power of the gospel is seen chiefly today through the opening of blind eyes and deaf ears, spiritually speaking. However, when applying the context of each reference to the gospel of the kingdom, the commonality is the miracles of Jesus, revealing Jesus, not the believer's power to do signs and wonders, such as healing miracles. The greatest of all miracles is to become born again, which you must be to inherit the kingdom of God (Jn. 3:3).

The reference to the gospel of the kingdom in Matthew, chapter twenty-four (v. 14) contextually applies to the gospel being preached in a time of tribulation by those who are resisting false teachers (Matt. 24:11) and enduring unto the end (Matt. 24:13). Many will die for their faith in Christ (Matt. 24:9), yet most will fall away (Matt. 24:11). Therefore, contextually speaking, the second most significant miracle in the tribulation, following coming to faith in Jesus Christ, will be remaining free from deception (Matt. 24:11, 24) and enduring to the end (Matt. 24:11).

Within the New Testament, there are ninety-three references to the word 'Gospel', clearly outlining what it is and how it is to be responded to. Paul's summary in First Corinthians (1 Cor. 15:1-6) is one of the clearest examples of Jesus, His death, and His resurrection. Within the chapter, Paul addresses the resurrection of Christ and believers (1 Cor. 15:12-24). As Jesus ascends again, so will those who truly followed Him! For those still alive, when Jesus returns for the church (Jn. 14:2-3, 1 Thess. 4:16, Rev. 4:1), they will be caught up in the air (1 Cor. 51-52). They will escape the things to come, being removed or raptured before the tribulation commences (Lu. 21:34-36, Rev. 3:10, 4:1). Until then, there is an interval between each event, leading to Jesus delivering the kingdom of God to His Father (Matt. 13:41-43). Within the separate events leading to that day, there is an order of things to come (1 Cor. 15:23):

1. Christ is first resurrected (1 Cor. 15:4)
2. The dead saints will be resurrected (1 Cor. 15:51-52, 1 Thess. 4:16)
3. Those still alive will be resurrected (1 Cor. 15:51-52, 1 Thess. 4:16)
4. After seven years of tribulation, Jesus will return, He will deal with the devil, and then set up His millennial kingdom, and hand over to the Father (1 Cor. 15:24)

Between the resurrection of Jesus Christ and the saints, there is a two-thousand-year gap. The parable of the good Samaritan provides a clue to the timeframe where the Samaritan (representing Jesus) provides and pays for the welfare of a dying man (Lu. 10:33). The Samaritan placed the dying man in the care of an 'Inn' (Lu. 10:34), paying two-denarii, instructing the innkeeper to look after him until He returns (Lu. 10:35). Two denarii represent two days' wages (Matt. 20:2), and the inn represents the church. The Samaritan also told the innkeeper that he would reimburse for any further cost (Lu. 10:35).

Clearly, within the parable, the gospel is taught with a clue to the timeframe of Christ's return. Jesus is the Good Samaritan, as the Good Shephard (Jn. 10:11), who paid the price for our sin, securing (Sozo) salvation for those who believe, repent, and remain (Sozo means compete life, healing, and deliverance). Two days' wages were given, representing two thousand years (2 Pet. 3:8), with a promise, anything more would be reimbursed when He returns. The reimbursement could be counted as a reward on judgement day (1 Cor. 3:14). However, those failing to do as

Jesus instructs will suffer loss (1 Cor. 3:10-15). In sum, Jesus will return after two days (two thousand years) for the ones He saved. Again, as seen in Paul's description of the gospel, there is an order of events (1 Cor. 15:23), beginning with Christ's going away for 'two days' (two thousand years) before returning to collect and compensate.

As mentioned above, there is an order of events regarding the gospel of the Kingdom, with the first phase being Christ's death and resurrection. The second phase is Christ returning, leading into the third, which is the millennial reign, and then there, death will have been dealt with (1 Cor. 15:25-26, cf. 55), not before. Death will be dealt with in the millennium because the destroyer is no longer with us; instead, he has been thrown into the pit (Rev. 20:1-3). The destroyer is Satan (Isa. 16:4). Once Satan has been dealt with, the saints will then rule and reign in glorified bodies (Phil 3:21) under Jesus (Rev. 1:6, 2:26, 5:10, 11:15, cf. Isa. 9:6, Rev. 20:4).

Therefore, the biblical position is Kingdom 'THEN' not Kingdom 'NOW!' Until then, the faithful follower of Christ is in danger (1 Cor. 15:30-32, 2 Cor. 1:8-9, 6:4-5, cf. 11:23-28), which runs in the opposite direction to Kingdom Now teaching, stating the believer has total authority and dominion over the whole earth. Nonsense!

Scripture reveals Satan deceives the whole world before Jesus returns (Rev. 12:9), and the entire earth is deceived by (Satan's) sorcery (Rev. 18:23). The Greek word for sorcerer is 'Pharmakeia,' meaning 'drug' or 'spell.' Twice more, the book of Revelation uses the word 'Sorcerers' (Rev. 21:8, 22:15), stating, anyone involved in sorcery will not inherit the Kingdom of God. This is due to rejecting, and or not meeting the requirements of the gospel of the Kingdom (Matt. 24:14). One leads to the other. The gospel of the Kingdom leads to the Kingdom of God.

The problem today was also the shared problem for Israel (Jer. 27:9). The whole world has now been placed under a hypnotic spell due to listening to the wrong voices. An excellent example of this is COVID-19. The world, including many churchgoers, has been put under a satanic spell, deceived, and coerced into taking the jab, which has set the stage for the antichrist. Today, many pulpits are filled by 'pastors' denouncing and even scoffing (2 Pet. 3:3, Jude 1:18) at warnings seen through the signs of the times, leading to the coming tribulation. The blind lead the blind, too blind to see despite the obvious. The current global deception relates to the injection linked to digital passports, preparing the way for the Mark of the Beast (666) and the New World Order.

Regardless of how blind you are in these last days, the current situation hardly supports the ideology Kingdom Now subscribers promote but rather confirms the theology of Kingdom (God's coming dominion, rule, and reign) Then (later), not Now!

On the matter of 'Kingdom THEN' theology, Paul reinforces that in this life, you will have trouble due to Satan being the god of this world (2 Cor. 4:4), supported by Jesus, referring to him as the ruler of this world (Jn. 12:31, 14:30). Satan, not the church, has dominion over this world here and now and will do so until Jesus returns, contradicting Kingdom Now ideology.

Again, Satan will rule until Jesus returns, confirmed by Paul, who repeats himself (1 Cor. 15:27-28 & 57), stating Jesus will take dominion from Satan when He returns. That is, Jesus will take away the antichrist's (who is empowered and embodied by Satan) God-given dominion (2 Thess. 2:8-11) after his appointed time (seven-year tribulation) has ended. Daniel says the same (Dan. 7:9-12, 23-27), confirmed by John (Rev. 19:11-21-20:1-6). Until then, we hold fast (1 Cor. 15:2), we remain immovable (1 Cor. 15:52), and we run the race, being careful not to become disqualified (1 Cor. 9:24-27); being careful also not to lose heart through affliction and persecution (2 Cor. 4:16-18). Persecution, not prosperity!

For the faithful follower of Christ, until Jesus returns, trouble in this world is the expectation (Jn. 16:33): that is the gospel! Contrary to the gospel, false teachers and false teaching do not have a theology of suffering, which can lead many astray, and away, becoming disqualified due to losing heart when trouble comes. The worst of false teaching is to deny the resurrection of Christ, and, subsequently, the believer's resurrection, resulting in careless living (1 Cor. 15:33-34, cf. Lu. 21:34-36), which is why Paul said to avoid false teachers altogether (2 Cor. 6:14-7:1). False teachers boastfully claim excellent knowledge yet are ignorant of God (1 Cor. 8:2), yet still, they deceive many (2 Cor. 11:3).

In the same way, Eve was deceived, many are today, with the same lie. It proclaims, "You can be like God!" Little gods, even - do it your way, and have dominion over the earth! Satan tried to deceive Jesus with the same nonsense, promising all the world's kingdoms if He falls down and worships him (Matt. 4:8-9). Essentially, what Satan attempted to do with Jesus has similarities with Kingdom Now 'theology', especially when incorporating the 'little gods' doctrine.

In sum, the gospel is one of suffering and sacrifice, persevering under pressure and persecution, with eyes fixed on Jesus, resulting in power, standing firm remaining faithful (1 Cor. 15:1-2, 58), and remaining free of deception. Those who do, they (alone) will escape the things to come (Lu. 21:34-36, Rom. 5:9, 1 Cor. 15:51-52, 1 Thess. 1:10, 4:16, 5:9, Rev. 3:10, 4:1). But, those who miss the rapture, will get another chance to endure for Christ in the tribulation. Through them, the gospel of the kingdom will be preached to the whole world as a testimony (through their martyrdom) to all nations.

As mentioned under the section addressing persecution, with and through persecution comes powers. During the tribulation, a great power will be seen and experienced, even dwarfing anything seen in the book of

Acts, and will continue until Jesus returns, confirmed by the words, "And then the end will come" (Matt. 24:14).

To conclude, the gospel of the Kingdom points to Jesus (alone), His sacrifice and suffering, shared by those that follow Him (Rom 8:17, 2 Cor. 1:5-7, 2 Tim. 1:8, Phil 1:29, 3:10, 1 Pet. 4:13, 16). When Christ returns, those who shared in His sacrifice and suffering, they (only they) will share in His rule and reign. WHEN HE RETURNS, not before, THEN the faithful follower of Christ will rule and reign, having dominion on this earth. Before then, we must endure suffering.

Persecution has always been a part of the salvation package this side of the millennium, which is the believer's wilderness experience before reaching the Promised Land. Currently, we are in the wilderness, on the way to the Promised Land, proclaiming Christ. That is, declaring 'the gospel,' which includes resisting and rebuking false teaching that promises (false) peace and prosperity, packaged in dominionism: 'Your Best Life Now.'

The proclamation of Christ will continue into the tribulation by those deceived, left behind, and then awakened. Many left behind will be due to following another Jesus by accepting a different gospel. Some will even be deceived by strange fire (counterfeit miracles) flowing from those coming in Jesus' name, just as Jesus warned (Matt. 24:4-5, 11, 23-26).

Throughout the tribulation, the gospel will be proclaimed to the whole world by the 144,000 Jewish evangelists and those who come to faith in Jesus through their witness (Rev. 7, 14:1-5). It will also spoken by the two (Jewish) witnesses (Rev. 11), and through angels (Rev. 14:6-13). Those who hear and receive the gospel, who fear God and worship Him alone (Rev. 14:7), during the tribulation will most likely die (Rev. 6:9-11, 7:6-14, 12:11, 13:10, 15, 14:13, 20:4). Actually, it would be better for them to die early than endure the seven-year ordeal (Rev. 14:13) - the earlier, the better!

At the end of the seven-year event, then Jesus will return - He will establish His Kingdom and execute His will on the earth, as it is in heaven (Matt. 6:9). When His kingdom comes His command will be done on earth as it is in heaven.

'The Great Tribulation'

(Matt. 24:15-28)

The midway point of the tribulation, leading into the great tribulation, is marked by the abomination of desolation (Matt. 24:15). This is where the antichrist announces himself to be God, from the third temple, the tribulation temple (2 Thess. 2:4). Persecution will be an increasing and continuing sign within the seven-year period; however, the first half will not compare with the second. Before the second half of the tribulation, being the great tribulation, during the tribulation (first half), hatred, betrayal, court cases, imprisonment, and beatings will be common, now, death is more likely. For this reason, the Jews flee the Holy Land (Matt. 24:16). Again, there will be a significant increase in false teaching, accompanied by lying signs and wonders (Matt. 24:24). Many will be deceived in those days. The great tribulation will end with the battle of Armageddon and Jesus returning (Matt. 24:27-28).

The Abomination of Desolation

'Ripe for Harvest'

(Matt. 24:15)

Previously, the gospel of the Kingdom was addressed with a comparison against false gospels, being 'Another gospel' (2 Cor. 11:4) and a 'Different gospel' (Gal. 1:6). Within the timeframe of the first half of the tribulation, the topics of the gospel and gospels, false teachers, and false teaching were covered. These false gospel will continue to lead many to fall away (Matt. 24:11). Even before the tribulation commences, there will be the great falling away (2 Thess. 2:3) resulting from false teaching, preparing the apostates for the coming antichrist, whom God sends (2 Thess. 2:11). Remember, the antichrist will be only revealed after the tribulation commences (2 Thess. 2:6).

The great falling away before the tribulation commences is another end-time sign. Before the tribulation, churchgoers will depart from the faith because they followed the doctrines of demons (1 Tim. 4:1). Included alongside those following doctrines of demons are the churchgoers who have itching ears and want only to hear what suits their passions (2 Tim. 4:3).

As revealed many times before, the apostates have not departed the church, but they, and their churches, have departed from the faith, proclaimed, and only gained through sound biblical teaching. The apostates are attending and even leading many liberal churches today, and they are rapidly increasing in numbers.

It is important to note that those falling away have fallen from grace (Gal. 5:4) and subsequently fallen away from Jesus due to following false teachers, preaching a different gospel (Gal. 1:6). The other gospel is either one of perverted grace (Jude 1) or void of grace (Gal. 5:4). The hyper-grace gospel and a gospel void of grace are two opposite extremes - they are two ditches on either side of the narrow road.

False grace, like false peace, is deadly, whereas biblical grace is essential, for, without it, there is no hope of redemption (cf. Eph 2:8-9), but instead, the curse of the Law remains (Gal. 3:10-14). Where any fail in any part of the Law, just one time, they, thereby, stand condemned (Ja. 2:10). No one can keep the Law (Rom. 3:23), not one (Rom. 3:10), except for Jesus. Therefore, any outside of Christ are condemned already and eternally unless repentance comes first.

Jesus was the only sinless 'man' to ever walk this earth, which is why it is essential to come to God, through Him, alone. Through Christ alone, we are saved (Jn. 14:6, Acts 4:12). There is simply no other way, and there is no other name to call on to be saved. That is the gospel - Christ is the gospel!

Most churchgoers are ignorant of the gospel, deceived by the self-help, self-serving version promising 'Your Best Life Now'. As for those who have had some introduction to the gospel, multitudes will, and are falling away from the foundation and the fundamentals of the faith because they are now following doctrines of demons, introduced, and promoted through popular, celebrity preachers. Many wannabe megachurch pastors have departed the gospel, trading it for the 'success model' introduced by certain men who have crept in unnoticed (Jude 1:4-5).

Doctrines of demons, or seducing spirits, are taught in the church through false teachers masquerading as 'ministers' of the gospel, yet they belong to Satan (2 Cor. 4:14). While many of Satan's agents started as being sincere, they lost their way because their conscience became seared (1 Tim. 4:2), leading to apostasy, leading others also into apostasy. Contextually, doctrines of demons refer to legalism, where restrictions were implemented to acquire salvation. Paul addressed a 'works-based' gospel with the church of Galatia, calling it a "Different gospel" (Gal. 1:6), a "Distorted gospel" (Gal. 1:7), and a "Gospel of man" (Gal. 1:11). A simple and subtle distortion of the gospel, such as what Satan did with Eve (Gen. 3) and attempted again with Jesus (Matt. 4:3-11), is a distorted gospel birthed from doctrines of demons.

When you add or take away, or change in any way, you no longer have the gospel of the Kingdom, but instead, another and a different version of the gospel. By tampering with the gospel, you place yourself under a curse (Deut. 4:2, Rev. 22:18-19), in the same way as when you depart from Christ, who redeemed you from the curse (Gal. 3:10). By doing so, you are thereby, and by default, eternally cursed.

Those who tamper with the gospel do so because their consciences are seared (1 Tim. 4:2), implying they have continually gone against the God-given witness in their hearts (Rom. 2:15) until they are numb to His Word and His Spirit. As a result, they are thereby abandoned by God (Rom. 1:24, 26, 28). Where the conscience is seared, it has been rendered insensitive to God, no longer having any means of knowing right from wrong, thus having no way of return.

For this reason, apostasy is so very dangerous that once a person is fully apostate, there is no way back (Heb. 5:4-8, 10:29). For that person, there remains no longer any hope. It is essential to note - however, no one becomes apostate overnight. Apostate in the Greek means 'away' and 'apart,' translating, 'standing away' applying desertion, or withdrawal of the faith. Apostasy can only apply to those who once stood with and for the truth and with those holding fast to the truth (Jesus). Like a runaway, derailed train, leaving the track one wheel at a time, so is the apostate, with many warnings blaring along the way with a screech of each departing wheel before the train finally arrives at the point of no return.

Another essential point here is, *IF you are worried you are apostate, with no hope of return, then you are not by definition, you are concerned about it. Once fully apostate, that person will have no fear over the matter, no consideration of Christ, and no desire to get right with Him. Those afraid of apostasy evidently prove that they are not. Fear is healthy, but when there is no fear, that is a most fearful state within itself! Instead of being apostate, the fearful person may be backslidden, leading to apostasy (Matt. 26:41) - therefore the backslidden condition should be addressed quickly.

The difference between being backslidden and apostate is that the backslider has relapsed in their faith - whereas an apostate has renounced the faith. To the backslider, God says, return (Isa. 44:22, Jer. 3:12, 14, 22, 4:1, 15:19, 18:11, Joel 2:12, 13, Zech. 1:3, 4, Mal 3:7. Rev. 2:5) and do it fast (2 Cor. 6:2, cf. Isa. 45). If not, then prepare for harvest, prepare to meet your God (Amos 4:12, cf. 3:11-15)!

The positive term 'Ready for Harvest' (Matt. 9:37, 38) refers to those ready to enter the Kingdom of God through the gospel of the Kingdom. However, the negative application refers to those who have rejected the biblical Jesus, revealed through sound biblical preaching. They have been conditioned, prepared, and made ready for a harvest of another kind of harvest (Matt. 13:30, 39, Rev. 14:14-19). The judgement harvest is reserved for those who have been distracted, deceived, and derailed, and for those who refused to love the truth and be saved. Soon, God will send them the strong delusion (the antichrist) so that they may (fully) believe what is false, so that all may be condemned who did not believe the truth (2 Thess. 2:11-12). Again, God sends the antichrist at the appointed time, confirmed by Daniel (Dan. 7, 11:35).

The appointed time begins with the tribulation, where the antichrist is revealed (2 Thess. 2:6). Next, the antichrist will be revealed through the signing of the false seven-year peace treaty (Isa. 28:15, 18, Dan. 9:24-27), and again when he announces himself to be God from the rebuilt third (tribulation) temple (2 Thess. 2:4). From there, he will command that all must worship him, and only him (Rev. 13:1-18), like Nebuchadnezzar (Dan. 3) and Darius (Dan. 6) did. Antiochus did the same (Dan. 11). All were antichrist types in their behaviours, albeit Nebuchadnezzar and Darius proclaimed God as the one true God (Dan. 4:1-3, 34-37, 6:25-27). Antiochus, however, like the antichrist will - never did. Antiochus, like the antichrist, was exposed and revealed to the wise by defiling the temple (Dan. 11:31-33). The antichrist will be revealed by doing the same thing (2 Thess. 2:4).

Another sign revealing the antichrist is his resurrection from the grave. While some say the antichrist was not resurrected but rather resuscitated, scripture confirms the former. In the book of Revelation, chapter thirteen states the antichrist receives a mortal wound, killing him (Rev. 13:3, 12, 14), and from which he will be resurrected (Rev. 17:8, 11). Therefore, the beast (antichrist) was and is not and is again about to rise from the bottomless pit. The same is confirmed in Revelation, chapter eleven, where the beast (antichrist) rises from the bottomless pit (Rev. 11:7). Also, notice the counterfeit comparison of the words "Was, and is not, and is again" with those referring to Jesus (Rev. 1:4, 8, cf. 5:6, 16:5). There is only one way you can be in the bottomless pit, and that is to die without Christ. Nothing good goes into or comes out of the bottomless pit.

Much speculation comes about how the antichrist receives his mortal wound. But, when reading Revelation, chapter eleven, the context suggests the two witnesses 'may' have killed him. The two witnesses are preaching from the rebuilt tribulation temple (Rev. 11:1-3), consuming their foes with fire (Rev. 11:5), as Elijah did (1 Kgs. 18, 2 Kgs 1). The one problem with the suggestion that two witnesses kill the antichrist is that the antichrist is killed with a sword (Rev. 13:14), not by fire. The only references to being killed with a sword in the tribulation, besides the antichrist (Rev. 13:14), refer to Jesus judging the church (Rev. 1:16, 2:12, 16) and the nations (Rev. 19:15, 21), and with the red horse (Rev. 6:4), combined with the white, black and pales horses, killing one-fourth of the population (Rev. 6:8). The martyred saints also perish by the sword from the antichrist (Rev. 13:10, 15).

The two-thousand-year-old reference to the sword probably translates to the modern equivalent. For an ancient observer, a discharged gun may indeed look like fire proceeding forth, resulting in death. Whichever way, the antichrist is probably not killed with an actual sword, causing a mortal wound to the head, but rather something else. Mass death will occur within the tribulation through natural (sword/gun/guillotine) and supernatural means (fire).

Another group killing people with fire proceeding from their mouths is the two-hundred million mounted troops (Rev. 9:17-18, cf. Joel 2:3). It has also been suggested that they deliver the antichrist his mortal wound. The two-hundred million mounted troops will oppose the antichrist in the second half of the tribulation, and the antichrist will oppose the two witnesses in the first half. After the two witnesses' testimony of Christ is finished, the antichrist will kill them, as God permits (Rev. 11:7). Then, after three days, God will resurrect the two witnesses from the dead. The killing of the two witnesses will be another sign revealing the identity of the antichrist.

Imagine now if the two witnesses are the ones who kill the antichrist (pure speculation). Then the antichrist rises from the grave and kills the two witnesses, and then the two witnesses rise from the grave and ascend into the air (Rev. 11:11-12); what a spectacular display of God's power that would be! There will be many competing signs and wonders, genuine signs and wonders versus counterfeit signs and wonders. The counterfeit will be so convincing that they will lead many astray, even the elect, if possible (Matt. 24:24).

None of the tribulation signs revealing the antichrist are more evident than when he announces himself to be God from the rebuilt tribulation temple. Remember, the left-behind population must be first conditioned for this event, rendered ripe for harvest, which is precisely what the spirit of the antichrist is doing in the church, and in the world today. Again, Revelation, chapter thirteen, referenced by Jesus in Matthew, chapter twenty-four (v. 15), where the antichrist commits the abomination of desolation. The abomination of desolation is first mentioned by Daniel (Dan. 9:27, 11:31, 12:11), referring to changing the Law of God and replacing God's Law with another. The changing of the Law refers to the temple sacrifice (Dan. 7:25), where the antichrist will do away with God's authorised sacrifice by introducing his own. The same was mentioned in the previous selection of this work, where Aaron's two sons brought strange (unauthorised) fire as a sacrifice at the altar (Lev. 10), resulting in them being consumed by the fire of God.

Satan will repeat the same through his son of perdition (2 Thess. 2:3), the antichrist (Rev. 13:11-18). The antichrist will attempt to do away with God's Law, also counterfeiting Jesus, thereby claiming he is the long-awaited Messiah, thus doing great signs and wonders, even calling fire down from the sky (Matt. 24:23-26, 2 Thess. 2:9, Rev. 13:13). The antichrist can do great signs and wonders due to being possessed by Satan (2 Thess. 2:9).

Again, when the antichrist is killed, Satan resurrects and embodies him. The antichrist is resurrected at the same time Satan is cast to the earth (Rev. 12:7-9, 13-14), at the halfway mark of the tribulation (Rev. 11:3, 12:6, 14, 13:5), which is when he announces himself to be God. It enforces his mark, commanding everyone receives it, and worship him (Rev. 13:11-18). The beast's mark (666) is another way of recognising the antichrist in the tribulation (Rev. 13:18). Remember, the antichrist cannot and will not be revealed before the tribulation (1 Thess. 2:6).

In sum, before the antichrist is revealed, there is no mark of the beast (666) - no beast, no mark (666). However, the COVID-19 passport has undoubtedly set the stage, indicating the nearness of the things to come. Another tell-tale sign is the recent construction of the image of the antichrist capturing the imagery of Daniel, chapter seven, and Revelation, chapter thirteen. The United Nations set up this statue and placed it in front of their New York headquarters (December 2021), under the banner of 'Peace and Security' (cf. 1 Thess. 5:3). Again, these signs are pointing at, even screaming - the end is near!

Like the COVID-19 passport, leading to social scoring and segregation, which is not the mark of the beast (666), these signs mentioned earlier have set the stage. They are preparing the spellbound global population, ripe for harvest, to be ready for the antichrist, whom God will hand-deliver them.

The COVID-19 passport is already evolving from a digital display on smartphones to a chip to be implanted into the hand of the deceived. No one can trade or travel without the mark (chip) (Rev. 13:16-17) or function within society. The beast's mark will become mandatory at the halfway point of the tribulation, following the antichrist's announcement that he is God. This announcement will fulfill the prophecy of the abomination of desolation (Matt. 24:15). The abomination of desolation commences the great tribulation (Matt. 24:21), lasting forty-two months.

Right now, Bible prophecy is being fulfilled at an alarming rate, yet those ready are not alarmed, but alert, ready and waiting for the words, "Come up here" (Rev. 4:1). Once the church has been removed, the tribulation commences (2 Thess. 2:6, Rev. 3:10, 4:1), and the antichrist is revealed, to those who are wise (Dan 11:33, 12:10). Everything required has already been set up, ready for the things to come, including:

1. False teaching and false teachers, now at an all-time high
2. Materials, artifacts, and religious ritual training for the third temple are in place
3. The Middle East Peace Treaty has been tabled and is gaining traction
4. The New World Order has been set up
5. A one-world, cashless cryptocurrency has been set up
6. A DNA altering injection is being forced upon the global population
7. Persecution and imprisonment (FEMA camps) for those who refuse to 'comply'
8. A 'mark' (COVID-19 passport) has prepared the way for the mark (666)
9. Wars and rumours of wars are escalating, globally (Russia and China)
10. An image of the beast, under the banner of 'peace and security' has been erected

The only thing we are waiting for now is the beast, the antichrist. He is, again, revealed only after the church has been removed (raptured) in the tribulation, preparing the faithless and the rebels for harvest (judgement). When the antichrist does appear, he will proclaim to have the answers to the world's greatest challenges, deceiving many, such as:

1. Climate change
2. COVID-19 (and the jab)
3. The global economy (socialism)
4. Currency (cash replaced with cryptocurrency)

5. War and civil unrest
6. Religious differences
7. Mortality

The stage is set, the global community is ripe for harvest. Due to rejecting Jesus Christ, they are ready to receive and worship their antichrist and receive his mark (666).

Flee

'Let the Reader Understand'
(Matt. 24:16)

The previous section discussed the antichrist, pinpointing the midway point of the tribulation, being the great tribulation, said to be a time worse than any before or will be again (Matt. 24:21). The midway point of the tribulation is marked by the abomination of desolation (Matt. 24:15), which is when the antichrist takes his place in the rebuilt tribulation temple (third temple), changes the Law of God (Dan. 7:25), and proclaims to be God (2 Thess. 2:4). When the antichrist declares to be God, he will demand everyone worships him, as Nebuchadnezzar did (Dan. 3).

Of the entire Jewish population and other nations and languages (Dan. 3:4, 7), only a handful, with fingers to spare, refused to worship Nebuchadnezzar's golden image. The image was of Nebuchadnezzar, the same way the antichrist's image is of himself, causing the global population to worship the beast (Rev. 13:14-15). Few, just a remnant, will refuse to bow down and worship the antichrist and receive his mark (666) when the time comes. Most will have and already have been conditioned to accept him.

The evidence is seen where the global population is and has been already prepared to go with the flow. They accept whatever narrative the world spins (e.g. COVID-19 with associated 'vaccinations' and resulting passports, restricting, and segregating the population, further developing into social scoring, concluding with the beast's mark).

The global population has been prepared over decades, mesmerized by the puppeteer mainstream media, to accept whatever spoonful of rubbish the world elites serve up next. One spoonful prepares you for the next, with each moving the spellbound further and further away from the truth, in preparation for the deceiver of all deceivers, the strong delusion (2 Thess. 2:11). Still, like the few who resisted Nebuchadnezzar by refusing to bow down and worship his image (Dan. 3:12), there will always be a remnant, as in the tribulation, refusing to worship the world system and the beast (Rev. 13:15). Like Shadrach, Meshack, and Abednego (Dan. 3:8-23), the remnant will be subject to persecution, even unto death (Rev. 13:10.15).

At the midway point of the tribulation, many of the wise (Rev. 13:18) will revolt against the antichrist. Not counted as the wise but still opposed to the antichrist are the two-hundred million mounted troops (Rev. 9:13-19, 16:12-16), who Gog and Magog join (Ezek. 38-39, cf. Dan. 11:40-45), and some Jews (Joel 3:116). They will collectively and or individually war against the beast, leading to Armageddon (Rev. 16:12-16, 19:11-21).

At the halfway mark of the tribulation, the antichrist first responds to armies from the South, probably returning from Europe into Jerusalem (Dam. 11:40). When the antichrist arrives in the Holy Land, he kills Jews in the tens of thousands. Before this, the antichrist signed a seven-year Middle East peace treaty that included the Jews (Dan. 9:24-27, cf. Isa. 28:15, 18). Three and a half years into the tribulation, the antichrist breaks that treaty by killing the Jews. The breaking of the peace treaty is when the antichrist changes the Law and announces himself to be God (Dan. 9:27).

In response to the antichrist's proclamation, demands, and murderous deeds, armies from the East (China and co.) and North (Russia and co.) invade Jerusalem (Dan. 11:40-45). More likely, these armies are attempting to liberate Jerusalem from the antichrist, yet also take the city for themselves. When Jerusalem is attacked by the kings of the East and the North, the antichrist shall go out to meet them with great fury, but he will not prevail (Dan. 11:45).

When the antichrist turns against the Jews, killing tens of thousands of them, they are told to FLEE (Matt. 24:16). Those fleeing will be delivered from the antichrist by God (Dan. 11:41). John saw the same event, as described in the book of Revelation, chapter twelve (Rev. 12:6, 14). Again, the timeframe of this event marks the midway point of the tribulation (Rev. 12:6, 14b). The first and second half of the tribulation are marked by the beast now proclaiming he is God (Rev. 13:5), which he cannot while the two witnesses are alive. For forty-two months, the two witnesses are preaching Christ (Rev. 11:3), making it tricky for the antichrist to claim he is the Messiah.

Forty-two months into the tribulation, the antichrist received a mortal wound (Rev. 13:3, 12, 14) and is then resurrected by Satan (Rev. 17:8, 11), who has been cast to the earth (Rev. 12:7-13). At the midpoint of the tribulation, Satan possesses the antichrist, giving him his power (Matt. 24:24, 2 Thess. 2:9, Rev. 13:13-14). Then, through the antichrist, and his armies, he goes after the Jews fleeing from Jerusalem (Rev. 12:13-15). The fleeing Jews will be made up of those now proclaiming Christ (Rev. 12:11, 17) and calling for His return (Matt. 23:39).

A similar event to the above mentioned occurred when Antiochus took his seat in the temple (Dan. 11:36). In contrast, he too changed the Law and set up the abomination of desolation (Dan. 11:31). In the same way, the antichrist will win over many, initially, with flattery - Antiochus did likewise (Dan. 11:32a). Antiochus flattered those into breaking the covenant with God rewarding them with position and possessions (Dan. 11:39b), peace, and security (cf. 1 Thess. 5:3), and fought against those who remained faithful to God (Dan. 11:32b, 1 Mac. 1:30). Those enduring, thereby resisting Antiochus, and remaining in the city, were slain (Dan. 11:33-34, 1 Mac. 1:50), which is repeated in the tribulation under the antichrist (Rev. 13:10, 15).

When Antiochus forced the Jews to violate their covenant with God, many, yet still a remnant, fled into the hills and were cut down by their faithless brothers (1 Mac. 1:53, Dan. 11:33). Most of the Jews violated their covenant with God by erecting and worshipping and sacrificing to idols and by profaning the Sabbath (1 Mac. 1:43). The faithless also caused others, under coercion, to do the same. Those who stayed in Jerusalem, who refused to submit to Antiochus, and violate their covenant with God, were killed (1 Mac. 1:62-64), which will be repeated in the tribulation. For this reason, Jesus said, when the time comes, "Flee to the mountains" (Matt. 24:16).

Many times, throughout the Old Testament, God's people are told to flee from an enemy. However, in the New Testament, believers are only told to flee from the enemy sin, e.g., sexual immorality (1 Cor. 6:18), idolatry (1 Cor. 10:14), the love of money (1 Tim. 6:9-11), and youthful passions (2 Tim. 2:22). Never in the Bible is the Christian told to take flight from their enemy, Satan, but rather Satan would flee from the faithful believer who is submitting to God (Ja. 4:7). The exception to that rule is in the tribulation, perhaps because the church is now gone. During the tribulation, the believer is referred to as the saint.

However, it is the Jew who Jesus had in mind when providing the details of Matthew, chapter twenty-four. Specifically, in the second half, the Jew residing in Jerusalem is told to flee (Matt. 24:16), namely from Satan, who is operating through the antichrist.

From the Old Testament, the prophet Zechariah has more to say on the topic (esp. Zech. 14:2, 5), predicting that half of Jerusalem's population will flee the city (Zech. 14:2), leading up to the day of the Lord. The half fleeing makes up the elected Jews (Matt. 24:22, 24, 31).

Like with the antichrist returning to Jerusalem, killing tens of thousands of Jews, another sign is when the earth shakes (Zech. 14:5). When Jerusalem shakes, the faithful Jews are to flee in haste, without delay, not looking back to gather possessions (Matt. 24:17-18), not looking back at what is lost (remember Lot's wife: Lu. 17:32). When the earth shakes, it is due to the antichrist defiling the temple, as King Uzziah did. (Amos. 1:1, 2 Chron. 26:16). Again, the earthquake is another sign for the watchful Jews to flee from Jerusalem - to flee fast! Jesus said, when the time comes, do not go back to gather goods, for it will be difficult enough without having to worry about saving and transporting possessions (Matt. 24:19-20). For the elected Jews, keeping the Sabbath will also be of great importance; therefore, Jesus refers to that potential challenge by saying, "Pray that your flight may not be on the Sabbath" (Matt. 24:19). In other words, accept the fact, you are going through the tribulation - however, I will be there with you!

As mentioned earlier, as Antiochus did, the antichrist will change the Law relating to the Sabbath and temple sacrifice. However, the fleeing Jews will hold fast to the Law, and God will supernaturally provide their needs (Rev. 12:6, 14, cf. Ex. 16, Isa. 41:17-20, Mic. 2:12). He will give them 'wings' (Rev. 12:14, cf. Ex. 19:4, Deut. 32:10-12), as with Israel in the wilderness. Still, Satan will be hot on their trail (Rev. 12:13).

When the time comes, the Jews flee to Bozrah, a region in southwest Jordan, where the ancient fortress city of Petra is located (cf. Jer. 49:13-14). Isaiah (63:1-3) reveals, from Bozrah, Jesus will take revenge on the nations pursuing the remnant of Israel, hidden away (Zeph. 2:3), which occurs at the end of the forty-two months, known as the 'Day of the Lord'.

During the tribulation Israel's false prophets will continue to respond negatively to God's judgements. After the tribulation, God turns everything around (Isa. 26), and then they will sing with joy. In the millennium, the song of salvation, sung by Judah, considers all that God has done. God has turned Israel's misfortune around (Isa. 25), which includes dealing with death (Isa. 25:8) through their long-awaited salvation (Isa. 25:9).

Note, Judah's salvation only comes through tribulation, which includes the judgement of Jerusalem (Isa. 24:12-13, 25:2), and follows the judgement of the nations (Isa. 25:10-12). Until that time, and during the great tribulation, Israel will be hidden away from the halfway point (Isa. 26:20-21).

Again, although hidden away, Israel will not be safe until the millennial dispensation, and they will only be safe in the millennium because Jesus is on the earth, ruling and reigning from Jerusalem. Therefore, not only will believing Israel enter the millennium but all and any, from every nation, who are found righteous in and through Christ Jesus (Isa. 26:2).

During the millennium, and even now, Jesus will be the Rock of salvation (Isa. 17:10, 44:8), for those trusting in Him. It is the opposite of those trusting in themselves (Isa. 26:5-6), and their cities. Instead of salvation, God will destroy the wicked (Isa. 25:12). Only those who humbled themselves, through repentance (Isa. 26:3-5), during the tribulation will be saved (Isa. 26:6-12).

There is deliverance, during the tribulation, but only for the ones who respond to God's judgements (Isa. 26:7-21). Only through judgement will the wicked respond (Isa. 26:9-10), albeit most will not see God's raised arm even when it is right in front of them (Isa. 26:11). God then levels the way, for those who respond to Him, through His findings. Those turning to

God, through judgement, look to Him (Isa. 26:8-9) and learn righteousness (Isa. 26:9). Those coming to God through His judgements (Isa. 26:9) during the tribulation previously failed to come to Him through His grace (Isa. 26:10), leaving them behind to endure the time of trouble.

Those turning to God, through judgement, were previously under and trusting in world governments and their governance of others, contrary to God, these people God will destroy (Isa. 26:13-14). God will destroy the cities and the world leaders of those cities who failed to humble themselves before and during His judgement. As for those who perished under their rule, who resisted them, and were instead trusting in God, they shall again live (Isa. 26:19, cf. 25:8). Still, judgement comes before joy (Isa. 26:16-18).

During the tribulation, Israel will be so distressed, like a woman in labour (Isa. 26:17-17, cf. 13:8), that their prayers will be merely whispered out (Isa. 26:16), and even though praying for deliverance, death will result for many (Isa. 28:19). On the contrary, those still trusting in themselves, shall not live (Isa. 26:14), and instead of whispered prayers, they will writhe, producing only wind (Isa. 26:18). The haughty will respond to God's judgement, albeit essentially blind to it (Isa. 26:11) in the same way that brought about the judgement in the first place, by trusting in themselves.

Again, Israel will be hidden away (Isa. 26:20-21) from the halfway point of the seven-year tribulation. For forty-two months, God will supernaturally sustain them (Rev. 12:6, 14), still many millions will die (Rev. 12:11), yet shall live again (Isa. 26:19, Dan. 12:2) because they put their trust in God.

While the Jews are hidden away, Jerusalem will be plagued by war from God (Zech. 14:12-15, 12:4), ending with the gathering for the battle of Armageddon (Rev. 16:16). The battle or campaign of Armageddon is prevented by Jesus, who returns before all flesh is destroyed (Matt. 24:22).

However, the return of Jesus is a most frightening day for those not prepared (Rev. 6:12-17). Chapter fourteen of the book of Zechariah addresses the coming day of the Lord (Zech. 14:1), described by Zephaniah (1:14-18). Leading up to that day, God gathers the nations to battle against Jerusalem (Zech. 14:2, cf. 12:2-9, Isa. 34:2, Obad. 15, Ezek. 38:4, 16b, 39:2, 11, Rev. 9:11, 16:12-16), and then once assembled, He 'goes out' (Zech. 1:3) to fight against them (cf. Ex. 15:3; Isa. 42:13; Rev. 19:11–21). Jesus Christ, not the antichrist, defeats the invading armies (cf. Dan. 11:45, Rev. 19:11-19). The term 'On that day' is seen eighteen times in the book of Zechariah from chapter nine onwards. Chapter fourteen contains seven references to the phrase, 'On that day', alone (Zech. 14:4, 6, 8, 9, 13, 20, 21).

Before Jesus returns, the faithful Jews will be supernaturally taken care of by Jesus and through those sacrificially committed to Him. Matthew, chapter twenty-five (vv. 31-46) contextually follows chapter twenty-four, stating that any who care for the Jews during the tribulation, will be likened to caring for Jesus (Matt. 25:35-40). In contrast, any who confess to following Christ, who do not take care of the Jews, will be judged as denying Christ (Matt. 25:41-46). Those who fail to care for the Jews do so to save their lives. Those caring for the Jews do so at the cost of their lives. Those who try to save their lives will lose them, and those who lay down their lives will save them (Matt. 10:39, 16:25). The same will be true of the Jews who do not flee Jerusalem when the time comes.

In sum, the reader who understands the signs of the times through the scripture will know when the antichrist returns to Jerusalem. It will be in response to an invading army from the South, killing tens of thousands of Jews. Thereby the peace treaty will be broken, and then defiling the temple by changing the Law, and proclaiming to be God. This will force the global population to take his mark (666), signified by an earthquake, then they must flee. Another sign indicating it is time to flee is when the antichrist is resurrected, and the two witnesses are killed, resurrected, and ascend into heaven (Rev. 11:7-12).

Following the ascension of the two witnesses with the words, "Come up here" (Rev. 11:12), there is a great earthquake (Rev. 11:13). There is also an earthquake when the antichrist defiles the temple (Zech. 14:5). When the earthquakes occur, the wised-up Jews (cf. Dan. 11:33, 12:10) will flee Jerusalem at the midway point of the tribulation, commencing the great tribulation. Half of the Jewish population residing in Jerusalem at that time flee to the mountains; however, not all within that company will be saved (Dan. 11:34). Only a remnant, by comparison, will be (Rom. 9:27-28, cf. Isa. 10:20-22), as it is also true of those confessing to be Christian (Matt. 7:21-23).

Important note: Today, many end-time watchmen are preparing to escape to the hills due to the writing on the wall, specifically seen through COVID-19 and the associated vaccinations and passport. However, Christians are not told to flee from the enemy other than from the enemy of sin. The only exception to this is seen in the early church, where believers fled persecution that spread the gospel (Acts 8:1, 4, 11:19). For the most part, what the early church experience will be repeated during the tribulation, for those left behind. Those who miss the rapture, who then repent of their sin, spread the gospel, like wildfire, throughout the whole world (Matt. 24:14). The coverage of the gospel, under persecution, will be, and already is, another significant end-time sign. Therefore, the call to escape the city does not, contextually, apply to this side of the tribulation.

Let the reader understand when we see these signs; you will know the end is near (Matt. 24:15b, 33, Lu. 21:31).

Tribulation like Never Before, or will be Again

'Judgement Before Joy'

(Matt. 24:21)

In the previous sections, commencing the great tribulation, the abomination of desolation (Matt. 24:15) was addressed, resulting in another topic, fleeing. When the antichrist announces he is God from the rebuilt tribulation temple, the Jews will flee Jerusalem (Matt. 24:16). The halfway point of the tribulation is marked and known by these events (Matt. 24:15-16). From this point onwards, Jesus said it would be a time like none other before it or afterward (Matt. 24:21).

The great tribulation is directly mentioned three times in the Bible (Jer. 30:7, Dan. 12:1, Matt. 24:21), with another reference found in the book of Joel (Joel 2:2, cf. 1:2). Each reference states the same; never in the history of the world has anything like what is to come, ever been seen before, or will be again. Although the topic of great tribulation was previously addressed under the heading of 'great oppression,' this section will dive deeper into the phrase's origin.

The book of Jeremiah (30:7) is the original place prophesying the great tribulation, confirmed by Daniel (12:1). When Jesus discussed the signs of the times, He narrowed in on the commencing sign of the great tribulation, which is the abomination of desolation. In doing so, He referenced Daniel as the source (Matt. 24:15). Daniel's reference is rooted in Jeremiah, whom Daniel was quite familiar with (Dan. 9:1-2, cf. Jer. 25:12). In the same way, Jeremiah predicted Judah's tribulation (cf. Lam. 3:5), and ours, Daniel also predicted the time of trouble for this last generation (Dan. 7:7-27, 9:24-27, 11:40-45, 12), and Jesus confirmed it (Matt. 24:21).

On the subject, Jeremiah starts with a positive note, "For behold, days are coming, declares the Lord, when I will restore the fortunes of my people, Israel and Judah, says the Lord, and I will bring them back to the land that I gave to their fathers, and they shall take possession of it" (Jer. 30:3). Note that the promise is addressed to Israel and Judah, not the church. The church has not and will never replace Israel. The land (Israel) is the Jew's promised inheritance forever. The land refers to Israel, the location, not any other nations, as some today suggest, naming and claiming whichever country as their inheritance, where they would rule and reign like kings in this life. Nonsense! As for the timing of Israel fully possessing the holy land, as God intended, contextually, that happens when Jesus returns, implying after the great tribulation. Before then, there will be trouble, great trouble, then blessings for those who respond.

Although the chapter (Jer. 30) speaks of the worst possible time the planet has ever seen or will again (Jer. 30:7), the message is one of hope (Jer. 30:3, 8-22). God will restore! God will restore, but not before judgement comes first. God's unstoppable, irreversible judgement (Jer. 30:24) will come on 'the day' (Jer. 30:3) appointed, set to occur after the great tribulation. Jeremiah referenced "the day" several times throughout his book (cf. 5:18; 7:32; 9:25; 19:6), always speaking of a day of destruction where God will judge Israel and Judah for their sin. Like the promised inheritance, the promise of judgment (on this occasion) is aimed at the Jews. If those within the church still want to claim the Jew's inheritance, they must accept, and share in their judgement, as they go together, one following the other.

While "the day" was fulfilled after Jerusalem fell to the Babylonians, the secondary application is eschatological, applying to the time of the antichrist. After the appointed time of the antichrist (Dan. 7), God will restore Israel (cf. Deut. 30:1-10), and judge the Gentile nations (cf. 3:16, 18; 16:14; 23:5, 7, 20; 30:3, 24; 31:27, 29, 31, 33, 38; 33:14–16; 48:12, 47; 49:2, 39; 50:4, 20; 51:47, 52).

Israel is first judged in the tribulation, and then the nations will be judged. The church is being judged now (1 Pet. 4:17) through shaking, testing, and separating. Those holding fast, enduring until the end, do not go through the tribulation (Rev. 2:25, 3:10). Those failing and falling will go through the tribulation (Rev. 2:16, 22, 3:3, 16).

Throughout the book of Jeremiah, the prophet saw the soon-to-be fulfilled events, such as the Babylonian invasion, and the events further out, as in the great tribulation. Although these events are far apart, Jeremiah included them as a continuous series of happenings. It is not uncommon for the Bible to treat the separate judgements as one, seen several times throughout the book of Daniel (chapters 2, 7, 9, 11, and 12).

Another example is when the prophet Isaiah referenced Jesus' first and second events as one event (Isa. 61:1-2). Jesus read the words of Isaiah, announcing His arrival, stopping short of the portion referring to His second coming (Lu. 4:18-19). Another example from Isaiah is seen in chapter nine (vv. 6-7), referring to Jesus returning to set up His government on the earth.

Again, before God restores Israel (Jer. 30:3, 17, 18), a time of great distress must first occur (Jer. 30:4-7). Jeremiah describes this as a time of panic and terror, not peace (Jer. 30:5), as the false prophets proclaim (Jer. 6:14, 8:11, 14:13, 28:9). Such terror will fall that men's faces will turn pale (Jer. 30:6), a great day of distress, yet through it, Israel will be saved (Jer. 30:7). The same 'day' is referred to by the prophet Zephaniah, who describes the utter dread of it (Zep. 1). Terror, not peace, will be the experience! Although the day will come when many say peace and security (1 Thess. 5:3).

Jeremiah further describes that day when men will clutch themselves as a woman in labour (cf. 4:31; 6:24; 13:21; 22:23; 49:24; 50:43), echoed by Paul (1 Thess. 5:3), and Jesus (Matt. 24:8). The same was referenced by John (Rev. 12:2), having both literal and allegoric meanings. Although the time will be like none seen before, and like a woman in labour, out of it comes great joy. Through tribulation, God will save Israel (Jer. 30:7, 10, 11); out of tribulation shall come a song of thanksgiving (Jer. 30:19, 31:12-13, 33:11).

As mentioned previously, the time of trouble Jeremiah references points to the coming tribulation and return of Christ. Some suggest the passage was fulfilled with the Babylonian invasion; but, they overlook that it only affected Judah's southern kingdom, not the northern kingdom, Israel. However, what Jeremiah predicts affects both (Jer. 30:3). The unparalleled persecution Jeremiah prophesies (Jer. 30:7, Dan. 9:27; 12:1; Matt. 24:15–22) refers to the tribulation and narrows in on the conclusion of the latter half. The later forty-two months will conclude when Jesus appears to rescue His elect (Matt. 24:22, Rom. 11:26) and establish His kingdom on the earth (Matt. 24:30–31; 25:31–46; Rev. 19:11–21; 20:4–6). The book of Revelation lists Jesus' return as 'the third woe' of the tribulation (Rev. 8:13), which is the seventh trumpet (Rev. 11:15-19), and seventh bowl (Rev. 16:17-21).

The return of Christ, for the unrepentant and unprepared, will be the most frightening day of all time. For the repentant and the prepared, the greatest time of distress will conclude with the most significant time of joy. "For His anger is but for a moment, and His favour is for a lifetime. Weeping may tarry for the night, but joy comes with the morning" (Ps. 30:5).

When Jesus returns to rescue His elect, He will break the yoke of bondage (Jer. 30:8). Israel's deliverance did not come as the false prophets predicted, and neither will peace come to this world before Jesus returns. So likewise, Israel and the church will not have dominion on this earth until Jesus sets up His government, no matter how much 'Kingdom Now' subscribers declare and decree it. The kingdom is not now, albeit soon to come, but not before the tribulation comes first. During the tribulation, Israel will seek Jesus (Hos. 3:5) - they will call on His name (Matt. 23:39) and be saved (Rom. 11:25-32). Then, when Jesus does come, Israel shall be, once more, God's people (Jer. 30:22).

No matter how far Israel had strayed, and no matter how far Israel had been scattered (Jer. 30:3, 10, 12-15), God will gather them (Jer. 30:3), heal (save, Jer. 30:7b, 10, 11) and restore (Jer. 30:3, 17, 18). No sin is too great, and no place is too far for God to reach those who seek Him, repent and return. However, God's discipline comes first, turning the sinner from sin (Jer. 30:11c). In the same way, God judged Israel He will judge her again (Jer. 30:12-15)., God will save the faithless nation through judgment, albeit just a remnant of them (Rom. 9:27) who respond (Rom. 10:5-21, 11:25-32).

When God saves Israel through suffering, He will restore their fortunes (Jer. 32:44; 33:11, 26; cf. Deut. 30:3), including the rebuilt temple during the millennium and the city of Jerusalem (Jer. 30:18). Again, the promise is to Israel, not the church, and the promise will be fulfilled in the millennium, following Israel's repentance during the tribulation and only after Jesus returns. On that day, Israel will serve God and no other (Jer. 30:9), and the other nations will recognise it. Once again, before Israel's situation is turned around, terror must come first (Jer. 30:23-24).

Jeremiah concludes the chapter by repeating a previous chapter (Jer. 23:19-20), echoing, before the blessing, judgement comes first. Chapter twenty-three deals with the lying prophets (vv. 9-39) who led Judah astray (Jer. 23:23) with their false promises of peace and prosperity (Jer. 23:16-17), leading the Jews into adultery and idolatry (Jer. 23:13-14, 26-27)). If God had sent the false prophets, they would have carried His word of warning, demanding Judah to repent (Jer. 23:22).

The evidence of the true prophet is seen and heard in his words (Jer. 23:28), likened to fire and a hammer (Jer. 23:29). Instead, the false prophets preach fluff, vain hope (Jer. 23:16), copying one another (Jer. 23:30) while declaring the Lord said it (Jer. 23:31). As an alternative of bringing the burden (word, cf. Jer. 23:36) of the Lord, they are the burden (Jer. 23:32). In response, and in time, God will repay the lying prophets (Jer. 23:39-40), which did happen through the Babylonians, as a foreshadow of the things to come. During the tribulation, God will repay the false prophets within Israel and the church.

Reapplying the exact words from chapter twenty-three (vv. 19-20), Jeremiah aims at the nations that opposed and oppressed Israel (Jer. 30:16-20). The fierce anger previously poured out on Judah (Jer. 23:19-20) will again be poured out on the nations (Jer. 30:23-24).

Like Jeremiah, Daniel addresses the same event with similar words, "There shall be a time of trouble, such as never has been since there was a nation, till that time. But at that time your people shall be delivered" (Dan. 12:1). During that time, many who are slain for their faith in Jesus (Dan. 12:10, cf. Rev. 12:11) shall rise again (Dan. 12:2). Those who lead others to faith in Christ during the tribulation will shine like the brightness of the sky above and like the stars forever (Dan. 12:3). During the tribulation anyone who comes to faith in Jesus will be counted as blessed, gaining access to the millennial kingdom (Dan. 12:12).

Jesus repeats the same (Matt. 24:21), and like Jeremiah, He narrows in on the false prophets (Matt. 24:5, 11, 23-26), stating only the elect will be saved (Matt. 24:23), enduring (Matt. 24:13) and remaining free of deception (Matt. 24:24). Again, when Jesus returns (Matt. 24:27), after the tribulation (Matt. 24:29), then He will judge the nations (Matt. 24:30-31) who oppressed Israel and rejected His salvation. Any confessing follower of Christ who failed to support Israel during the tribulation will also be judged (Matt. 25:41-46).

In conclusion, the verses referenced (Jer. 30:7, Dan 12:1, Matt. 24:21) clearly talk about Israel. In no way can they be applied to the church; but, the lukewarm will suffer the same for the same reasons. When considering the application of the mentioned verses, within context, applied primarily to Israel for the purpose of salvation, then if confessing Christians insist on stealing Israel's future promises of prosperity, they must also share in their coming sufferings through the great tribulation. Through the great tribulation, God will save His rebellious people. Salvation through suffering applies to all, here and now, and through the time of trouble, for those left behind. Remember, Jesus came seeking to save the lost (Lu. 19:10), and He will use any means possible to achieve His redemptive plan.

While the concept of the things to come was difficult for Jeremiah to understand, in the latter days, understanding will come (Jer. 23:20, 30:24). The same was said to Daniel; the wise will understand, through increased knowledge (Dan. 12:4) in the latter days (Dan. 12:10), bringing others also into an understanding (Dan. 11:33). The understanding to come revolves around the knowledge of Jesus and sin. During the tribulation, many (albeit still a remnant) will repent of their sins and be saved (Rev. 7:9-14). Although the verses referred to are aimed at Israel, the promise of salvation is extended to all (Rom. 10:9-10).

Seen through the verses of Jeremiah, chapter thirty (vv. 12-15), no matter what anyone has done, no matter how badly any have strayed, and how long they have been away, Jesus is always seeking to save the lost (Jer. 7, 10, 11, 22). That same message is relayed repeatedly throughout the scriptures, perhaps nowhere better than through the parable of the parodical son (Lu. 15:11-31). When a sinner comes to faith in Jesus, through repentance, all of heaven rejoices (Lu. 15:7, 10, 20-24), and so it will be throughout the tribulation, as the saints above watch on (cf. Heb. 21:1), rejoicing in song over the victories of the Lamb (Rev. 11:17-18, 16:4b-7, 19:1b-3, 5, 7-8).

False Prophets and False Messiahs

'Purge the Evil from Among You'

(Matt. 24:23-25)

Adding to the aforenoted, another sign of the end times is an increase of false prophets performing lying signs and wonders during the mid-tribulation. Several times now, the topic of false teachers and false prophets has been addressed, and necessarily so, as Jesus repeated the same, "I have told you this beforehand" (Matt. 24:15). Furthermore, Jesus addressed the topic of false teachers/prophets more than any other end-time sign when warning of the signs of the things to come (Matt. 24:4-5, 11, 23-26). False teachers and false prophets are addressed so often because they are so numerous, and so dangerous, leading so many people astray (Matt. 24:11), even the elect, if possible (Matt. 24:24). False teachers condition their audience for the antichrist, whom God sends because people refused to love the truth (2 Thess. 2:10-11).

The antichrist is the ultimate false teacher, whom his sidekick, the false prophet, prepares the world for (Rev. 13:11-14). So serious is the problem of false teachers and false prophets in the church every New Testament writer addresses them, warning they will increase as we near the return of Jesus, and increasingly they have! Today the challenge is finding a Bible-preaching church, fearing/pleasing God more than man, or finding a 'Christian' television network that does not promote false teachers.

Although it is prophesied that false prophets will increase in the last days (Matt. 24:4-5, 11, 24, 1 Tim. 4:1, 2 Tim. 2:3), they were also the number one problem plaguing Israel in the Old Testament. Because Israel and Judah followed the false prophets, they went through a version of the coming tribulation, foreshowing the things to come. God judged Israel harshly to deal with false teaching/teachers and turn them around and away from idols; God will do the same again through the coming tribulation (Isa. 26:9-10).

Again, so severe is the problem of false prophets, under the Old Covenant, God commanded they be dealt with by stoning them to death (Deut. 13:10, 18:20). Today, under the New Covenant, Christians are commanded to have nothing to do with them (2 Jn. 1:9-11). The command for Christians is not to bring anything false into your life and home, whether in person, through 'Christian' television, the internet, recordings, or through their books, and do not attend the gatherings/meetings of false teachers. In other words, the believer is to separate themselves from anything and anyone false!

As previously stated, the problem of false teachers/prophets is nothing new and was addressed several times throughout the Old Testament. The book of Deuteronomy (Deut. 12:1-13:1-18) contains one of the most considerable portions of scripture outlaying the rules of entering, and remaining in the Promised Land, prewarning Israel not to entertain anything false. The opening verses (Deut. 12:1-4) state that the people of God are not to worship Him through a mix of means that the world (pagans) practice. God's people were to submit every area of their lives to Him, to be totally dependent on Him, primarily expressed through worship. Verses one to four warn Israel what not to do these things... followed by verses five to seven, eleven to eighteen, and twenty to twenty-seven, instructing Israel to take care (Deut. 12:19, 28) in how to worship God, with remembrance and with thanksgiving (Deut. 12:7). On the condition that Israel obeys God, things will go well for them (Deut. 12:28), which was not their experience due to their disobedience.

Until Israel entered the Promised Land, everyone had done what they saw fit in their own eyes (Deut. 12:8), which needed to change. The strict requirements placed on them were to preserve them and the purity of worship. Sadly, history confirms Israel failed to follow God's instructions, doing again as they saw fit (cf. Judg. 17:6, 21:25), eventually removing them from the Land and being temporally disqualified (Rom. 9, 11). Like the church (in many cases), Israel never learned the seriousness of God's commands.

On entering the Promised Land, Israel was to remove every idol and false god, which would eliminate any means of temptation and prevent any way of them defiling their worship unto God. By eliminating false gods from the Land, God would cut evil from off His people (Deut. 12:29). This instruction comes with another 'Take care'. "Take care that you be not ensnared to follow them (false gods) after they have been destroyed before you and that you do not inquire about their gods" (Deut. 12:30). Twelve times the words 'Take care' are recorded in the book of Deuteronomy, and each time refers to worship and or remembering God. The New Testament likewise provides the same caution:

"Take care, brothers, lest there be in any of you an evil, unbelieving heart, leading you to fall away from the living God" (Heb. 3:12).

"You, therefore, beloved, knowing this beforehand, take care that you are not carried away with the error of lawless people and lose your own stability" (2 Pet. 3:17).

Peter's reference is particularly interesting, following the passage addressing the return of the Lord, focussing on the scoffers not looking or believing that day will come (2 Pet. 3:1-13). Peter continues with, "Beloved, since you are waiting for these things, be diligent to be found by Him (Jesus) without spot or blemish, and at peace" (2 Pet. 3:14). Again, the contrast is clear, while one group is not looking for Jesus, the other is looking and waiting (2 Pet. 3:12, 13, 14) for Him, followed by a warning to those who twist the scripture (2 Pet. 3:16).

Following verse sixteen comes the instruction to 'Take care' (2 Pet. 3:17), not to be caught up in false teaching, and not to twist (tamper with) the written word. As with the writer of the book of Hebrews (Heb. 3:12), Peter's warning instructs the believer not to follow false and failing teachers. Again, the author of the book of Hebrews makes an example of Israel, who was disqualified from the Promised Land for their rebellion (Heb. 3:7-11, 16-19, 4:2-3, 6-7), encouraging the reader to "Strive to enter that rest, so that no one may fall by the same sort of disobedience" (Heb. 3:11). Israel's disobedience included forgetfulness, unbelief, ungratefulness, rebellion, and idolatry, leading to child sacrifice.

For the reasons mentioned above, God instructed the generation of Israelites who did enter God's rest (the Promised Land) to have nothing to do with worldly (pagan) worship. Be careful not to make the same mistake your ancestors did. Sadly, Israel did far worse than the disqualified generation once in the Promised Land. Child sacrifice to Molech exceeded their former sins. Israel was prewarned not to do this (Lev. 18:21; 20:2–5; 2 Kings 23:10) but did it anyway (Jer. 32:35).

Today's equivalent of child sacrifice is abortion, with particular 'Christian' denominations 'blessing' institutions performing this murderous act. Like the false prophet, the penalty for child sacrifice is death (Lev. 20:2–5). With confidence, one can assume that the same spirit connected to the false god Molech is behind the modern-day practice of abortion. Because of child sacrifice, Israel was removed from the Promised Land (2 Kings 17:6, 17). Israel's evil religious practice led to their disqualification and destruction.

Chapter twelve of the book of Deuteronomy concludes with, "Everything that I command you, you shall be careful to do. You shall not add to it or take from it" (Deut. 12:31). The warning is like that of Peter's, as mentioned earlier. 'Do not twist the written word!' The best way to avoid being tempted to twist scripture is to have nothing to do with false teachers. Instead, remove them from your life (2 Jn. 1:9-11), in the same way Israel was told to remove every idol and every false pagan practice of worship from the Land.

After breaking down and removing idolatrous practices from the Land, Moses warned Israel of three ways they could return: 1). Through false prophets (Deut. 13:1-5), 2). Through someone close (Deut. 13:6-11), and 3). Through worthless fellows (Deut. 13:12-18). In Moses' example, the worthless fellows led an entire town into apostasy. In the New Testament, the word worthless is used by Jesus, Paul, and Jude to describe an individual condemned to hell (Matt. 25:30, Rom. 3:12, Jude 3-5).

The first of the three groups is of particular interest given in the opening text of this section, where Jesus warned of false prophets who operated in signs and wonders (Matt. 24:23-25). The same was true of those Moses warned about (Deut. 13:1-5). While signs and wonders confirm the word of God (Mk. 16:20, 2 Cor. 12:12, Heb. 2:4), Satan does the same through lying signs and wonders (2 Cor. 11:13-14, 2 Thess. 2:8-9, Rev. 13:13-14, 16:13-14, 18:23, 19:20), which is why we are to test every spirit to see whether they are from God (1 Jn. 4:1-6). The importance of the warning is that signs and wonders were never meant to be a 'test of truth.' The standard of truth is not the miraculous, but rather the written word of God, taught contextually, correctly, and concisely, as in, to the point.

Today, many have already been led astray by false words of knowledge, false dreams, and visions, and counterfeit miracles because they did not test those manifestations by and through the scriptures. These counterfeit signs and wonders are described by Paul as the mystery of lawlessness already in operation within the church (2 Thess. 2:7). Each test is designed to examine your faithfulness to God, as it did with the Israelites, who failed terribly, and paid the price. The penalty of disobedience, in their case, was death (Deut. 28:15-68) versus obedience resulting in life (Deut. 30:15-20). Obedience is to hold fast to God, and His word (cf. Deut. 10:20; 11:22; 30:20), which was also the command given to the churches of Smyrna, (Rev. 2:13), also the remnant within the church of Thyatira (Rev. 2:25), and the church of Philadelphia (Rev. 3:11).

Again, for those leading people astray and away, the death penalty applies (Deut. 7:26), and will be reapplied by divine stoning (Rev. 16:21) to purge the people of God from evil. Nine times Moses said to purge the evil (false prophets) from them (Deut. 13:5; 17:7, 12; 19:19; 21:21; 22:21–22, 24; 24:7), which include those close to you.

Following the address of false prophets doing signs and wonders, verses six to eleven of Deuteronomy, chapter thirteen addresses 'loved ones' who lead astray. "If your brother, the son of your mother, or your son or your daughter or the wife you embrace or your friend who is as your own soul entices you secretly, saying, "Let us go and serve other gods, which neither you nor your fathers have known you shall not yield to him or listen to him, nor shall your eye pity him, nor shall you spare him, nor shall you conceal him. But you shall kill him. Your hand shall be first against him to put him to death, and afterward the hand of all the people. You shall stone him to death with stones because he sought to draw you away from the LORD your God, who brought you out of the land of Egypt, out of the house of slavery" (Deut. 13:6-10).

The instruction not to listen to such a person means to give him no hearing, no plea for mercy, no compassion, and no pity. Give them no opportunity to cover up their sin, and do not 'shield' (protect) them as a loved one. In other words, do not let your emotions get in the way, but rather deal with them as God commands (cf. Zech. 13:3).

Here, the words of Jesus should come to mind, "A man's enemies will be the members of his own household. Anyone who loves his father or mother more than Me is not worthy of Me; anyone who loves his son or daughter more than Me is not worthy of Me, and anyone who does not take up his cross and follow Me is not worthy of Me" (Matt. 10:36-38).

When confronting a false prophet, the one that casts the first stone testified foremost to that which is false. Those who then join the first to throw a stone form an alliance, witness the truth against evil, resulting in fear (Deut. 13:11). Acts, chapter five (v. 11) serves as a New Testament example of God dealing with false witnesses. Here, God struck down two confessing followers of Christ for bearing false witness, producing great fear within the church (Acts 5:5, 11). The danger of not dealing swiftly with a false witness is that they will lead a multitude astray, as with Moses' third example (Deut. 13:12-18).

Moses' final example of how evil can re-enter the Land is through 'worthless fellows' saying, "Let us go and serve other gods, which you have not known" (Deut. 13:13). While the other gods were known to Israel; they were not experienced as their God was through deliverance. Moses' ultimate example of apostasy involves a whole town being led astray due to not executing the judgement as commanded in the first and second examples, which is relevant to Jesus' warning (Matt. 24:26). Now, the entire city was to be destroyed, including every man, woman, child, and beast (Deut. 13:15). Even the spoils were to be burned before God (Deut. 13:16), that nothing could ever be rebuilt. Nothing was allowed to remain of the wicked city, that nothing may stick to anyone's hand (Deut. 13:17), meaning no matter how valuable an item may be, it cannot remain. If an item was to remain, God's anger would be directed at the disobedient for holding onto what God said was defiled. Disobedience attracted death, on the other hand - obedience to the command attracted God's mercy and compassion (Deut. 13:17b-18). Again, the command was to purge the evil from among them!

The chapters mentioned above introduce the temptation to participate in false worship through false prophets/teachers, loved ones, and worthless fellows, leading whole towns (and denominations) astray. In each case, they are to be purged from within. Have nothing to do with them (2 Jn. 9-11)! Because Israel failed to obey God by removing the false within, they followed and practiced evil, resulting in their disqualification and destruction.

Jesus warned of the same, for the same reasons, where many will be led astray by those coming in His name (Matt. 24:4-5), by the false prophets (Matt. 24:11), and even by false christ's performing signs and wonders (Matt. 24:24). Those deceived by the false are so because they failed to follow God's command, to test every spirit, and to purge the evil from within. The importance of testing every spirit is due to the deceptiveness of those operating with false signs and wonders that even the elect, if possible, would be led astray (Matt. 24:24b). Jesus warned of this from the beginning (Matt. 24:25).

Jesus' reference to false christ's refers to another Jesus, proclaimed through a different gospel (2 Cor. 11:4). In the last days, it is predicted there will be a particular focus on self-serving gospel suited to lovers of self and lovers of money (2 Tim. 3:2, cf. 1 Tim. 6:5). Promoters and followers of this gospel will appear godly but will deny its power (to rule over sin). Paul says to "Avoid such people" (2 Tim. 3:5). Like with Moses' third example, such people have 'crept into households' and 'led astray by various passions' (2 Tim. 3:6). Those who promoted this self-serving gospel have become disqualified regarding the faith (2 Tim. 3:8), and disqualify those who follow them.

Notice, these worthless fellows, devoid of truth, believing godliness is a means of financial gain (1 Tim. 6:5), have crept in, promoting another Jesus suited to the passions (lovers of self and money) of those accepting, tickling their itching ears (2 Tim. 4:3). In other words, they are promoting 'Prosperity Jesus,' and what better version of the 'gospel' to promote in a perceived time of 'Peace and Security' (1 Thess. 5:3). Jesus warned against chasing after prosperity, saying, "Take care, and be on your guard against all covetousness, for one's life does not consist in the abundance of his possessions" (Lu. 12:15). Like Moses, Jesus reminds His followers to take care not to be attached to the things of this world, warning elsewhere, "You cannot serve God and money" (Matt. 6:24).

Of the seven churches addressed in the book of Revelation, the church of Laodicea was most guilty of worldly worship, best defined as a prosperity driven church. They say, "I am rich, I have prospered, and I need nothing" (Rev. 3:17a), little realising they were wretched, pitiable, poor, blind, and naked (Rev. 3:17b). Unless repentance comes first, such a church will find themselves vomited out (Rev. 3:16) 'into the tribulation.' Such a church has been led astray by false teachers promoting a different gospel, becoming so vile to God, that they are in danger of being violently spewed out of His mouth. In other words, they are in danger of being destroyed, such as the towns Moses described who had accepted the worthless fellows.

Remember, five of the seven churches addressed by Jesus had strayed from Him, through false teaching or a lack of intimacy. All of which were in danger of judgement, explicitly pointing to the coming tribulation (Rev. 2:16, 2:22, 3:3, 3:16), unless repentance came first. What was true for Israel is also true for the church. How God treated Israel is how He will also respond to the church for the same level of unfaithfulness (Rom. 11:22). Soon, many confessing believers will find themselves left behind due to following and incorporating false teachers and practicing worldly worship.

In the same way, faithless Israel was disqualified from the Promised Land, the lukewarm church will be disqualified from entering it. It will wake up in the tribulation, where they will have another opportunity to repent and be restored. The purpose of the tribulation is to test, shake and separate. Every false thing is to be purged from the lives of those professing to follow Christ, which will come at the cost of their lives (Matt. 10:38-39, Rev. 12:11).

The surest way to avoid falling away (Matt. 24:4-5), and thus into the tribulation, following repentance, is to 1). Purge false teaching/teachers, 2). Distance yourself from loved ones who aim to deceive, and 3). Remove 'worthless fellows' who creep in secretly, promoting other gods, and another way through a different gospel.

Remember, the test of truth is not through signs and wonders, for even the unsaved can operate with miraculous power in Jesus' name (Matt. 7:22). The antichrist will also operate in signs and wonders (2 Thess. 2:8-9, Rev. 13:13-14, 16:13-14, 18:23, 19:20). The test of truth is through the written word, where scripture interprets scripture (Isa. 28:10). Scripture is not subject to someone's interpretation, but rather the written word of God in its contextual setting and often through its literate application. The easiest way to identify a false teacher is where they do not place a priority on God's words, majoring instead on dreams, visions, and miracles, and therefore do not handle the Bible correctly. Another way to identify a false prophet is when their 'word' does not come to pass (Deut. 18:22) - however, it still may, where God is testing you (Deut. 13:3).

The evidence then, and again is where the false prophet strays from God's word. When a 'prophet' strays from God, so does their word - instead of giving a word in season, preaching repentance, they spout a sugar-coated substitute (Jer. 23:22). Adding to the above mentioned, a false prophet is also identified when they are not looking for Christ's return, preaching a message of preparedness, but rather distracts with a version of 'Your Best Lifer Now.' To avoid temptation, avoid such people, and even purge them from your life, including their material, therefore their influence!

The Campaign of Armageddon

'That they will Know Me.'

(Matt. 24:6-7a, 27-31)

As mentioned, a few topics back, the Jews fleeing Jerusalem occurs at the midway point of the tribulation, commencing the great tribulation. The Jews fleeing will be triggered by the abomination of desolation, resulting in international conflict. Many will resist when the antichrist announces that he is God and that all must take his mark (666). Egypt, followed by China and Russia, will be included in the nations (Dan. 11:40-45) that reject the antichrist's claim as the one world leader over the New World Order. With his European armies, the antichrist will wage war against the invading nations, Egypt, China, and Russia. Ten nations will empower the antichrist from the Revived Roman Empire, which is European, and Rome's centre.

The Revived Roman Empire is referenced in Daniel, chapters two (v. 33) and seven (v. 20); John also mentions it in the book of Revelation, chapter seventeen (vv. 12-14). The ten kings that John revealed are modern-day world leaders (Rev. 13:1), appointed and positioned today to war against Jesus Christ (Rev. 17:14) after warring against the saints for the latter three and a half years (Dan. 7:21, Rev. 13:7). Although the latter half of the tribulation will exceed anything of the former, there will be persecution, civil unrest, and international conflict all the way through.

In Jesus' opening statement, following that warning of false prophets (Matt. 24:4-5), He said during the tribulation and even leading into the tribulation there will be wars and rumours of wars, that nation will rise against nation, and kingdom against kingdom (Matt. 24:6-7a). By these signs, we are expected to know the times (Matt. 16:3).

Today, we are seeing both, through civil and international uprisings. On a civil level, COVID-19 and the forced 'vaccine' have brought about civil unrest on a global scale. Millions of otherwise law-abiding citizens are protesting their governments worldwide, and the government responds with military force, which is unprecedented in democratic countries. What started with 'We are all in it together' and 'It is for your health' quickly became the makings of a New World Order. In fact, the term 'New World Order' has become common language, and the very slogan defines the new age.

Alongside civil unrest, there are international conflicts, with some age-old power struggles now at boiling point; the most obvious is China, closely followed by Russia, with many minor clashes in-between. For example, the China versus Taiwan conflict has now involved the United States and therefore, by default, the United Kingdom, New Zealand, and Australia. Under the Trump administration, the United States supplied Taiwan with weapons to defend itself against hostile neighbours. Obviously, China is Taiwan's greatest threat. China is reclaiming Taiwan as a part of its southern region, to be governed as one nation under two political systems. Due to the United States' involvement, China warned them, and even threatened them with war if they continued. Unmoved, the United States remain committed to Taiwan.

In the north, there is an escalating conflict between Russia and Ukraine. In 2014 Russia seized part of southern Ukraine and is now threatening the west, with the United States making threats of their own towards Russia. US intelligence predicts an invasion of Ukraine from Russia as early as this year (2022), which would then involve the United States. Like the China-

Taiwan situation, the Russia-Ukraine conflict would force the United States to respond, potentially resulting in WWIII.

There is also the ongoing Israel and Iran conflict with threats from both sides to wipe the other off the map. Unlike the above mentioned, where the issues revolve around land, the problem for Israel is Iran's push for nuclear power. The international concern is that if Iran becomes a nuclear power, Saudi Arabia, Turkey, and Egypt are likely to follow suit. Again, the United States is involved, protecting their Middle East interest and their Middle Eastern ally, Israel. The United States wants to achieve peace in the Middle East, primarily through the Middle East Peace Treaty but has also threatened Iran with war if need be.

The latest Middle East Peace Treaty was released in June 2019, otherwise known as the Trump Peace Plan, or Abrahamic Accord. Although Donald Trump was the then US President formalising the peace plan, his son-in-law, Jarrod Kushner, tabled it and has since been heavily involved. Recently, Kushner raised three billion dollars for a new investment firm called Affinity Partners. Kushner hopes to create 'an investment corridor' between Israel and Saudi Arabia by working with Israeli and Gulf companies and investors, with plans to set up his headquarters in Israel soon. Interestingly, Kushner is an American-Jew practicing Judaism, and he is the grandson of a Holocaust survivor. Kushner is a successful businessman, specialising in real estate, with his best-known acquisition being 666 Fifth Avenue in Manhattan, which he bought for $1.8 billion in 2007.

Jarod Kushner is an interesting person to watch regarding current and unfolding global events. Remember, the person who signs off on the Middle East Peace Treaty is the antichrist, and the signing of that (false) peace treaty triggers the tribulation. The peace treaty will be signed for seven years, yet broken halfway through the time of trouble, resulting in an all-out war. (Isa. 28:15, 18, Dan. 9:24-27). The resulting conflict will escalate and conclude with the battle of Armageddon (Rev. 16:14-16). Triggering war (Dan. 11:40-45, Matt. 24:6, Rev. 6:3-4, 9:15-16, 12:7-17, 16:12-16, 17:12-14, 19:11-21) is the release of the red horse, which is a significant sign of the end times. Global war is signified by the release of the red horse (Rev. 6:3-4). The red horse, accompanied by the pale and white horses (Zech. 1:8), and the black horse (Zech. 6:2) were first revealed by the prophet Zechariah and interpreted as winds (Zech. 6:5) and spirits (Zech. 1:10-11, 6:7-8). The horses are also known as 'Horns' (Zech. 1:18-21) that scatter and terrify Judah. Horns symbolise power, kings, and rulers (Dan. 7). As discussed above, partly resulting from an outbreak of war, the Jews flee Jerusalem midway through the tribulation.

As seen through the book of Revelation, chapter six, following the breaking of the seals (chapter five), the four apocalyptic horses appear, one after the next, and together kill a quarter of the earth's population (Rev. 6:8). The white horse is first released (Rev. 6:2), symbolic of the antichrist, followed by the red horse, symbolic of war (Rev. 6:3-4). Although Zechariah reveals these spirits will terrify Judah (Israel), causing them to flee half-way through the seven-year event, they will be released at the beginning of the tribulation, evident by the tribulation being triggered by the antichrist signing the peace treaty. Furthermore, the antichrist cannot be revealed until the tribulation commences, following the removal of the church (2 Thess. 2:6-8). The four winds, or spirits, are spiritual and literal, evidenced by the antichrist being a literal man while possessed and empowered by a demonic spirit (wind).

Until now, the four winds have been patrolling the earth (Zech. 1:10-11, 6:7), awaiting their appointed time. Again, their appointed time commences with the triggering of the tribulation. As mentioned there will be continual conflict; however, the great tribulation will be a time like never before (Jer. 30:7, Joel 2:2, Dan. 12:1, Matt. 24:21). The reference made by the prophet Joel (Joel 2:2) refers to a supernatural army, seen again in Revelation, chapter nine, which is the sixth trumpet judgement. The sixth trumpet (Rev. 9:13-19) is the second woe of the tribulation (cf. Rev. 8:13), pointing to the two hundred million mounted troops that kill a third of the remaining population (Rev. 9:18).

Revelation, chapter sixteen reveals that when the sixth bowl judgement is released, super-soldiers march towards Jerusalem, from the east, being China and co. (Rev. 16:12-14). The sixth trumpet and the sixth bowl are the same judgement. Revelation chapter nine reveals these literal soldiers are also led by demons (Rev. 9:14). In the same way, the antichrist is a literal man; he is possessed by Satan (2 Thess. 2:9).

The army of super-soldiers, amounting to two hundred million, will war against the antichrist after he proclaims to be God from the rebuilt tribulation temple (2 Thess. 2:4). The army from the south will first attack Jerusalem, followed by troops from the east and the north (Dan. 11:40-45), causing the antichrist to return to Israel, probably from Europe, killing tens of thousands of Jews on arrival (Dan. 11:41). When the antichrist slaughters the Jews, he naturally breaks the peace treaty (Isa. 28:18, Dan. 7:27).

Specifically, Daniel's prophecy speaks of Egypt (south), China (east), and Russia (north); however, there are other players involved. Armies from the Middle East, made up of a ten-nation confederation (Ps. 83:6-8), joined as one (Ps. 83:3, 4, 5) also attack Israel (Ps. 83), to whom God will respond, that they may know Him (Ps. 83:15-18). Before the attack, the ten-nation confederation will be in covenant with Israel under the Middle East Peace Treaty. The covenant will be broken with Israel (Isa. 28:15, 18, Dan. 9:27), as mentioned previously, and replaced by another excluding the Jews, "With one mind they plot together; they form an alliance against you—the tents of Edom and the Ishmaelites, of Moab and the Hagrites, Byblos [Gebal],

Ammon and Amalek, Philistia, with the people of Tyre. Even Assyria has joined them to reinforce Lot's descendants." (Psalm 83:5–8).

While these groups are no longer identifiable by their ancient names, Bill Salus, author of 'Israelistine and Psalm 83: The Missing Prophecy Revealed' ascertains the modern-day equivalents/descendants of these coalition members as the following:

- Tents of Edom: Palestinians and Southern Jordanians
- Ishmaelites: Saudis (Ishmael is the father of the Arabs)
- Moab: Palestinians and Central Jordanians
- Hagrites: Egyptians (Hagar is the matriarch of Egypt)
- Gebal (Byblos): Hezbollah and Northern Lebanese
- Ammon: Palestinians and Northern Jordanians
- Amalek: Arabs of the Sinai area
- Philistia: Hamas of the Gaza Strip
- Tyre: Hezbollah and Southern Lebanese
- Assyria: Syrians and Northern Iraqis

While the nations mentioned above are not yet in coalition with each other, they still all come under the umbrella of Islam. The Psalms eighty-three prophecy will occur during the great tribulation, arguably joining the kings from the south in their attack against Israel (Dan. 11:40-43). Another prophecy yet to be fulfilled, and probably will be at the same time as those mentioned above, is found in Isaiah, chapter seventeen, appointed to be fulfilled on 'That day' (Isa. 17:4), which will be 'a day of grief and incurable pain' (Isa. 17:6).

The day of grief and incurable pain follows a time of (false) peace and security (1 Thess. 5:3). Through the Arab invasion, the Jews will look to their Maker (Isa. 17:7), no longer considering any other god or other means to deliver them (Isa. 17:8). Like with the Asaph's prophecy (Ps. 83), the purpose of the time of trouble is to make God known. The same is true with the Ezekiel prophecy; God will bring Russia and co. (Gog and Magog) against Israel, that the nations will know Him through His vindication (Ezek. 38:16, 21, 23, 39:4, 6, 7, 13, 21, 27).

The armies from the South, East, Middle East, and the North are all drawn out by God, stating that God is sovereign overall. Nothing, absolutely nothing can happen unless God allows it, and He does allow it for the purpose of making His name known. Isaiah, chapter twenty-six, reveals that unless God pours out His judgement, the wicked will not repent (Isa. 26:9b-10). God's mercy is seen and experienced through His judgements. The day Isaiah speaks of (Isa. 26) refers to the great tribulation, where Israel will be hidden away (Isa. 26:20-21) for forty-two months (Rev. 12:6, 14).

The above-mentioned transpired for a period of forty-two months, leading to a single day of judgement. Hence, the term 'campaign' of Armageddon is more appropriate than 'battle.' Essentially, on that last day, when the armies meet at Megiddo (Rev. 14:20, 19:19), there is no battle at all but only slaughter by God. On that day, Jesus Christ will strike down every man, woman, and beast with the sword of His mouth (Rev. 19:15) unless repentance comes first. The prophet Zechariah narrows in on the same.

The message given through the prophet Zechariah is the same as every other prophet. "Return to Me, and I will return to you" (1:3). The announcement echoed throughout scripture (for example, Mal. 3:7, Isa. 55:7, Jer. 3:12, 22, Ezek. 33:11, Joel 2:12, etc.) is a strange notion for most today, even for those standing behind pulpits. Zechariah, chapter twelve narrows in on 'That day'. The phrase 'On That Day' is mentioned five times in chapter twelve (v. 3, 4, 6, 8, 9), three more times in chapter thirteen (vv. 1, 2, 4), and seven more times in chapter fourteen (vv. 4, 6, 8,

9, 13, 21, 22). Throughout prophetic literature, 'That day' always refers to Jesus' second coming and His judgement. On that day, everyone who had previously rejected Jesus will recognise Him. As mentioned earlier, the event will take place at the plain of Megiddo (Zech. 12:11b), which is the location of the Battle of Armageddon.

The Battle of Armageddon is further described in chapter fourteen of Zechariah. Even at this late stage, leading right up to Jesus' return, people will still be able to repent due to God's extended grace and mercy. According to Zechariah, chapter twelve, and verse ten, even when Jesus is seen with the naked eye, at His appearing, salvation is still on offer. It is expanded through verses ten to fourteen, at the appearance of Jesus (v. 10). As always, an individual response is required through repentance and mourning. In chapter thirteen such a response secures salvation, confirmed again (v. 1), "Where comes the cleansing of sin and uncleanness." Meaning, that forgiveness is granted to repentant sinners because of God's grace and mercy.

Joining the prophet Zechariah, the prophet Joel states the same, "The day is near" (Joel 1:15, 2:1). The day is exceedingly great and very awesome (Joel. 2:11), where God gathers the nations to the valley of Jehoshaphat to enter His judgement (Joel 3:2, 12). The Valley of Jehoshaphat, or the Valley of Decision today is the Kidron Valley. The Kidron Valley as it is known today runs north and south and separates the Mount of Olives on the east and the Old City of Jerusalem on the west. There, multitudes will gather (Joel. 3:14), where Jesus will execute His judgement (i.e., the valley of decision) according to how people responded to His work of salvation through the cross. The outcome of that day is later discussed under the heading, "Wherever the corpse is, there the vultures will gather" (Matt. 24:28).

Throughout this section, we have seen that God uses judgements to make Himself known, to draw people to repentance, and to save. The point and purposes of the coming tribulation are to test, shake and separate. War will serve that purpose where through it, some will turn to God and be eternally saved, albeit most will continue to reject God and be slain, thus, being eternally dammed. Those being eternally saved through repentance are not immune to the bulk of the judgements during the time of trouble, any more than followers of Christ are immune from trials today.

During the tribulation, the time of testing (Rev. 3:10) will last seven years. Nevertheless, the Campaign of Armageddon occurs over the last half, being forty-two months, concluding with the return of Jesus Christ.

Vultures Will Gather

'Where the Corpse is'
(Matt. 24:28)

Following seven years of unprecedented deception (Matt. 24:5, 11, 23-26), throughout the tribulation (Rev. 12:9, 18:23, 19:20, 20:10), so deceptive that even the elect could be led astray, if possible (Matt. 24:24), Jesus returns, and when He does an unmatched level of carnage follows. The location where this takes place is Megiddo, also known as Armageddon (Rev. 16:14-16). The antichrist, false prophet, and demons perform signs to deceive and assemble the kings of the whole world at Megiddo (Rev. 16:14).

As mentioned previously, the battle of Armageddon is no battle at all but rather a massacre of the rebellious with a spoken word (Rev. 19:11-15, 21), where Christ alone tramples the nations (Isa. 63:3-6). Those struck down by Jesus when He returns include the antichrist, the false prophet

(Rev. 19:20), the antichrist's armies (Rev. 17:14, 19:19), and the kings of the whole world (Rev. 16:14, 17:14). The armies of the antichrist consist of ten united nations (Rev. 17:12-14) that enforce the New World Order, which is is the seventh kingdom (Rev. 17:10). The seventh kingdom gives way to the eighth, the antichrist's (beast) kingdom (Rev. 17:11). On this topic, Daniel, chapter seven, should be compared with Revelation, chapter seventeen.

Daniel, chapter seven (vv. 7-8, 17-25) describes the antichrist's dominion, lasting seven years, supported by chapter nine (Dan. 9:24-27). Like the book of Revelation, chapter seventeen, Daniel also refers to the ten nations (Dan. 7:20), led by the 'other horn' that had eyes and a mouth that spoke great things (Dan. 7:8, 20) for forty-two months (Rev. 13:5-6). Forty-two months refers to the great tribulation (Matt. 24:21), which is the second half of the seven-year ordeal (Rev. 13:5), following the abomination of desolation (Matt. 24:15). The abomination of desolation signifies the antichrist setting himself up in the newly built tribulation (third) temple, proclaiming to be God (2 Thess. 2:4), fulfilling his predicted blasphemous nature. The antichrist will be full of blasphemy (Rev. 13:5-6), partnered with another, the false prophet, who is head of the one-world religious system, which is also full of blasphemy (Rev. 17:3). The one-world religious system is an all-inclusive ecumenical arrangement, like ancient Rome. In Rome, all gods were accepted providing they did not conflict with the Roman gods, where Caesar was 'lord.' Of course, this presented a problem for the Christians, resulting in their deaths. How Christianity started is how it will end.

Before Jesus returns to judge the nations, the false prophet will set up a similar arrangement to that of Rome in submission to the antichrist. All gods will be accepted, as long as the antichrist is 'lord,' for the first forty-two months. After the abomination of desolation, the antichrist and his armies will turn against the one-world religion, the harlot, or prostitute, made up of many nations (Rev. 17:15) that ride the beast (Rev. 17:1-2). The one-world religious system is connected to the New World Order.

The end-time religious system, made up of the deceived during the tribulation, that were led astray and fell away (Matt. 24:11), is further misled by the false prophet until they have served their purpose. Then, once the antichrist has no more need for the one-world religious system, the whore, he destroys it, making her (the harlot tribulation church) desolate and naked, devouring and burning her (Rev. 17:16).

The harlot church will include those refusing to repent during the tribulation (Rev. 9:20-21, 16:9, 11). Those who celebrate the deaths of the two witnesses by exchanging gifts (Rev. 11:10), and who participated in the murder of the martyred saints (Rev. 3:10., 6:10, 7:14, 13:10, 15, 14:13, 16:6, 17:6, 18:24, 19:2, 20:4), countless millions of them (Rev. 7:9, 14). Interestingly, the end-time worldly church was previously pronounced naked by Jesus Christ (Rev. 3:17), thereby left behind, unless repentance came first. During the tribulation, the harlot church will be made naked by the antichrist sometime after the midway mark (Rev. 17:16).

Jesus judged the lukewarm church as naked due to being full of the world, therefore, empty of Him. In the end, the harlot church, which replaced Jesus with the things of this world, will be stripped of everything the antichrist promised and provided. The same promises offered to Jesus by Satan (Matt. 4:8-9) are offered to the church, summed up as the prosperity 'gospel.'

During the tribulation, Jesus warns those left behind with these words, "Behold, I am coming like a thief! Blessed is the one who stays awake, keeping his garments on, that he may not go about naked and be seen exposed!" (Rev. 16:15). Again, the reference to being naked is used. Those who have the garment of salvation are clothed, and not exposed. Notice here the blessing, to the one who stays awake, and keeps his garment on. In other words, even in the tribulation, after being awakened, one can again fall asleep, and become exposed, repeating the sin of the church of Sardis (Rev. 3:1-6), which would result in them being left behind unless repentance came first (Rev. 3:3).

Members of the harlot church, who perished during the tribulation at the hand of the antichrist, will be resurrected at the end of the millennial dispensation (Rev. 20:5) to stand before the great white throne (Rev. 20:11-15). As for those remaining, who made war against Jesus Christ, they will be conquered when He returns (Rev. 16;14, 17:14). Alongside the armies warring against Jesus are the religious ones, referenced by Jesus in Luke's gospel, chapter seventeen, under the header 'The Coming of the Kingdom' (Lu. 17:20-37). There, Jesus warned the Pharisees not to focus on 'signs' pointing to the coming kingdom (Lu. 17:20) but instead to pursue Him (Lu. 17:21). The Kingdom was in their midst, then, because Jesus was present, standing among them.

The window of opportunity for the Pharisees to receive Christ was closing (Lu. 17:22) and soon to be counterfeited by false christ's (Lu. 17:23), for a time before Jesus returns (Lu. 17:24). For the gap between Christ's first appearance and His second, He warns, "Do not follow them (the false prophets and false messiahs)" (Lu. 17:23b). Notice, those looking in the wrong places for Jesus, are still seeking Him yet will be deceived by false prophets (Lu. 17:23). They are deceived due to following a man, and not God, through His word. The deceived are biblically illiterate confessors of Christ who make easy prey for false prophets. These are the same caught up in false signs and the things of this world (Lu. 17:27-32), falling victim to the trickery of false prophets and false teachers. The false prophets of Jesus' day included the Pharisees, who claimed to know and represent God but rejected Jesus, even when He was standing in their midst. False prophets today do the same, only instead of altogether rejecting Jesus, they present another (2 Cor. 11:4).

In the same way, the Pharisees rejected the suffering Christ, the religious generation following have and will do the same (Lu. 17:25-30). Even up until Jesus returns suddenly (cf. Lu. 17:30), many will be blinded by the things of this world, seeking to save their natural lives and possessions, moreover their eternal souls (Lu. 17:31-34). These are the ones 'taken' when the Lord returns (Lu. 17:35-37).

When hearing these words (the one taken), the disciples asked, "Where Lord?" (Lu. 17:37), and Jesus answered, "Where the corpse is, there the vultures will gather" (Lu. 17:37). Many have mistakenly interpreted this for the rapture when reading the words, "One will be taken and the other left" (Lu. 17:34). The rapture, however, will take place seven years before this event (Rev. 3:10, 4:1), where the one now taken is killed. Those killed will then be food for the vultures (Lu. 17:37).

The ones 'Taken' at this point include the armies of the antichrist and the religious (Pharisees and harlot church) who reject Jesus. The antichrist and the false prophet are not killed, thereby being food for vultures; instead, they are cast alive into the lake of fire one thousand years before any other (Rev. 19:10, 20:10). There, they are eternal food for the everlasting worm (Mk. 9:48).

Many nations will gather at Megiddo, for the "Great supper of God" (Rev. 19:17).

These include the armies of the antichrist, consisting of ten nations from the revived Roman Empire (Europe and northern Africa), Russia (Ezek. 38-39), and China (Rev. 16:12), among other Middle Eastern nations (Dan. 11:40-45), and include the kings of the whole world (Rev. 16:14).

Following the great supper of God, the marriage supper of the Lamb commences. All who have not taken the mark of the beast (666) are invited

(Rev. 19:9, 22:17); the great supper of God occurs first. The great supper of God is where the birds of the air gather to feast on the flesh of kings, captains, mighty men, horses, and their riders, the flesh of all men, both free and enslaved person, both small and great (Rev. 19:17-18). The banquet primarily consists of the armies gathering at Megiddo; however, it also includes the religious, and those following in the footsteps of Lot's wife, seeking to save their natural lives and possessions (Lu. 17:27-33).

Apart from those mentioned above, suffering the all-inclusive judgement, one of the most apparent links to the great supper of God, is found in Ezekiel's prophecy (Ezek. 38-39), referring to God and Magog. Ezekiel (39:17) prophesies something like Jesus' prediction (Lu. 17:34-37), stating when the Messiah returns He will destroy the nations that come up against Israel (Ezek. 39:4). He elaborates further in verse seventeen: "And you, son of man, this is what the Lord God has said, "Say to every kind of bird and every beast of the field, 'Assemble and come, gather from all around to my sacrifice that I am slaughtering for you, a great sacrifice on the mountains of Israel; and you will eat flesh and drink blood'" (Ezek. 39:17). The fulfillment of Ezekiel's prophecy is revealed further through John's revelation (Rev. 19:17-18), where those who gather at Armageddon are slain by the sword that came from the mouth of Jesus (Rev. 19:15, 20) - they are then gorged upon by the birds (Rev. 19:21). Hence, they are the great supper of God (Rev. 19:17).

When Jesus returns, He is not just slaying the rebel armies, which include the armies of the antichrist, Russia, China, and the Middle East, but the 'Nations' (Rev. 19:15), which consist of "All men, both free and slave" (Rev. 19:18, cf. 6:15b). The free could refer to those without the mark (666), leaving the enslaved to be those who have taken it (Rev. 19:20b).

Remember, the armies of the south (Egypt), the north (Russia), and the east (China) war against the antichrist and his armies rejecting his claim of being

God and thereby resisting his demand to receive his mark and worship him (Dan. 11:40-45). Because the opposing armies of the antichrist have refused to worship him, the beast, they are still free, to some degree. Those who have taken the mark are eternally dammed; they are without hope of redemption (Rev. 14:9-11). Whether a free or enslaved person, any facing Jesus at the plains of Megiddo is slain and gorged on by the birds when He returns.

As mentioned earlier, deception is a primary end-time sign, leading into and continuing throughout the tribulation. During the tribulation, "The nations are deceived by sorcery" (Rev. 18:23). The Greek word for sorcery is pharmakon, where the English word 'pharmacy' comes from, also translated, 'drugs.' Reworded, the verse (Rev. 18:23) could say, "Drugs deceived the nations." On this, think COVID-19 and associated vacci-nations (drugs) resulting in the global inoculated population receiving a passport allowing them to 'buy and sell' (cf. Rev. 13:16-17), 'no shot, no shop.' Those who have taken the jab are now enslaved to governments, the world system, with a false sense of freedom, conditional upon receiving the next mandated booster. The jabbed are only 'fully vaccinated,' providing they have received the latest shot. Once jabbed, the 'vaccinated' are locked in, digitally tracked, and traced. Essentially, the nations have been deceived through COVID-19 and associated vaccinations, setting the stage for the introduction and even enforcing the beast's mark (666).

At the midway point of the tribulation, those already enslaved by the world system, and the free will be required to worship the beast and receive his mark (Rev. 13:16). However, as mentioned earlier, some will resist and perish (Rev. 13:10, 15), while others go to war against the New World Order and the antichrist (Dan. 11:40-45). Again, for those who war against the antichrist, regardless of whether any have taken his mark (666) or not, they are still deceived by him, the false prophet, and demons, by being assembled for the battle of Armageddon (Rev. 16:14-16).

The battle of Armageddon is like a winepress (Rev. 14:19-20, 19:15), and the armies assembling are like grapes, who are gathered by the angels (Rev. 14:18). Outside of the battle of Armageddon, the angels gather the wicked at the end of the age (Matt. 13. 30, 40, 40), and also the righteous (Matt. 24:31). The difference between the angels gathering of the rebellious in Matthew, chapter thirteen, and Revelation, chapter fourteen is that Matthew's account does not mention bloodshed. There (Matt. 13), the wicked are bound and cast into a place of weeping and gnashing of teeth. When Jesus slays the rebels, as recorded in Revelation, chapter fourteen, the bloodshed will flow, "From the winepress as high as the horse's bridle, for 1,600 stadia" (Rev. 14:20). One thousand six hundred stadia are about one hundred and eighty-seven miles.

Jesus, who slays the armies with the sword of His mouth (Rev. 19:15, 21, cf. 2:16, 1:16, Isa. 66:15-16), is clothed in a robe dipped in blood (Rev. 19:13). Jesus is clothed with the blood of the slaughtered! On Jesus' first arrival, His blood was shed. On His second, those who refused His sacrifice, through the cross, their blood will be shed. In fact, on His return, Jesus makes the rebels drink their own blood, which is what they deserve for shedding the blood of the saints (Rev. 16:6, 7).

The prophet Isaiah pronounces, "Those that afflict you (Israel) will be made to drink their own blood and eat their own flesh, that they would know God" (Isa. 49:26). Isaiah's warning will be fulfilled through the prophecy recorded in the book of Revelation, chapter sixteen (Rev. 16:6). In fulfilment of this prophecy, the martyred saints' prayer will be answered (Rev. 6:10); they are now revenged and redeemed (Rev. 7:15-17, cf. Isa. 66:17-21).

The pouring out of the blood is more than mere death; it indicates suffering (cf. Rev. 6:6-9-10, 12:11). As the saints suffered for accepting Jesus, now the rebels will suffer for rejecting Him. Although the angels gather the rebels for harvest, Jesus alone tramples them (Isa. 63:3-6, Joel 3:13), as He did before with Judah (Lam. 1:15).

Like before (i.e., Noah's generation, Sodom and Gomorrah, and Judah), most today claim God will not judge His creation. However, scripture clearly states, what God did then, He is about to do again. As mentioned previously, the Jesus returning at the end of the age is hardly the one known, and 'worshipped' today in many churches.

In sum, Luke's gospel (Lu. 17:27, 29, 20) and John's revelation (Rev. 19:17-18) describe the same event, as does Ezekiel's prophecy (Ezek. 39:4, 17). While Ezekiel refers explicitly to Russia and accompanying nations, Luke and John's account includes all nations and men, being everyone remaining and unrepentant (Rev. 6:15b). All predictions state that when Jesus returns, He will destroy all as He did with Noah's generation (Lu. 17:29) and Sodom and Gomorrah (Lu. 17:29). In the same way as with Noah's generation, and those living in Sodom and Gomorrah, those left behind, and surviving the tribulation judgements to the end, who have still not submitted to Jesus Christ, are 'Taken' (Lu. 17:34, 35, 36) and then fed to the birds.

A direct link and application of the above-mentioned are seen with the church of Thyatira (Rev. 2:18-29), which mainly tolerated Jezebel's teachings (Rev. 2:20). Remember, literal Jezebel met her end by being thrown down by Jehu (name meaning: He is God), then trampled by horses, before being eaten by dogs (2 Kgs. 9:32-37). The church of Thyatira had followed in the footsteps of Jezebel by corrupting their worship of God, except for a few (Rev. 2:24). Those failing to repent will be thrown into the great tribulation (Rev. 2:22), while those who do repent and or holdfast (Rev. 2:25b) are removed before the hour of trial (cf. Rev. 3:10).

Those waking up in the tribulation (cf. Rev. 3:3) will be given another opportunity to repent, which is the purpose of the judgement (cf. Isa.

26:10). Again, most, however, will not repent and therefore will make up the harlot church of Revelation, chapter seventeen. They are members of the one-world religious system that rides the beast during the final seven years of this age. The harlot prophetess, Jezebel, previously deceived the church members, conditioning them for the false prophet who will hand them over to be destroyed by the antichrist and his armies once they have served their purpose (Rev. 17:16). Despite all the promises of prosperity and dominion, they are slain and then gorged upon by birds (Rev. 19:17-19, 21) gathered for God's great supper (Rev. 19:17).

In conclusion, answering the disciple's question, "Where is the one taken?" Jesus essentially says they have been taken to hell! The judgement of the rebels results in the shedding of their blood, the gorging of their flesh, followed by suffering in a place of weeping and gnashing of teeth. Once the rebels are slain, they go into the grave, fully conscious for one thousand years, before being resurrected (Rev. 20:5) to face the great white throne judgement (Rev. 20:11-15). When resurrected, they will receive 'glorified' bodies, referred to as the resurrection of the unjust (Dan. 12:2, Jn. 5:28-29, Acts 24:15), for the purpose of everlasting torment. Because they sinned with the body, they will be eternally punished in the body. On earth, their mortal bodies will feed the birds (Matt. 24:28), and in hell, their eternal bodies will feed the worms (Mk. 9:48, Isa. 66:24). In contrast, the just (saints) receive a glorified body (1 Cor. 15:52-53, Phil. 3:21a) for everlasting joy, while the sinner suffers eternal, visible sorrow (Isa. 66:24).

'Immediately After the Tribulation'

(Matt. 24:29-31)

Immediately after the tribulation, there will be signs in the sky and on the earth - everything will be shaken (Matt. 24:29). Jesus will be the most significant sign when He returns, made visible to all (Matt. 24:30, Rev. 1:7). On that day, He will send His angels out to gather up the nations (Matt. 13:41, 24:31) to separate the wheat from the chaff (Matt. 13:30, Lu. 3:17) and the sheep from the goats (Matt. 25:32-46). Jesus will also judge the 'stars' (fallen angels), which will include Satan (Rev. 20:1-3). When Jesus returns after the seven-year ordeal, it will be likened to a thief (Matt. 24:42-43, 2 Pet. 3:10, Rev. 16:15). When Jesus comes for His bride (the church) it will be like a thief in the night (1 Thess. 5:2, Rev. 3:3), and again when He returns, seven years later, to judge those who have been left behind to endure the tribulation.

CHAPTER FOUR

Immediately After the Tribulation
'Heaven and Earth Shaken'
(Matt. 24:29)

Shortly after the world's armies assemble at Megiddo for the 'battle' of Armageddon (Rev. 16:16), Jesus Christ returns to judge the nations (Matt. 25:31-46). As mentioned in the previous section, there is no battle, no WWIII, other than Jesus slaying humanity with the sword of His mouth (Rev. 19:15, 21, cf. 2 Thess. 2:8) and trampling them like grapes (Rev. 14:17-20, Isa. 63:3, Joel 3:13). The imagery captured in the referenced verses was the looming threat John saw when Jesus appeared in chapter one of the book of Revelation (Rev. 1:16), which terrified him (Rev. 1:17), and will again the rebellious (Isa. 13:13-14, 24:17-18, Rev. 6:17).

Sections of the same imagery seen in chapter one were injected into each letter to the seven churches, relaying the same vision and meaning John saw (Rev. 2-3). The message and warning of the things to come contained within the book of Revelation are first and foremost to the church, then to Israel, and then the rest of the world. The threat to all is, "Unless you wake up, I (Jesus) will come like a thief, and you will not know at what hour I will come against you" (Rev. 3:3). Jesus will first come for His faithful church, snatching them out of the way before the tribulation commences (Rev. 3:10), and then He will come again to judge the nations. This section will deal with His seconding coming.

Matthew, chapter twenty-four (v. 29) deals with the event concluding the tribulation. However, the disturbance of cosmos is seen throughout the whole tribulation, particularly through the trumpet and bowl judgements, but none more so than then when Jesus appears. When Jesus returns to the earth, His return will be complemented by an extraordinary exhibition in the heavens (v. 29; cf. Isa. 13:10; 34:4; Joel 2:31; 3:15–16). The exhibition in the heavens will be complemented with His 'sign' in the sky (Matt. 24:30). The manifestation of 'the sign' will cause the remaining population to mourn (cf. Rev. 1:7) and be terrified (Rev. 6:17).

Here, we should be reminded of what God said through the prophet Jeremiah, "The prophets prophesy falsely, and the priests rule by their own authority. My people love it so, but what will you do in the end?" What will they do? They will not do anything - precisely nothing, that is what! They will be too terrified to do anything but flee. These terrified, on that day, are the same who said God would not judge (Zeph. 1:12). Yet God says that judgement is coming, with the statement, moreover the question, "What will YOU do?"

Important to note is the false prophets were not denying God's existence but were instead adding to or taking away from the law of God. They were twisting God's word to suit their own purposes, focused on lining their own pockets (Jer. 7:8-11). During His first arrival, Jesus dealt with the same issue (Matt. 21:12-13). In sum, the religious were merchandising God and the people of God for their own greedy gain, which was seen again through the writings of Paul (2 Cor. 2:17) and Peter (2 Pet. 2:3, 14) also with Jude (Jude 1:11).

The problem of apostasy and prosperity is also the primary prophesised concern with the last church (Rev. 3:15), with a prophetic timeline from the 1900s until Jesus returns. Those who fail to take God's word seriously will be first left behind, and then still failing to repent during the tribulation, will suffer the wrath of the Lamb on His return (Rev. 6:16-17). Then, when standing face-to-face with the One, they have mocked, the statement is made to them, "What will you do, now?" John answers Jeremiah's question by providing another rhetorical statement, "On that day, who can stand?" The answer is None, except for those found and hidden in Christ

(Phil. 3:7-11, Col. 1-11). Those living for themselves by seeking their 'Best Life Now' hardly qualify!

Alongside the false prophets and lukewarm 'Christians,' there will also be those rejecting God favouring the antichrist. Although it could be argued all groups fall into this category, there will be many who go to war against Jesus Christ during the tribulation (Rev. 17:12-14), made up of every people, nation, and language (Rev. 17:15). However, the one thing all groups have in common, is false worship. While some are worshipping another Jesus (2 Cor. 11:4), others are worshipping other gods (Rev. 9:10); and others again are promoting themselves as the Messiah (Matt. 24:14). All by default, are under the influence of Satan through the antichrist.

As seen through previous sections, the primary issue now and then is worship. The same concern is addressed in each of the seven churches in the book of Revelation (Rev. 2-3). For this reason, when Jesus returns, He will deal with every false form of worship. "Immediately after the tribulation of those days the sun will be darkened, and the moon will not give its light, and the stars will fall from heaven, and the powers of the heavens will be shaken" (Matt. 24:29).

The cosmic signs accompanying Jesus' return can be considered literal and supernatural. In particular, the sign of the 'stars'. Within the context, sun, moon, and stars, there is the literal application of planets. However, there is also the mention of 'The powers of the heaven' in context with the stars, suggesting a supernatural application, signifying angels.

The Greek also supports a celestial being, as in an angel, and in this case, fallen angels (Rev. 12:4), so the supernatural position is favoured. Yet, whether literal or supernatural, the issue is false worship, as star worship is condemned as idolatry (Deut. 4:19; 17:2–5). Failing to obey God, Israel worshipped the stars (Amos 5:26), as did Judah (2 Kgs 23:4–14), promoted by Manasseh (2 Kgs 21:3–5; 2 Chr. 33:3). The worship of the stars attempts to predict the future (Isa. 47:13) - see also Jer. 10:1–2), which is forbidden in scripture.

Recently, some end-time ministries did the same, arguing there was an astronomical alignment on September 23, 2017, which fulfilled the first two verses of Revelation, chapter twelve. Supporters claim that an astronomical alignment involving Virgo and Leo's constellations, the sun, moon, and planets Mercury, Mars, Venus, and Jupiter that occurred in September 2017 fulfilled the prophecy of Revelation, chapter twelve (vv. 1-2) word-for-word. Besides the verses mentioned above forbidding such practice, the other obvious criticism is that the interpretation of the Apostle John says that "There appeared a great wonder in heaven." He does not say, "There will be a great wonder in heaven." In agreement with the rest of scripture, John does not tell us to 'look for a great wonder in heaven' to interpret the signs of the times.

Likewise, the number one sign of the end times referred to by Jesus is an increase of false teachers and false teaching, and using lying signs and wonders to deceive. The above interpretation of Revelation, chapter twelve (vv. 1-2) leans more towards false teaching. The counterargument might be the star signalling the birth of Jesus is found only in Matthew's Gospel (Matt 2:1–12), which led the Magi from the East to Jerusalem and then to Bethlehem. Regardless, as already stated, consulting with the stars and star worship are forbidden by God.

The sun, moon, and stars have been worshipped by humanity throughout the ages, identified as gods, but when Jesus Christ returns, all will submit to Him. The prophet Isaiah confirms every cosmic host will fall when Jesus appears (Isa. 34:4). Matthew, chapter twenty-four (v. 29) seems to best fit Isaiah's prophecy, where God will literally roll back the sky and cast down the fallen angels (Isa. 34:4). Isaiah's prophecy is supported by the prophet Haggai (2:6-9, 21), cited by the author of the book of Hebrews (Heb. 12:26), and repeated by John (Rev. 6:12-17).

Again, in the book of Revelation, the sky being rolled up (Rev. 6:14) and the stars falling (Rev. 6:13) is in context with the kings of the earth being slain (Rev. 6:15). Haggai's prophecy adds, "The silver is mine, and the gold is mine, declares the Lord of host" (Hag. 2:8). In other words, everything is subject to God. The very things that man worshipped, or claimed for themselves, distracting them from God, God says, belong to Him. Even the hosts of heaven (angels) belong to Him. Haggai ends with, "The latter glory of this house shall be greater than the former,' says the Lord of hosts'" (Hag. 2:9).

Often verse nine is misquoted to support false teaching, stating the church will see God's glory greater than what was experienced in the temple. Contextually, the verse does not support that, but rather when Jesus returns, then His shekinah glory will also be experienced, greater than any time in the past. The same false teaching mentioned above presents the notion that the 'best is yet to come.' Isaiah addresses that also calling promoters dumb dogs (Isa. 56:10), greedy for gain, who are void of understanding (Isa. 56:11), those who declare tomorrow will be better than today, greater beyond measure (Isa. 56:12). In part, they are correct, only not as they suspect. Instead of prosperity, it will be judgement, beyond measure for them. God's outpouring of judgement on the nations is balanced by His glory; one is never without the other. On that day, not and never before, when Jesus sets up His kingdom on the earth, the saint's THEN rule alongside Him (Isa 24:23). But not before the judgement comes first.

Additional references supporting the text (Matt. 24:29) are found in Isaiah (13:10; 34:4) and Joel (2:31; 3:15–16). Isaiah, chapters thirteen to fourteen (vv. 1-27) go together. There, the prophet saw the oracle (burden) concerning the coming judgement of the nations, notably on Babylon, and

Assyria, before the restoration of Israel. The occurrence Isaiah predicts has a double reference, prophetically speaking.

While both Babylon and Assyria have already been defeated, they will be again, allegorically speaking for Babylon, at the conclusion of the tribulation. Assyria, now northern Iraq, south-eastern Turkey, north-western Iran, and north-eastern Syria may well join Russia and Turkey as kings from the north (Dan. 11:40-45), fulfilling Ezekiel's prophecy (Ezek. 38-39), summonsed to invade Israel, for their destruction.

On the other hand, Babylon is not a literal nation but a system. The Babylon beast-system is described in Revelation, chapters seventeen (religious) and eighteen (political). From the midpoint of the tribulation, forty-two months in, the kings of the east and the north will war against the antichrist, therefore against the beast system, Babylon (Dan. 11:40-45). Russia is the king of the north, China is the king of the east, and God summons both. They are His armies (Isa. 13:3, cf. Joel 2:25), albeit led by demons, to do as God pleases (cf. Rev. 9:13-19, 16:12-16, Isa. 13:4).

The term 'The Day of the Lord is near' (Isa. 13:6) and 'The day of the Lord comes' (Isa. 13:9, cf. 22b) makes it clear, Isaiah's prophecy is still yet to be fulfilled. The coming judgement will affect the whole world (Isa. 13:11), causing all inhabitants extreme distress like a woman's labour pains (Isa. 13:7-8, cf. Isa. 21:3; 26:17; Jer. 4:31; 6:24; 13:21; 22:23; 30:6; 48:41; 49:22, 24; 50:43; Mic. 4:9–10). On that day, God will pour out His anger (Isa. 13:3, 13), cruel wrath, fierce anger (Isa. 13:9, 13b) on sinners, to destroy (Isa. 13:9), punishing the proud, pompous, godless, and boastful blasphemers (Isa. 13:11; cf. v. 19; 10:6, 12–13). So awesome will that day be, the heavens will shake (Isa. 13:10).

As seen in the text (Matt. 24:29), Isaiah states, "On that day, God will shake the heavens" (Isa. 13:10). In the same way, the world will tremble, the heavens will also. Besides here, and the text (Matt. 24:29) many times throughout scripture, this coming event is prophesied (Isa. 24:18, 34:4, Joel 2:10, 30–31; 3:15-16, and Hag. 2:6–7, 21–22), contextually supporting God's judgement on the stars, that is, fallen angels.

At that time, due to the severity of the tribulation judgements, people will be rarer than fine gold (Isa. 13:12). And, on that day, they will plead for mercy and pity, and find none (Isa. 13:18), and although many will flee (Isa. 13:14b), none will escape (Isa. 13:14a), including infants and wives (Isa. 13:16), young men and children (Isa. 13:18). On that day, no amount of money will save the rebellious (Isa. 13:17), the rich will perish alongside the poor, for both rich and poor worshipped the beast (Rev. 13:16), and now they must also die together (Rev. 6:15, Isa. 2:19, 21).

Isaiah, chapter twenty-four states the same, that. the people, priest, slave master, maid, mistress, buyer, seller, lender, borrower, creditor, debtor, kings and even the host of heaven (Satan) will be punished together (Isa. 24:2-3, 21-23), and none will escape (Isa. 24:17-18). Again, so severe will be the judgement, that few will survive (Isa. 13:12, 24:6).

So severe is the judgement, Babylon will never be inhabited again (Isa. 13:20). Clearly, the ancient city of Babylon, being Iraq, is inhabited today, thereby disqualifying the prophecy's fulfillment with it being historically conquered. As mentioned earlier, the future fulfillment of this prophecy refers to the beast-system (Rev. 18), which will be destroyed in a single day (Rev. 18:8, cf. Jer. 50:1-51:58), in a single hour (Rev. 18:10b, 17, 19b), being then, no more, no more, no more, no more, no more, no more (x6, Rev. 18:21b-23).

Again, the reason God destroys Babylon and everyone in it is due to their sin (Rev. 18:2-3, 5-6) and arrogance, claiming God will not judge (Rev. 18:7). FOR THIS REASON (Rev. 18:8a), a day of death, and morning and famine, and fire is coming (Rev. 18:8b), but not before one last call, where God says: "COME OUT OF HER, MY PEOPLE" (Rev. 18:4).

The words, "Come out of her, My people," prophetically speak to today's generation of lukewarm believers who will find themselves waking up in the tribulation. These ones lacked the fear of God and therefore compromised and corrupted their worship of Him. In response, God will shake everything that can be shaken to wake some up. Hebrews, chapter twelve (vv. 18-28) confirms that God is about to shake the planet and the heavens one more time. Then, both people and angels will be judged by Jesus Christ on His return (Heb. 12:26-27). Therefore, the timeless message is to fear God (Heb. 12:21), who is a consuming fire (Heb. 10:26-27).

As with those who have already been judged, including people and angels (Jude 1:5-11), Jesus Christ is coming again with ten thousand of His holy ones to execute judgement on sinners (Jude 1:14-16) and angels (1 Cor. 6:3, cf. Isa. 24:21-22, 2 Pet. 2:4). Afterall, if we endure with Christ, we also reign (and judge) with Him (2 Tim. 2:12). Like Isaiah, chapter thirteen, chapter twenty-four also describes that day (vv. 24:23), confirming that few will survive it (Isa. 24:6). When the earth is violently shaken (Isa. 24:19), those attempting to flee the terror will end up in the pit (Isa. 24:17-18). On that day, God will punish the host of heaven and the kings of the earth (Isa. 24:21).

As mentioned above, the hosts or stars of heaven refer to fallen angels, and the chief star is Satan (Isa. 14:12) who took a third of the stars (angels) with him when he was kicked out of heaven (Rev. 12:4). When Jesus appears, He will deal with Satan, and his angels. Satan will be cast into the bottomless pit for one-thousand years (Rev. 20:1-3). Following Satan's defeat, Jesus will set up His millennial kingdom; THEN, when the world and cosmic powers are put to shame, the saints will rule with Christ on the earth (Isa. 24:23). Only those who survive the concluding tribulation judgement, by submitting to Jesus Christ (Zech. 12:10, 13:1), enter the millennial kingdom (Zech. 14:16).

To summarise - when Jesus returns, He will judge the heavens and the earth. This is the biblical Jesus, not often heard about today. Instead, most focus on their version of the 'Good News' Jesus came to bring (Isa. 61:1-2a), neglecting the latter part of verse two (b). When Jesus commenced His ministry, He read from Isaiah (Isa. 61:1-2a, Lu. 4:18-19), deliberately leaving out verse two (b). The latter part (Isa. 61:2b) will be fulfilled when He returns, as described throughout the above mentioned. On that day, those looking for Him will be comforted (Isa. 61:2b-11, 65:17-25, 66:22-23), and they will reign with Him (Isa. 24:23), while those rejecting Him, will be trampled by Him (Isa. 63:1-6, 66:15-16, Rev. 14:20).

The Sign of the Son of Man

'All the Tribes of the Earth will Mourn.'

(Matt. 24:30-31)

In the previous section, immediately after the tribulation, the judgment of the stars (angels) and the wicked was addressed. When Jesus returns to the earth to judge the nations and fallen angels, the saints will return with Him, from heaven, to also judge, rule, and reign with Christ. It is at this time within the seven years of trouble that Luke's record of Jesus' words contextually applies. "Now when these things begin to take place (the signs in the heavens), straighten up and raise your heads because your redemption is drawing near" (Lu 21:28). While the nations are perplexing over the calamity (Lu. 21:25), fainting with fear with foreboding of what is coming on the world (Lu. 21:26), the saints rejoice!

Up until now, the rebels have been warned many times to repent (cf. Rev. 9:20-21, 16:8, 10), through the one-hundred and forty-four thousand Jewish evangelists (Rev. 7, 14:1-5), also through the two Jewish witnesses

(Rev. 11), and again through the angels (Rev. 14:6-13). Many others have heard the gospel through those who have come to faith through the afore-mentioned groups and ministries.

In sum, throughout the tribulation judgements, many come to faith in Christ Jesus, who would not have otherwise (cf. Isa. 26:10). However, the salvation of their souls will come at the cost of their natural lives (Rev. 6:9-11, 7:9-14, 11:13, 12:11, 13:10, 15, 14:13, 15:2 20:4, 22:14). In business terms, this is called a trade-off. One thing will cost you the other. Failing to lay down their lives, metaphorically speaking (Matt. 16:24-25), this side of the tribulation, they will have another opportunity to do it, literally, during the tribulation.

On this side of the tribulation, members of the church are told to 'lay down their lives' and 'endure until the end' (Matt. 10:22). The same con-cluding message was given to each of the seven churches in the book of Revelation, using the word 'Conquer' or 'Overcome' (Rev. 2:7, 10-11, 17, 26, 3:5, 12, 21). The churchthat has an ear to hear what the Spirit is saying (Rev. 2:7, 11, 17, 29, 3:6, 13, 22) is told to conquer, and remain conquer-ing, which is to endure. Those having ears to hear (Mk. 4:9, 12, 20) are those that Listen (Mk. 4:3), Perceive (Mk. 4:12), Understand (Mk. 4:12, 13), Accept, and Bear Fruit (Mk. 4:20). They Endure (Mk. 4:17).

Those who endure do so through tribulation (Mk. 4:17) and are not caught up with the cares of this world (Mk. 4:19). Those enduring (Rev. 1:9, 2:2, 3:10), by remaining faithful, this side of the tribulation, will be removed (raptured) before the tribulation commences (Rev. 3:10, cf. Lu. 21:34-36), and those who do not, will be left behind. Again, while in the tribulation, the left behind will be commanded to lay down their lives and endure until the end to be saved (Matt. 24:12, Rev. 13:10, 14:12), or else perish. Most will perish!

Most within the tribulation, as now, will seek to save and improve their lives (i.e Your Best Life Now). While some will start out the right way, as seen through the parable of the sower (Mk. 4:1-20), as soon as tribulation or persecution comes, they fall away (Mk. 4:17), or consumed by the things of this world (Mk. 4:19), like Demas (2 Tim. 4:10). Important to note - those falling away were once enduring for the gospel, for a while (Mk. 4:17), before departing.

The same is seen within each of the five failing churches in the book of Revelation (Rev. 2-3), requiring repentance or else they will face judgement. Like Israel, the church is plagued with false teachers and increasing, who claim God will not judge. But He did judge Israel, and He will judge them again, and He will also judge the lukewarm church.

Regarding the verse at hand (Matt. 24:30) and the signs of the times (Matt. 24:3), Jesus listed several, yet none will be more confronting and frightening than seen through the rebels' response when He returns (Matt. 24:30). When Jesus returns, the whole world will mourn! Not some, all! All the tribes of the earth will mourn (Matt. 23:30). Jesus' words echo that of the prophet Zechariah (Zech. 12:12), only with Zachariah's prophecy, the land of Israel, and not the world, mourns. Jesus' prophecy in the book of Matthew (24:30) includes Israel but focuses on the rest of the world. Undoubtedly, unlike Zechariah's reference, the world mourning refers to grief at the expectation of judgment rather than a mark of repentance. The image of the coming judgement was first seen by John, which terrified him (Rev. 1:17).

John also reveals when Jesus returns, the whole earth will mourn (Rev. 1:7). Here, and once more, we are reminded of the words of Jeremiah "What will you do when the end comes?" (Jer. 5:31). Throughout the previous sections, we have seen the answer to Jeremiah's question, or statement, where the wicked flee and are terrified when the end comes. In this section, see that they mourn! The whole world mourns in terror and fright-ful expectation of judgement!

While the world mourns in terror of expected judgement, believing Israel and anyone else trusting in Jesus will be comforted, receiving grace and mercy. As mentioned previously, even at this last stage of the tribula-tion, in fact, after the tribulation (Matt. 24:29) Jesus affords an opportu-nity to be saved (Zech. 12:10), by being cleansed from all sin (Zech. 13:1). Those who respond in the required way to Christ's invitation enter the Millennium (Zech. 14:16, cf. Rev. 22:17).

While the message of 'grace and mercy' is often misused and abused today, Zechariah provides the proper application through the introduc-tion of sin and suffering. This leads to supplication and repentance, with mourning, when coming face to face with the living God. By addressing sin, the passage and the prophet takes into view Jesus Christ, "Whom they pierced on the cross" (Zech. 12:10). The prophet is not so much taking into consideration the crucifixion of Jesus - instead, he looks well past that event, even two thousand years further on, to the return of Jesus after the tribulation (Zech. 12:11, cf. Matt. 24:29). Verse eleven (Zech. 12:11) clar-ifies with the words, "On that Day…" On that day, Jesus will appear from the heavens and judge the righteous and the wicked alike.

Throughout prophetic literature, 'That Day' always refers to Jesus' sec-ond coming and judgement. On that day, everyone who had previously rejected Jesus will recognise Him. On that day, those who look to Him will mourn in repentance (Zech. 12:10), while those resisting Him will mourn in terror (Matt. 24:30-31, Rev. 1:7). The event referred to will take place at the plain of Megiddo (Zech. 12:11b), which is the location of the Battle of Armageddon. The Battle of Armageddon is further described in chapter fourteen of the book of Zechariah and again in the book of Revelation, chapters sixteen and nineteen, among other places.

As mentioned many times before, during the tribulation, following the rapture of the church, the awakened Jews (cf. Rom. 11:25-36) will come to faith in Jesus (Rev. 7, 14). They will bring about a mass revival, converting multitudes from every nation, all tribes, peoples, and languages (Rev. 7:9). This tribulation revival will be ongoing throughout its seven years, concluding with Jesus' return. Again, and unbelievably, even at this late point, leading right up to Jesus' return, people will still be able to look into the face of Christ and repent due to God's extended grace and mercy. According to verse ten (Zech. 12:10), even when Jesus is seen with the naked eye, salvation is still offered.

As seen in verses ten to fourteen (Zech. 12:10-14), at the appearance of Jesus (Zech. 12:10), as always, an individual response is required, through repentance, and mourning. Such a response secures salvation, confirmed by chapter thirteen, verse one, "Where comes the cleansing of sin and uncleanness." This means that forgiveness is granted to repentant sinners because of God's grace and mercy, which Peter confirms (2 Pet. 3:9), among others.

Again, the appearance of Jesus is expanded on further in the first chapter of the book of Revelation (1:7), saying, "He is coming with the clouds, and every eye will see Him— even those who pierced Him. Moreover, all the tribes of the earth will mourn because of Him. So shall it be! Amen." The word 'mourning' as seen in Zachariah, chapter twelve, (v. 11), and the book of Revelation (1:7), is eschatological and contextually supports the phrase 'On that Day', indicating, and even confirming again, as to when this event takes place.

On that day when Jesus returns, multitudes are gathered, collectively and individually saved. The evidence is seen through the words 'families' and 'wives,' and by 'themselves'. This suggests many individuals from all nations will come to faith in Jesus during the tribulation, and even just after it, through mourning and repentance, even at the time of His appearing (Zech. 12:10-14).

As seen above, there will be two responses to Jesus when He returns. Contrary to those who receive grace and mercy, responding to Jesus' last invitation for salvation, there are those, in fact, most, who would instead call for the rocks to fall on, and hide them from the wrath of the Lamb (Rev. 6:14-17). The two different responses to Jesus when He returns, are seen through many parables. Matthew, chapter thirteen (Matt. 13:24-30, 36-43) is of particular interest, showing the wheat (righteous) and weeds (wicked) remain together until it is time for harvest, which occurs at the end of the age.

The parable reveals two types of yields (wheat and weeds), two sowers (Jesus and Satan), and two different times to sow (day and night), into the same field. At harvest time, first, the weeds are gathered and destroyed, then the wheat is assembled into the barn. The parable represents 1). The good seed (Jesus); 2). The field (the world where Jesus is proclaimed); 3). The wheat (the sons of God); and 4). The weeds (the sons of Satan).

The harvest occurs at the end of the age (Matt. 13:49), which concludes this age, ending when Jesus returns after the tribulation (Matt. 24:30). Therefore, the parable covers the time from Jesus' first appearing until His next. The point of Jesus' teaching is that when He returns, then He will deal with the 'weeds' by sending out His angels to gather them and throw them into judgment (Matt. 13:40–42; cf. vv. 49–50; 2 Thess. 1:7–10; Rev. 19:15). The judgement refers to the millennial period, before the great white throne judgement (Rev. 20:11-15), where still there will be weeping and gnashing of teeth (Matt. 13:42, cf. Matt. 8:12; 13:50; 22:13; 24:51; 25:30).

Here 'Weeping' suggests sorrow and grief, corresponding with mourning at Christ's return (Matt. 24:30), and grinding of one's teeth speaks of pain and suffering (physical agony in hell). Through the verses listed, the teaching of Christ confirms that hell is a literal place of eternal physical and mental anguish When Jesus returns, contrary to the wicked suffering, the parable also teaches that the righteous will shine like the sun in the kingdom of their Father (Matt. 13:43; cf. Dan. 12:3). When Jesus returns, He will send out His angels with a loud trumpet call, and they will gather His elect (Matt. 24:31).

On the topic of Jesus' return, there is much more to say - so, in the next section, we will dive deeper into the two judgements, including the resurrection of the just and the unjust. To conclude this section, the sign of Jesus' return, going by those mentioned above, is that the whole world will mourn at His appearance; some over their sin through repentance, and others over the fearful expectation of judgement. Both, however, have the same opportunity, the same invitation to be saved, yet each group chooses very different paths. Some even start well yet fall away due to tribulation and persecution or are distracted by the things of this world. Here, the words of Jesus are a timely reminder, "Blessed are those who mourn, for they will be comforted" (Matt. 5:4). The faithful follower of Christ should expect trouble in this life (Jn. 16:33); those left behind, coming to Christ in the tribulation will suffer far worse.

Here, and again, the reader should also be reminded of the opening words to this section: "Now when these things begin to take place (the signs in the heavens), straighten up and raise your heads because your redemption is drawing near" (Lu 21:28). While the nations are perplexed over the calamity (Lu. 21:25), fainting with fear with foreboding of what is coming on the world (Lu. 21:26), the saints rejoice! During the tribulation, the saints will be morning, but shortly afterward, their mourning will be turned into joy (cf. Jer. 31).

The Angels are Sent Out
'Lord, Lord'
(Matt. 28:31, cf. 13:30, 41, 49)

As seen in the previous section, the most significant sign of the end times is that after the tribulation, the remaining earth's population will mourn the return of the Son of Man. All the people of the planet will mourn for one of two reasons, 1). They will either mourn over their sin in repentance, or 2) they will mourn in fearful expectation of judgment. Those submitting to Jesus, even as late as when He returns (cf. Zech. 12:10), will alone enter His rest, being the millennial kingdom (Zech. 14:16). Those still resisting and rejecting Jesus will be slain.

At the end of the age, the wicked are gathered first by the angels (Matt. 13:30, 41, 48), before the righteous are gathered (Matt. 24:31), who enter the new world. Only those who have submitted to Jesus will enter His rest, and only those who have followed Him will rule and reign with Him (Matt. 19:28). In the new world, Jesus will be its God, having removed and replaced its former god (2 Cor. 4:4), ruler, and prince (Jn. 12:31, 14:30, 16:11, Eph 2:2). The removal of Satan and the judgement of sinners will occur between the conclusion of this world and the commencement of the next. Some refer to this period as the seventy-five-day interval. The seventy-five-day interval theory is gained from Daniel's prophecy (Dan. 12:11-12).

The understanding of the seventy-five-day interval follows the latter one thousand, two hundred and sixty days of the tribulation, being the great tribulation. The great tribulation will commence from the time of the abomination of desolation, when the antichrist announces he is God. The antichrist's short-lasting rule and reign in the newly formed new world order will end when Jesus Christ returns, replacing the antichrist's New World Order, or beast system, with His new world.

In Daniel's passage (Dan. 12:11-12), the seventy-five-day interval comes from a figure of one thousand, two hundred and ninety days, making a difference of thirty days following the latter one thousand, two hundred and sixty days of the great tribulation. Alongside the figure of one thousand, two hundred and ninety days, there is also a mention of one thousand, three hundred and thirty days, making a difference again of forty-five days after the great tribulation. The two additional amounts make seventy-five days, which, again, is where the seventy-five-day interval theory comes from. However, it is also argued the two additional amounts of thirty days and forty-five days refer to two different times. The first relates to the setting up of the antichrist's throne, and the second refers to the setting up of Jesus Christ's throne. The latter is the favoured position and expounded on further in the book Daniel's Divulgement.

Within the period, argued to be forty-five days between Jesus' return and the commencement of the millennial dispensation, Jesus will remove the abomination of desolation, the third temple, the false prophet, and the antichrist (Dan. 12:11). He will also judge the stars (angels) and cast Satan into the bottomless pit (Rev. 20:1-3) and then He will gather and judge the nations. Those who survive the tribulation, and come to Christ through it, receive a special blessing (Dan. 12:12). Unfortunately, John's revelation almost contradicts Daniel's predicted blessing by saying that, during the tribulation, the blessed ones die early (Rev. 14:13).

The meaning of John's record of the angel's proclamation is that the tribulation will be such a troublesome time; any who die in Christ will be blessed due to being delivered from the rest to come. The longer anyone lasts during that time, the more difficult it will be, particularly for those following Jesus. Daniel refers to the blessing of those who survive the tribulation, indicating that they enter the millennium along, being the Messianic Kingdom (cf. Zech. 14:16).

Dwarfing the number of people now following Christ at the end of the tribulation, there will be those still resisting, albeit a remnant by comparison of those left behind (cf. Isa. 23:3, 7). These will be the ones even surviving the battle of Armageddon, or at least, its conclusion (cf. Rev. 16:16, 19:11-15). Those surviving the tribulation judgments, concluding with the battle of Armageddon, will be gathered for judgement (Matt. 13:30, 41, 49), one thousand years short of the final judgement, which is at the great white throne (Rev. 20:2, 10, 11-15).

Within Matthew's account of the gospel, there are two end-time gatherings, one of the righteous (Matt. 24:31) and the other of the rebels (Matt. 13:41, 49). Both are gathered by the angels sent by Jesus when He returns (Mat. 25:31-32). As mentioned earlier, the rebels are gathered first. The prophet Joel further describes that event (Joel 3:1-3). The very place of the battle of Armageddon is where the judgement of the Gentiles (rebels) takes place, resulting in them being cast out (before the millennial kingdom) into a place of weeping and gnashing of teeth.

The judgement of the Gentiles will be based on how they responded to Jesus and how they treated the Jews during the tribulation (Matt. 25:32), whether favourable (Matt. 24:34-40) or not (Matt. 25:41-46). At that time, the tribulation survivors will be judged and referred to as either sheep or goats (Matt. 25:32). The sheep will be the blessed ones entering into the millennium (Matt. 25:34, Dan. 12:12, Zech. 14:16), and the goats will go into eternal punishment (Matt. 25:46).

Following the judgement of the goats is the resurrection of the saints, or the righteous (Isa; 26:19, Dan. 12:2, Jn. 5:28-29, Acts 24:15, Rev. 20:4), where they will receive their reward for remaining faithful unto God. This resurrection will consist of those who laid down their lives for Jesus during the tribulation (Rev. 12:11, 20:4). These will be the resurrected referred to as the 'Friends of the bride' (Jn. 3:29), who also partake of the wedding feast and the millennial kingdom blessings. The resurrected will likewise receive their glorified bodies, as the raptured saint did seven years earlier (1 Cor. 15:35-58, Phil. 3:21).

Everyone left behind in the tribulation is invited to the marriage supper of the Lamb (Rev. 19:9, 22:17), but to enter and remain, they must respond appropriately. Sadly, some will come close yet fall short in the end (cf. Matt. 22:11-12). The wedding feast will most likely commence during the forty-five-day gap between Jesus' return and the instigation of the millennial dispensation. Again, everyone following Jesus is invited to the wedding feast, although many will not experience it (cf. Matt. 25:1-13). "Many are called, but few are chosen" (Matt. 22:14).

When comparing the parables following the Olivet Discourse (Matt. 241-31), Jesus warns of the danger of not being ready for His return multiple times (Matt. 24:42, 44, 50, 25:13). In doing so, He further warned those who are wicked that they would be cut into pieces and put with the hypocrites, in that place of weeping and gnashing of teeth (Matt. 24:48-51). Jesus also warned the foolish virgins that they will be shut out (Matt. 25:11) of the marriage feast and, therefore the millennial kingdom. The reason being, stated by Jesus, "I do not know you" (Matt. 25:12). The words "I do not know you" should be compared with a similar rebuke, where Jesus told His confessors, "I never knew you" (Matt. 7:21-23).

The stark warning of Matthew, chapter seven (vv. 21-23), is one of the most startling of all scripture. The warning is aimed at those who confess Jesus' name, even doing signs and wonders in His name, yet never 'knew' (experienced) Him. They knew about Him, but did not enter His covenant, as they remained 'Lawless' (Matt. 7:23). In the same way, the lawless knew about Jesus, He also knew about them and their works. While the lawless will say to Jesus, on that day, "Lord, Lord, did we not do works in Your name?" Jesus prewarned those trusting in works, by saying, "Not everyone who says Lord, Lord will enter My kingdom." The kingdom referred to is the millennial kingdom - therefore, these verses will be fulfilled when Christ returns after the tribulation.

Those standing before Jesus, hearing the rebuke, mentioned above will be the same surviving the tribulation. The false teachers and false prophets even doing signs and wonders in His name, leading many astray (Matt. 24:23-24). Anyone else falling into the category of lawlessness who perish before Jesus returns will go directly to the place of weeping and gnashing of teeth (cf. Lu. 16:19-31), where they will await the final judgement (Rev. 20:11-15). Those perishing, either before the tribulation or in it, do not have an opportunity to respond to Jesus (i.e., Lord. Lord). When they are resurrected after the millennial dispensation (Rev. 20:5) to face the final judgement, there is no evidence of any discourse there (Rev. 20:11-15). However, as seen through the parable of Matthew, chapter twenty-five, among other places, there is discord of those facing Jesus when He returns, yet to no avail. On each occasion the wicked called Jesus, "Lord" (Matt. 7:21-22, 25:11, Lu. 6:46, 13:25).

To summarize, when Jesus returns at the end of the tribulation, He will judge the nations, including those confessing to follow Him. The word for 'nations' refers to Gentiles. The Jews will be judged first, and then the Gentiles. The parables following the Olivet Discord include both Jews and Gentiles claiming to be followers of Jesus Christ during the tribulation. Some continue as if Jesus was not returning; therefore, they will not be ready (Matt. 24:36-44). The same is applied to the five foolish virgins (Matt. 25:8, 13). Then there is the wicked servant, the self-consumed lawless man who pleased himself (Matt. 24:48-50), like the wicked, slothful, and worthless servant (Matt. 25:24-30), and again the goats (Matt. 25:41-46).

On each occasion, those rebuked respond to Jesus with an excuse or some form of justification. Again, there is no such opportunity to dialogue with Jesus, for those who perished before He returns, or any evidence again of a plea for mercy at the great white throne judgement (Rev. 20:11-15) - therefore, the parable warnings best apply to those surviving the tribulation. However, everyone here and now should pay careful attention.

Anyone failing to enter covenant with God through Jesus Christ will experience eternal suffering. Many will think they are/were saved when, according to the parables, most are not. Many will fall short due to resting on their works, name, position, ministry, followers, and credentials, overlooking their apparent failure to obey. Those failing, and being cast out, are workers of lawlessness (cf. Matt. 24:23) rather than being servants of righteousness.

Today, goats masquerade as servants of righteousness, but they are actually servants of Satan (2 Cor. 11:15). Satan's servants fill pulpits and occupy television ministries the world over, deceiving, and leading millions astray, continuing, and escalating into and throughout the tribulation (Matt. 24:24). These ones failed to know Jesus, and made evident by their works and words.

Jesus' warning in Matthew, chapter seven (Matt. 7:21-23) is the conclusion of a sermon, commencing in chapter five, called 'The Sermon on the Mount.' There, Jesus lists the requirements for entering heaven (Matt. 5:2-12). Access to the kingdom of heaven is extended to:

1. The poor in spirit
2. Those who mourn
3. The meek

4. Those who hunger and thirst for righteousness
5. The merciful
6. The pure in heart
7. The peacemakers, and
8. The persecuted

The above-listed qualities are to be evident and on display for all to see (Matt. 5:13-16) yet can only be achieved through Christ (Matt. 5:17-20), highlighting the importance of being in a covenant (right relationship) with Him. No amount of religion will save the one outside of the covenant (Matt. 5:20) from judgement, although many will rely on their religious works, saying, "Lord, Lord, did we not do... in your Name!" (Matt. 7:21). On that day, not only will everyone's outward work be examined, but their heart also (Matt. 5:21-30). Every action, reaction, word, and thought will be judged (Matt. 5, 6), which is why Jesus said, amputate anything that causes you to sin (Matt. 5:30), for whatever was done, whether openly or in secret (Matt. 6:4) will be exposed and judged by the all-seeing Judge, Jesus.

While many will boast of their dead works on that day (Matt. 7:22), Jesus will judge them as lawless (Matt. 7:23) because they failed and or refused to obey. The Greek word for lawless is 'no law.' In other words, the lawless state that everything is acceptable, and nothing is forbidden. Therefore, they can do whatever they like, and it will be alright... Sound familiar!

Today this is known as 'hyper-grace,' or as Jude calls it, 'Perverted grace'. Grace is perverted by those who have crept in, promoting another gospel, and in doing so, they deny Jesus as the only way and means of salvation (Jude 1:4).

An interesting comparison is found between Matthew (7:13-14, cf. 21-23) with Luke's record of the 'Narrow Door' (Lu. 13:22-30). Notice again, like Matthew's account, by using the word 'Many', saying, "Many will come to Me on that day," Jesus is stating that MOST confessing to be saved will not be. Luke comes in from the opposite direction saying, "FEW will be saved" (Lu. 13:22). THEREFORE, "Strive to enter in through the narrow door" (Lu. 13:24). Luke then joins Matthew by saying, "Many will seek to enter and will not be able" (Lu. 13:24). Again, like with Matthew's account, those shut out also call Jesus, "Lord" (Lu. 13:25), as did the five foolish virgins (Matt. 25:11). These were those who were in God's presence (Lu. 13:26) yet cast away (Lu. 13:29) into the place of weeping and gnashing of teeth (Lu. 13:28) as workers of evil (Lu. 13:27).

In sum, ON THAT DAY, when Jesus returns, after the tribulation, many (most) will be caught out, deceived into thinking that they are right with God when they are not. The same could be said today by comparing the 70/30 percent ratio of the seven churches. The seven churches addressed in the book of Revelation (Rev. 2-3) represent the church collectively. Five (70%) of the seven were failing and needed repentance, or else! Unless repentance came first and fast, the five would not receive the reward. First and foremost, the reward is Jesus.

You have eternal life if you have Jesus (Jn. 17:3). If you do not have Jesus, you do not have eternal life, therefore, will not be raptured when He returns for His church. Still failing to secure Jesus in the tribulation, then the above mentioned will be the experience for those falling short, which is, being cast into the place of weeping and gnashing of teeth.

As always, whether this side of the tribulation or in it, Jesus is seeking to save the lost (Lu. 19:10), which is the purpose of judgement (Isa. 26:10). Therefore, those failing to know Jesus, securing Him as their Saviour, do so due to trusting in themselves, and their works. The question then remains, do we truly know Jesus, or do you merely know about Him?

The Thief

'Stay Awake, for you do not know on what Day your Lord is Coming'
(Matt. 24:42-43)

At the beginning of this series, two questions were raised and have since been addressed: 1). When would Jesus return? And, 2). What signs would signify His return? (Matt. 24:3). While most of the signs are reserved for the tribulation, there are also listed birth pain signs leading into the tribulation (Matt. 24:5-8), setting the stage for the antichrist (Matt. 24:15) and the New World Order (cf. Dan. 7:24, Rev. 13;1, 17:11-13).

As mentioned previously, the New World Order is already here, albeit in the shadows. Although the writing is on the wall, most cannot see it due to being spiritually asleep. The COVID-19 passport and associated buying and selling restrictions (cf. Rev. 13:16-17), are arguably the greatest evidence of the New World Order, where the very words (NWO) are now common language for the mainstream media, politicians, and chief medical officers.

As mentioned above, commencing this series was the consideration of two questions asked of Jesus, by the disciples (Matt. 24:4). The bulk of this work has already addressed the second question, relating to the signs of the end times. The first question, being the 'time' was also covered with the rebirth of Israel (Matt. 24:32-35), but still, more work needs to be done. Remember again, the disciples asked, "When will these things be?" (Matt. 24:3). The disciples' question was prompted by Jesus saying the temple will be destroyed (Matt. 24:2b).

Making the connection to the temple and the time is important due to the previous chapters revolving around it (Matt. 21-24), specifically its cleansing. After Jesus cleansed the temple of traders (Matt. 21:12-13), He connected Israel's faithlessness and fruitlessness with the cursing of the fig tree (Matt. 21:18-19). Jesus then addressed the faithless, fruitless scribes and Pharisees regarding His deity by asking, "What do you think about the Christ?" (Matt. 22:42). The religious leaders could not or dared not answer Jesus, resulting in Jesus' strongest recorded rebuke (Matt. 23). Jesus responded to the scribes and Pharisees by calling them hypocrites (Matt. 23:14, 15, 23, 25, 27, 28, 29), blind guides (Matt. 23:15, 24), blind fools (Matt. 23:17), blind men (Matt. 23:19), full of greed and self-indulgence (Matt. 23:25), blind Pharisees (Matt. 23:26), whitewashed tombs (Matt. 23:27), lawless (Matt. 23:28, 34), murderers (Matt. 23:31, 34, 35), snakes (Matt. 23:33), and persecutors of the prophets (Matt. 23:34). In His scolding rebuke, Jesus warned the religious leaders three times that they were going to hell (Matt. 24:13, 15, 32).

Following Jesus' eternal judgement of the scribes and Pharisees, He pronounced a natural sentence of death over them, blood for blood (Matt. 23:35-36), which was fulfilled, in part, in 70 A.D. Because the religious leaders shed the blood of the prophets, their blood will be required of them. Repeating the sins of the past, during the tribulation, the religious leaders will be the chief cause of persecution and death for the newly converted saints (cf. Rev. 6:10, 7:14, 12:11, 17:6 18:24), triggering Jesus to respond in a similar way He did to the scribes and Pharisees when He returns (Rev. 16:6).

Again, when Jesus addressed the scribes and Pharisees (Matt. 22:41-42) and answered the disciples (Matt. 24:4), the context revolved around the temple, commencing with Him cleansing it (Matt. 21:12-13). First, Jesus drove out all the moneychangers from the temple who were merchandising God and taking advantage of the people of God. Crooked men had turned the house of prayer into a den of thieves, a twisted place of business, repeating the sins of their forefathers (Jer. 7:11). And the scribes and Pharisees were in on the act, being full of greed, and self-indulgence (Matt. 23:25).

Matthew, chapter twenty-three, is a repeat of Jeremiah, chapter seven, where the religious leaders were also greedy for gain (Jer. 6:13, 8:10) and would not listen to God through the prophets (Jer. 7:13, 24, 28). As a result, the 'people of God' were cast out (Jer. 7:15, 29).

In the same way, Jesus accused the scribes and Pharisees of being robbers and murderers, God said the same of Judah's religious leaders (Jer. 7:25-26), promising the temple they trusted so much (Jer. 7:4, 14a), would be handed to another (Jer. 7:14b, cf. Lu. 19:41-44). Like Judah's religious leaders, much like today, the scribes and Pharisees thought they could do whatever they liked with, and within the temple, including turning it into a den of robbers (Matt. 21:12-13), not realising God was watching. But God was watching (Jer. 7:12), and due to their sin, He was looking to do them harm, not to do good (Jer. 44:27).

Due to Judah's short-sightedness, God reminds them, "What I did to your forefathers, I am about to do to you" (Jer. 7:14). He cast them out of His presence, which meant losing access to the law, the land, and the temple. In Matthew's account, Jesus is saying the same thing, warning the scribes and Pharisees the temple they had corrupted and placed so much trust in was about to be destroyed (Matt. 23:38, 24:2). They were also about to be cast out and would remain cut off until they called upon His name (Matt. 23:39). A similar warning was given to the churches in the book of Revelation (Rev. 2-3), where members had defiled the place of worship with greedy, self-indulged worldly practices.

The key and common sign of the times with Judah, the scribes, the Pharisees, and the church (being the temple of God), is the corruption of God's house. Similarly, Jesus rebuked the religious leaders of His day - He rebuked the churches, Sardis, and Laodicea (Rev. 3). The churches had repented of the greedy, self-indulgent sins of the Pharisees, specifically seen through the church of Laodicea, which prophetically represents the last church before Jesus returns. So corrupt was Laodicea - Jesus had nothing good to say about her.

Going by that mentioned above, the time of the signs is marked by absolute corruption, driven by greed, within the church (the temple of God), also known as the great falling away (2 Thess. 2:3). The great falling away (apostasy) refers to whole denominations and entire churches no longer following or enduring sound doctrine (2 Tim. 4:3); instead, they are lovers of self, and money (2 Tim. 3:2).

The great falling away must take place first before the faithful church is removed (2 Thess. 2:7), then revealing the antichrist (2 Thess. 2:6, 8), who sets himself up in the third temple (2 Thess. 2:4). During the tribulation the antichrist will set himself up as ruler and as God. Before the tribulation, members of the church of Laodicea also set themselves up as God (or, at least, little gods). Remember, the word Laodicea means, 'People ruling,' and indeed, they were/are.

Like the other signs, the next following the tribulation temple includes the millennial temple. When Jesus returns after seven years of tribulation, He sets up the millennial temple, which will never be defiled (Ezek. 40-48). Until then, each temple, including the church (1 Cor. 3:16-17), has been contaminated through corrupt, greedy, self-serving, man-centred worship. Again, the same rebuke as seen in Jeremiah, chapter seven, and Matthew, chapter twenty-three, is just as applicable today and chiefly seen in the letter to the Laodicean church (Rev. 3:14-22), prophetically representing the 21st century church. Although the church of Laodicea is the worst, the other four rebuked churches are also in danger of corrupting their worship of God and are warned unless repentance comes first and fast, judgement will (Rev. 2-3).

The warning addressed to the church of Sardis is noteworthy when considering the language, 'Wake up', and if not, then Jesus would come like a thief: "Wake up, and strengthen what remains and is about to die, for I have not found your works complete in the sight of my God. Remember, then, what you received and heard. Keep it, and repent. If you do not wake up, I will come like a thief, and you will not know at what hour I will come against you" (Rev. 3:2-3).

The reference to the 'thief' was previously seen in Matthew's account of the Olivet Discord (Matt. 24:43), picked up on twice more by Luke (Lu. 12:33, 39), again by Paul (1 Thess. 5:2, 4), and Peter. (Pet. 3:10), and John (Rev. 3:3, 16:15). Of the listed references, only one applies directly to the church (Rev. 3:3), with the rest aimed at those left behind. The reason could be that, at the time, Jesus' audience was Jewish, and the Jews will go through tribulation for rejecting Him (cf. Rom. 11:25-32). John's reference is to the church; therefore, the faithful Gentile believers, supporting that will be removed before the tribulation commences (Rom. 11:25, Rev. 3:10, 4:1), that is, providing they have 'Stayed awake' (cf. Rom. 11:22).

To understand the significance of those mentioned earlier, the Jewish idiom of 'Thief in the night' needs clarification. The term refers to the Jewish high priest who would come in the night to check on the temple guards to see if they were sleeping. When Jesus, Paul, and Peter were teaching, using statements like, 'The thief in the night,' their audience would have been aware of the phrase and its meaning. The consequences for being found asleep when the high priest came, at an hour they would not know, was being set on fire. When arriving to find sleeping guards, the high priest would take hot coals from the altar and set the guard's garments alight. Once realising their garments were on fire, the sleeping guards would awake, shed their clothing, and run through the temple courts naked, looking for new garments. Subsequently, the high priest was 'the thief in the night' for those found sleeping on the job.

The reference to the thief in the night was applied to the churches of Sardis and the church of Laodicea, albeit indirectly. Both churches were rebuked and warned of being asleep (Rev. 3:3) and naked (Rev. 3:17). To the dead church of Sardis, Jesus said, "Wake up" (Rev. 3:3a), warning, if they did not, He would come like a "Thief" (Rev. 3:3b). Jesus further warned the church if they did not wake up, He would come against them at an hour they would not know (Rev. 3:3c).

The same warning is applied to the lukewarm church of Laodicea, who were (spiritually) naked (Rev. 3:17). Jesus told them to stop buying from the world (the prosperity-driven church) and start buying from Him (Rev. 317-18). If they heeded the warning through repentance, then Jesus would cloth them in white garments (Rev. 3:18). The same white garments are mentioned in the church of Sardis, where a remnant had not soiled their clothing (Rev. 3:4-5). Those alone, who have white garments, their names are not blotted out of the book of life (Rev. 3:5).

In contrast, for those who have soiled their garments, their name is blotted out. Remember, to have soiled your garment, you first must have one. A similar promise is given to the church of Laodicea, where the one who conquers is joined with Jesus (Rev. 3:20-21), whereas the one who does not is spewed out (Rev. 3:16).

The members of the seven churches addressed by Jesus (Rev. 2-3) – particularly the churches of Sardis and Laodicea, who repent. and remain faithful and hold fast, receive, and keep their white garments. They are raptured when Jesus (the High Priest) comes at an hour they do not know. Further support for this statement is seen in Revelation, chapter four. Verse one signifies the rapture, with the words, "Come up here" (cf. Rev. 11:12), with the following verses detailing heaven. The raptured saints, who are now in heaven, wear white garments and have crowns on their heads (Rev. 4:4). The crown of life was promised to the two faithful churches, holding fast (Smyrna and Philadelphia), providing they continue to conquer (Rev. 2:10-11,

The raptured saints are seen in heaven in the following reference and are mentioned again in chapter nineteen (v. 14). The saints in heaven make up, "The armies of heaven, arrayed in fine linen, white and pure" (Rev. 19:14). Again, the saints are those who ascended into heaven when Jesus (the High Priest) came at an hour they did not know (the rapture), and seven years later, they return with Him, at an hour those left behind do not know. On this side of the tribulation, the church members are likened to the 'temple guards,' who are responsible for keeping the 'temple' clean (cf. Eph 5:14-15) by staying awake (Rev. 3:3). During the tribulation, those left behind, who come to faith through repentance, are also called to 'Stay awake', and keep their garment on (Rev. 16:15).

Paul further supports the above-mentioned by presenting the same warning in this first letter to the church of Thessalonica (1 Thess. 5:2, 4). Paul refers to the times and the seasons, directly referencing Genesis (1:14, 16). In Genesis, Moses records the creation story where God spoke into being two great lights, the sun, and the moon, which are a reference point for signs and seasons. The Hebrew word for 'seasons' is Mo'ed, defined as a feast or a divine appointment. Moses' reference in the book of Genesis should also be compared with another, found in the book of Leviticus, chapter twenty-three, addressing the feasts of the Lord. The same Hebrew word, Mo'ed, is used as with Paul's letter (1 Thess. 5:1). The significance is all three verses apply to the Lord's holy feast days, or years, otherwise known as the 'Shemitah', which is the seventh year, reoccurring every seven years.

In sum, when Paul wrote to the church of Thessalonica, he said there is no need to mention anything further about the signs and seasons, as you already knew about them, being the holy feast days. Because they knew about the holy feast days, "THAT DAY would not surprise them like a thief" (1 Thess. 5:4). The church of Thessalonica was faithfully watching, looking for the signs and the seasons, unlike the religious hypocrites (Matt. 16:3). Therefore, THAT DAY would not overtake them; and they would not be left behind to suffer the wrath of God, as hypocrites would be (1 Thess. 5:9).

Peter further supports Jesus, and Paul, stirring up and reminding his reader of the holy predictions and the commandments (2 Pet. 3:1-2), warning of scoffers in the last days (2 Pet. 3:3-7). Like Paul, Peter also looks back to the Genesis account (2 Pet. 3:8), confirming God will fulfill His promises (2 Pet. 2:9), albeit, for most, that day will come like a thief (2 Pet. 3:10a). Finally, Peter's reference is applied to the conclusion of the tribulation (2 Pet. 3:10b 13), encouraging his hearers to live holy lives (2 Pet. 3:11), "Waiting for and hastening the coming of the day of God" (2 Pet. 3:12), again, applied to the millennial dispensation (2 Pet. 3:3).

Several scriptural references encourage believers to stay awake and watch for Jesus' return. Through the signs of the times, like with the religious hypocrites of Jesus' time (Matt. 16:3), and the general population claiming to be the people of God, not knowing the time of visitation (Lu. 19:41-44), most of the church is distracted (not watching) and asleep. Most have fallen asleep, even soiling their garments (corrupted and contaminated by the world), and therefore will be surprised by 'The thief in the night'.

Consider the rebukes received by the five failing churches (70%), alongside the greatest sign leading into and during the tribulation. These are false teachers and false teaching (Matt. 24:5, 11, 24). So, it is no wonder Jesus urged His followers to stay awake (Matt. 24:42, 43), which would also be, 'stay free from the sugar-coated (hyper-grace, and prosperity) gospel'.

In Mark's account of the Olivet Discord, the words 'Stay awake' were recorded four times (Mk. 13:33, 34, 35, 37). Luke records it once with his account of the Olivet Discord (Lu. 21:36), yet twice more when warning of Christ's return (Lu. 12:37, 38). The call to stay awake applies to both this side of the tribulation and during the tribulation for those left behind. The parables of Matthew, chapters twenty-four and five, refer to those in the tribulation (Matt. 24:42, 44, 50, 25:13). During the seven-year ordeal, the one who stays awake will be counted 'Blessed' (Rev. 16:15). The blessed will be blessed due to being clothed with the salvation gown and the righteousness robe. The rest are naked and exposed; therefore, their sin is on full display, and they will be judged accordingly.

CHAPTER FIVE

The parable of the ten virgins is distinctly Jewish, as is Jesus' teaching of the Olivet Discord (Matt. 24, Mk. 13, Lu. 21). The ten virgins refer to the Jews left behind and awakened in the tribulation. Once the Jews realise that they are in the time of Jacob's trouble (Jer. 30:7), they prepare for the return of their Messiah.

The Ten Virgins
'Give Me Oil'
(Matt. 25:1-13)

The previous section addressed the "Day and the hour (that) no one knows" (Matt. 24:36), also discussing the meaning of the "Thief in the night" (Matt. 24:43, Lu. 12:39), urging the reader to "Stay awake" (Matt. 24:42, Mk. 13:36). The close of the previous section settled that the Jewish idiom of the 'Thief in the night' applies to this side of the tribulation and the conclusion of the great tribulation. The implication is Jesus (the High Priest) could come at any time; therefore, the hearer is advised not to be found sleeping while on watch.

Again, as determined in the preceding section, the reference to sleeping refers to being spiritually asleep, as the members of the church of Sardis were (Rev. 3:1-6). While the church of Sardis had a reputation of being alive, they were 'Dead' (Rev. 3:1) because they were in bed with the world. While the church was seen to be busy with activities, they were spiritually asleep (Rev. 3:2). Jesus warned the sleepy church, "If you will not wake up, I will come like a thief, and you will not know at what hour I will come against you" (Rev. 3:3).

In the letter to the church of Sardis, the words of Jesus applied to the church, this side of the tribulation. The church is not mentioned again within the tribulation period. The church of Sardis is both literal and symbolic of every sleepy church, albeit having a reputation of being alive (awake).

Today, many churches fit the exact description of Sardis, busy with bustling programs, professional bands and brands, celebrity preachers, and proficient speakers, yet are dead, as far as Jesus is concerned. The said dead church has departed the way due to being void of preaching Christ, therefore preaching repentance and warning of the things to come. 'Progressive' churches fitting the sleeping description are the same, loved by the world and loathed by the remnant faithful followers of Jesus Christ. Jesus even hates their works, being Nicolaitan in practice (Rev. 2:6, 15).

The Nicolaitans were a controlling, cult-like group of confessing believers who had infiltrated the church. The word, Nicolaitan, refers to clergy ruling over the laity, The Nicolaitans were authoritarian wolves spruiking prosperity and hyper-grace (false) teaching, precisely what is seen in many churches today, having a reputation of being alive.

Today, self-serving professional preachers control congregations through a hierarchy of henchmen. Like with the warning to the church of Sardis, Jesus told those holding to the teaching of the Nicolaitans to repent, or else He would come soon and war against them with the sword of His mouth

(Rev. 2:16). The warning to both the church of Sardis and the church of Pergamum was similar. To the church of Pergamum, Jesus said He would come at an hour they would not know and war against them. On both occasions, the reference to waring against the church refers to the tribulation (cf. Rev. 19).

A more obvious reference to the tribulation was given to the church of Thyatira (Rev. 2:22). The church of Laodicea received a similar rebuke and warning where Jesus said He would vomit them out of His mouth (Rev. 3:16), therefore, into the tribulation. The reference to being vomited out should be compared with Moses' writings, where God warned the Israelites, "If you do what the surrounding nations do, I will vomit you out of the Promised Land" (Lev. 18:25, 28, 20:22). The Israelites did do what the surrounding nations did, and God did vomit them out of the Holy Land.

The application for the church of Laodicea refers to the same, "If you do what the world does, I will vomit you into the tribulation," therefore out of the Promised Land. The rapture saints will be in heaven for seven years, and then they will return with Christ to rule with Him on the earth in the millennial kingdom. The millennial kingdom is the Promised Land for the church, applying, kingdom THEN, not, and never NOW.

Once the faithful virgin church has been removed, presented pure, and blameless before Christ (2 Cor. 11:2, Eph. 5:27) by way of the rapture, those remaining on the earth are left behind to endure the tribulation. Among those left behind are the Jews. The Jews will not wake up this side of that seven-year event, but only after many Gentiles come in (Rom. 11:25).

The church is Gentile; therefore, once the church reaches its total number, then Jesus takes it out of the way (Rev. 3:10). The same is true for the Jews during the tribulation; their number is complete when the faithful remnant of virgin Jews (brothers) confesses Christ (Rev. 6:11) and follows

Him wherever He goes (Rev. 14:4). Following Him wherever He goes implies total obedience, enduring until the end until Jesus returns.

Remember, the purpose of the tribulation is to wake up the sleepy confessor of God, who thinks they are alive (saved) but are dead. During the tribulation, a specific pre-determined yet remnant (Rom. 9:27) number of Jews will come to faith in Jesus and will be sealed by the Holy Spirit (Rev. 7:4-8), converting countless millions of left-behind Gentiles from every nation, from all tribes and languages (Rev. 7:9). During the tribulation, the gospel will be proclaimed throughout the whole world until Jesus returns (Matt. 24:14), primarily through the awakened Jews. Like now, during the tribulation, both Jew and Gentile must be awakened and must stay awake until Jesus comes.

The context of the parable of the ten virgins declares the same and revolves around the end of the age, which implies Jesus' return (Matt. 24:3, 14, 27, 30, 39, 44, 51). Therefore, the parable applies directly to the tribulation, explicitly speaking to the left behind Jews. Throughout the Old Testament, faithless Israel is called 'Virgin Israel' several times, specifically throughout Jeremiah's writings (Jer. 14:17, 18:13, 31:4, 31, Lam. 1:4, 15, 2:13). Yet, she was anything but a 'virgin,' likened better to a whore, referenced fourteen times by the prophet Hosea. The Hebrew word for 'virgin' also translates 'daughter' referring to Jerusalem as a city conceived by God. Due to Israel's faithlessness, God did and will again appoint whoring-Israel to the tribulation. The tribulation trial is aimed first at the Jews (Jer. 30:7, Dan. 12:1, Matt. 24:21) and then the rest of the world including the faithless church (Rev. 3:10, cf. Rom. 11:22).

Again, the purpose of the warning in the first place is to avoid the judgement (cf. Dan. 4:27); failing avoidance, then its purpose is to turn around (Isa. 24:10). The seven-year event will serve to shake, test, and separate the sheep from the goats (Matt. 25:31-46). Failing the test during the time of trouble, the goats will then go into hell when Jesus returns. As for the Jews passing the test, when Jesus returns at the end of the tribulation, they will be redeemed and restored (Ezek. 20:33–44; Zech. 13:1).

Another clue supporting that the parable of the ten virgins contextually applies to the tribulation are the words 'Marriage feast' (Matt. 25:10). The marriage feast occurs after the wedding ceremony in heaven when the raptured saints are taken out of the way. Jesus, who is the Thief, and the Bridegroom, at the trumpet blast, will return for His bride, the church, at an hour they do not know. If the bride is ready, the Son (Jesus) will lift her up (rapture) and carry her away to the Father's (God) house, where a place has been prepared (Jn. 14).

The rapture theory is in the precise pattern of a Galilean wedding. When Jesus and Paul reference the rapture, their hearer would have connected the language with a traditional Galilean wedding. Therefore, their audience understood, those missing out on the wedding ceremony have another opportunity to attend the feast, concluding that not everyone at the banquet will attend the ceremony.

Additional support for the statement mentioned above is in Revelation (Rev. 19:9), where the tribulation saints are called "Blessed" due to being invited to the marriage supper of the Lamb. The saints are blessed with the invitation to the banquet due to "Staying awake" (Rev. 16:15) and "Keeping the words of the prophecy" (Rev. 22:7). The invitation is given again at the end of the revelation/tribulation, where a voice from heaven, being the Spirit and the bride (the church), says, "Come" (Rev. 22:17) to those remaining on the earth. To all with ears to hear, the Spirit says, "Come to the marriage supper." The invitation extends to all, who have not taken the mark (666) during the hour of trial and are found ready and waiting when Jesus returns (Matt. 25:13).

The parable of the ten virgins contextually fits within the tribulation period, where the Jew's eyes will be opened once the church has been taken out of the way. The Jews will wake up in the tribulation realising they have missed Christ twice, knowing they will not see Him again until they call on His name (Matt. 23:39).

Remember, the Olivet Discord is addressed first to the Jews and then to the rest of the world. So, again, the Jews will first respond to Jesus during the tribulation, and then through them, people from every nation will come to faith in Jesus (Rev. 7).

The left-behind Jews will suffer seven years of tribulation, awaiting the return of the Bridegroom. Jesus will return with His bride at the end of the age (Rev. 19:6-8), when the tribulation is complete, to judge the nations, and the Jews (Matt. 24:29-31, 25:31-46), before setting up His millennial kingdom. The Jews, who are then invited to the marriage feast, will be guests or friends of the bride, but will never be the bride. Anyone missing the rapture will never be the bride but only and ever a friend of the bride.

In preparation for the marriage feast, , the Jews are to make themselves ready during the tribulation, to be found waiting for when Jesus returns (Matt. 25:13). The readiness requirement was to have oil in their lamps (Matt. 25:4, 8). Notice, all had lamps, which was the very thing Jesus threatened the church of Ephesus with; unless they repented, He would remove their lamps (Rev. 2:5). No lamp, no oil, results in no entry to the Promised Land (Rev. 2:7). While the ten virgins all had lamps, only five had enough oil to last. A lamp without oil is about as useless as a church building without Jesus (cf. Rev. 3:15-20). At midnight, on the announcement of the Bridegroom's return (Matt. 25:6), all ten virgins rose from their sleep and trimmed their lamps to meet Jesus (Matt. 25:7), yet the five foolish virgins had not enough oil (Matt. 25:8), and neither did the five wise virgins have enough to share with the foolish. Each was required to have enough oil for themselves; none would carry or cater for another.

Remember again; the Jewish ten virgins knew the season through the signs, namely the rapture and the revealing of the antichrist. They now recognised Jesus as their Messiah, yet still, all had fallen asleep, all ten of them, the wise and unwise alike (Matt. 25:5). Now awakened by the sound of the Messiah's return, the five foolish virgins went to buy oil for their lamps, while the five wise virgins entered the marriage feast (Matt. 25:10). However, when the five foolish returned, the feast was in progress, and they were denied entry (Matt. 25:11).

In sum, the parable of the ten virgins is a warning to Israel, left behind in the tribulation, who are cautioned, during the trial, Stay awake, watch, and be ready!" As mentioned in the previous section, Jesus will come in the middle of the night (Matt. 25:6), like a thief (Matt. 24:43), when the Jews least expect Him (Matt. 24:27, 39, 50), catching many asleep (Matt. 25:5, cf. Rev. 3:3). Those sleeping and having no oil are spiritually dead due to being in bed with the world (Matt. 24:37-49). The oil represents the Holy Spirit. While the five foolish, lacking oil, knew Jesus, calling Him Lord (Matt. 25:11), Jesus did not know them (Matt. 25:12, cf. 7:21-23).

While the awake left behind will know the season and time remaining, being seven years, the ability to stay awake and remain ready is still beyond them. The same was true of the disciples just before Jesus went to the cross. "Then Jesus returned to the disciples and found them sleeping. Were you not able to keep watch with Me for one hour?" He asked Peter. "Watch and pray so that you will not enter into temptation. For the spirit is willing, but the body is weak" (Matt. 26:40-41). Due to falling asleep, many fall into temptation, even during the tribulation.

To reiterate, on this side of the tribulation, the Jews and much of the church, are asleep and in bed with the world. When the faithful remnant is removed, then those left behind will be spiritually awakened. Again, first the Jews, and then the Gentiles, including the dead and lukewarm church. That said, the parable of the ten virgins speaks more towards the return of Jesus (Matt. 25:1, 6, 10, 12) than the tribulation itself.

After realising the left behind had missed the Messiah, five of the ten made sure they had enough oil to last (Matt. 25:4, 8). The five having oil did so due to having the Holy Spirit. They had the Holy Spirit because they had Jesus and were waiting for His return (cf. Jn. 14:15-31, 1 Jn. 3:24, 4:13, Rev. 14:4). Because they had Jesus, they were known by Him and were granted access to the wedding feast (Matt. 25:10).

Before the tribulation, those left behind did not have Jesus; therefore, Jesus did not receive them as His bride. At the commencement of the trial, the left behind then bought from Jesus without price (cf. Isa. 55:1, Rev. 3:18, 22:17) instead of buying (trusting) from the world. Once awakened, the five foolish virgins attempted to buy from the world, even though it was too late. Even if they had oil in preparation for Jesus' return, it still would have been from the wrong source (the world); therefore, resulting in the same end, "I do not know you" (Matt. 25:12).

In conclusion, the rapture trumpet (1 Cor. 15:52, 1 Thess. 4:16, Rev. 4:1) serves as the midnight cry and announcement, "Come out and meet Him" (Matt. 25:6). Any missing that event will be left behind and will need to get busy buying oil. Those who do not only acknowledge Jesus, but they make Him Lord, through obedience. While others may call Jesus Lord (Matt. 25:13), most (Matt. 7:21) fail to obey (Lu. 6:46), therefore, they are disqualified.

Even during the tribulation, many will be still in bed with the world. This is why the voice from heaven says, just before Jesus returns at the end of the tribulation, "Come out of her My people lest you take part in her sins and share in her plagues" (Rev. 18:4). Those remaining in bed with the world will share in her judgement. Those who break away from the world are invited to the wedding feast, which occurs on earth, after the tribulation, in-between Jesus judging the nations, then the Jews, and setting up the millennial kingdom.

Even at that late stage, many will say, "Lord, Lord" (Matt. 25:12, cf. 7:21-23), and Jesus will respond, "I do not know you" (Matt. 25:13), because they did not have oil (Matt. 25:3, 8). Like the five foolish virgins who did not have oil, and presuming after acquiring some from the world, they, did not have the right oil, due to being purchased from the wrong place, or source.

Many churches today are in the same predicament as the five foolish virgins, either having no oil, or the wrong oil (spirit). While they seem to have oil or a reputation of being alive, they are dead due to purchasing their oil from the world. The worldly churches of Sardis and Laodicea are excellent examples being alive and active today. While like churches have a reputation of being alive, but are dead, and rich, being full of the world, they are empty of Jesus.

The heart cry both now, and throughout the tribulation should be, "Give me oil!" That is, give me the Holy Spirit. The one who has the Spirit, has Jesus.

CHAPTER SIX

L ike the parable of the ten virgins, the parable of the talent is distinctly
Jewish. During the tribulation, Jews coming to faith in Christ Jesus
will be assigned talents and tasks to do. Those who do well will be rewarded
with more; those that do not, will be punished.

The Talents
'Rewarded According to Your Works'
(Matt. 25:14-30)

The second parable of Matthew, chapter twenty-five, is the parable of the
talents. Again, keep in mind that chapters twenty-four and twenty-five go
together and are in chronological order. Like the parable of the ten virgins,
the ten talents speak first to the Jews and point to the return of Jesus Christ
at the conclusion of the tribulation.

As a refresher, the Olivet Discord (Matt. 24) is an outline of the book
of Revelation, in the exact order, from chapters six to nineteen (Rev. 6-19).
The first four verses (Matt. 24:4-8) are applied to Revelation, chapters two
and three, addressing the church. These are the birth pains before the trib-

ulation commences, including persecution that the church must endure until the end. The birth pains serve to wake up the sleeping church and break her away from sin (worldliness). They also help motivate the church to get busy preparing for Jesus' return.

The birth pains lead to the tribulation; however, the hour of trouble will not commence until the church is first taken out of the way (2 Thess. 2:6-8). The faithful remnant is removed before the hour of trial that is coming on the whole world to try those who dwell on the earth (Rev. 3:10). Revelation, chapter four (v. 1), symbolises the church being removed from the earth before the tribulation commences.

Matthew, chapter twenty-four, verse nine and onwards, provides an outline of the following events. Verse nine is the commencement of the tribulation, and verse fifteen marks the midway point, with verse twenty-nine pinpointing the end. Verses thirty and thirty-one refer to the judgement of the Jews and the Gentiles when Jesus returns, which is expounded on through the parable of the virgins, and talents. The final judgement is further explained at the conclusion of Matthew, chapter twenty-five (vv. 31-46).

Again, the parable of the talents speaks of judgement, first to the Jews and then to the Gentiles, who have been left behind to endure the tribulation. The church was removed seven years earlier, and raptured into heaven (1 Cor. 15:51-52, 1 Thess. 4:16-17). Once the church has been removed from the earth, she will then be judged by Jesus. Her removal in itself is a judgement, judged, faithful, clean, and spotless, worthy to escape the things to come (2 Cor. 11:2, Eph. 5:27, Rev. 19:7). The judgement is known as the Bema Seat of Jesus Christ, spoken of by Paul, "For we must all appear before the judgment seat of Christ, so that each one may receive what is due for what he has done in the body, whether good or evil" (2 Cor. 5:10).

At the Bema Seat, every believer will be judged according to what they have done (Rom. 14:10, 12). As mentioned in the previous section, none can carry or cater for another. Again, the church has been raptured and therefore has already been judged righteous, implying the Bema (judgement) Seat of Jesus Christ is not unto punishment, but reward. Once more, following the rapture, the church will be rewarded for their actions (Matt. 16:27, Eph. 6:8). The rewards are given to believers according to their works. It is important to note that works do not save the believer, but the saved have done good works because they are in covenant with God the Father through Christ the Son. The initial salvation reward is being joined with Jesus and therefore removed from the hour of trial (1 Thess. 1:10, 5:9, Rev. 3:10).

Following the rapture (1 Thess. 4:13-18), the first reward, outside of avoiding the tribulation, is receiving glorified bodies, exchanging this earthy vessel for a heavenly one (1 Cor. 15:52-53, Phil. 3:21a). The believer's heavenly body will be like Jesus' resurrected body (1 Jn. 3:2). The rewards following the removal from the earth and receiving glorified bodies include crowns (1 Cor. 9:24-25, 1 Thess. 2:19, 2 Tim. 4:8, Phil 4:1, 1 Pet. 5:4, Rev. 2:10, Ja. 1:12), and authority (Lu. 19:17, 19, Rev. 1:5, 2:26, 5:10, 11:15), which will be disclosed on the day of judgement (1 Cor. 3:13). On that day, everyone's work will be tested by fire, where some works will be burnt up, and others will survive. The works surviving the test of fire are rewarded (1 Cor. 3:13-14), which all should work towards, being careful not to lose what any have worked for (2 Jn. 8, cf. 1 Cor. 9:24-27).

Not everyone at the judgement seat of Jesus Christ will be rewarded, some will suffer loss, but they will be saved (1 Cor. 3:15), which again supports that works save no one. Again, none standing before Jesus on that day will have anything to fear or be ashamed of (1 Jn. 2:28). Here, the verse "Perfect love casts out all fear" (1 Jn. 4:18) should be considered, implying the one who has God's (perfect) love has no fear of punishment on the day of judgement (1 Jn. 4:17). The reward given to raptured and resurrected believers on that day, is beyond anything anyone can imagine (1 Cor. 2:9). Albeit unimaginable for most, Paul did know something about what awaits the faithful followers of Christ, yet he was not allowed to talk about it (2 Cor. 12:4). A lot of people today 'say' they have been to heaven, sharing what they 'saw' and 'heard' (even making money from it), yet Paul did go to heaven and yet was not permitted to share it, other than to say, indirectly, he went. The unimaginable things Paul saw in heaven will be experienced by the rewarded, raptured, and crowned church (Rev. 4:10-11) in the very near future.

Likewise, those enduring the tribulation will be rewarded beyond imagination (Isa. 64:4, cf. Matt. 25:34). Paul's promise (1 Cor. 2:9) to the church ("What no eye has seen, nor ear heard, nor the heart of man imagined, what God has prepared for those who love him") is a direct quote from Isaiah (Isa. 64:4). It, in context, speaks of the tribulation, therefore applying the original promise to the left behind Jews.

Like Paul, Jesus also quoted Isaiah when referring to the age before the tribulation and His return (Lu. 4:18-19, cf. Isa. 61:1-2), stopping short of verse two (b), which will be fulfilled before His return, through the tribulation. The context (Isa. 60-66) describes the coming tribulation when, through it, a remnant of the Jews will come to faith in Jesus (Isa. 10:22-23, cf. Rom. 9:27); then, they will be remembered, restored, and rewarded.

Isaiah, chapters sixty-one through to sixty-six, is necessary to compare with the Olivet Discord and the book of Revelation to gain the correct theological framework, understanding what happens to who, when, and why. Clearly, the Jews are the focus, and Isaiah even prophesies the rebirth of Israel (Isa. 66:8). Israel is front and centre, and the nations are always in the background (Isa. 61:5-6, 9, 64:2, 65:1). While in the background, the

Gentiles will come in before the Jews (Matt. 19:30, 20:16) because they listened to God when Israel did not (Isa. 65:1). Israel refused to listen to God, to hear His voice (Isa. 65:12, 66:4) which is the reason Jesus said they would not see Him again until they called on His name (Matt. 23:39). The tribulation will serve that purpose, opening Israel's deaf ears, causing those who failed to tremble at God's word previously to shake during the time of trouble (Isa. 66:2, 5).

During the tribulation, faithless Israel will have an opportunity to be faithful to God once again. The parable of the talents revolves around faithfulness versus faithlessness. Luke provides a similar parable (Lu. 19:11-27) where three servants were trusted with an amount of money according to their ability. Although varying, both Matthew and Luke's accounts tell the same story; Jesus gave His servants money to invest on His behalf. Some did well and were rewarded. Others who did nothing were punished— those doing nothing, such as burying the money in the ground (Matt. 25:25) or wrapping it up in a handkerchief (Lu. 19:20), did so that they might keep it for themselves, should the Master not return.

If the money had been deposited in the bank (Matt. 25:27, Lu. 19:23) where it would have gained interest, there would have been a record of it; therefore, the faithless servant could not have claimed it for himself. Luke's account is more prominent, where Jesus said some would reject Him, not wanting Him to return or reign over them on His return (Lu. 19:14, 27). The talents and minas represent gifts and time. Time, in itself, is a gift.

On both accounts, Jesus called out the faithless servant, calling him slothful, worthless, and wicked (Matt. 25:25-27, 30, Lu. 19:22-23), before taking what he had, giving it to another (Matt. 25:28-29, Lu. 19:24) and then condemning him to hell (Matt. 25:30, Lu. 19:27). On the other hand, the faithful servants received a reward when the Master returned

(Matt. 25:19, Lu. 19:15). Similarly, both accounts record the words, "Well done" (Matt. 25:21, 23, Lu. 19:17).

Matthew's record reveals the praised servants receive an increase of money and Entered into the Master's joy' (Matt. 25:21, 23) instead of being cast out into a place of weeping and gnashing of teeth (Matt. 25:30). Luke's record reveals the praised servants receive authority to reign over cities (Lu. 19:17, 19). These cities are those in the millennial kingdom; therefore, the faithful servant has been given access to the coming kingdom, as opposed to the ones failing who have been slaughtered (Lu. 19:27) and cast out (Matt. 25:30).

Notice the commonality of both faithful and faithless servants calling Jesus, "Lord" (Lu. 19:16, 18, 20, 25) and the use of the word "Master" in Matthew's record (Matt. 25:18, 20, 21, 22, 23, 24, 26). And again, the reference to Jesus being a 'Hardman' (Matt. 25:24) and a 'Severe man' (Lu. 19:21, 22). Paul confirms that Jesus is severe to those who fall away (Rom. 11:22). Surely, this is not the same Jesus that many claim to know and promote today.

Alongside Matthew and Luke, Mark writes something similar (Mk. 13:34), urging the reader to "Be on guard, and keep awake" (Mk. 13:33). Following the command to keep awake three more times, Mark records the words, "Stay awake" (Mk. 13:34, 35, 37). With Matthew and Luke's records, the faithless servants had fallen asleep (spiritually), either not expecting or wanting the Master to return. Again, the unfaithful servants desired to keep the Master's property for themselves, repeating the sins of Judas, the thief (Jn. 12:6).

Mark's record adds another parable (Mk. 4:1-20), highlighting that for those who care more about the things of this world, the deceitfulness of riches and desire for other things, the 'word' in them is choked and they become fruitless (Mk. 4:19, cf. Lu. 21:34-36). Following the parable of the sower (Mk. 4:1-20), Mark records Jesus saying, "Pay attention to what you hear: with the measure you use, it will be measured to you" (Mk. 4:24). As with Matthew and Luke's recorded parables, Mark concludes with the same, "For the one who has, more will be given, and from the one who has not, even what he has will be taken away" (Mk. 4:25), repeated by both Matthew (Matt. 25:29) and Luke (Lu. 19:26).

As mentioned above, talents refer to gifts and time. Mark's account (Mk. 4:1-20, 21-25) could also include the 'Word' (seed), and 'Lamp' (testimony). God has gifted us with His word (the gospel) and has given us the time and anointing to share it (shine the light). What we did with the gospel, for ourselves, and how we share it with others will be judged.

As with the parables mentioned above, a similar promise is given to the faithful remnant with the church of Thyatira, providing they hold fast to the uncompromised gospel until Jesus comes, they would be given authority over nations (Rev. 2:26). When Jesus sets up His millennial kingdom, He will rule with an iron rod (Rev. 2:27, 12:15, 19:15), and the faithful saints will rule with Him. Again, the reference to the iron rod speaks of the hardness and severity of Christ to those who disobey (cf. Matt. 25:24, Lu. 19:21, 22). Those found to be faithless, from the church, therefore fruitless, are cast into the great tribulation (Rev. 2:22). Those remaining fruitless during the tribulation are cast into hell (Matt. 25:30).

While the parables recorded by Matthew, Mark, and Luke, mentioned above, speak first and foremost to the Jews, Luke's account is more inclusive. All must obey and be found busy in preparation for Jesus' return (Lu. 19:13b). Luke's account is still specifically aimed at the Jews, first, with the Jews best fitting the description of 'Citizens' (Lu. 19:14), referring to citizens of the Land, being Israel.

Regardless, as seen with the example of the church of Thyatira, the warning and promise apply to all, both the church this side of the tribulation and Israel, in the tribulation. First to Israel within the hour of trial, then the nations, including confessing Christians who have been left behind.

To summarise, the mentioned parables are eschatological and therefore intertwined with the book of Revelation, which commences and concludes with the words "Behold, I am coming" (Rev. 1:7, 22:12). The words are first aimed at the church (Rev. 22:16), where Jesus will reward her when He comes. Paul narrows in on the same with the warning to walk carefully (cf. 2 Cor. 5:10-11, Eph 5:15). The warning also applies to Israel, who is the subject of the parables. The warning within the mentioned parables is, "Do not fall asleep." "Do not seek to keep what is not yours," and 'Do not chase after the things of this world."

In conclusion, the raptured, awake believers forsook the things of this world, thereby escaping the things to come (Lu. 21:34-36). Every raptured believer standing before Jesus at the Bema Seat has no need to fear, for all are saved. Following the church, the words of Christ regarding His return are then aimed at Israel. Jesus says, "Be found ready and busy until I come" (Lu. 19:13, 15, 23).

Like now, during the tribulation, Israel will be called to forsake the things of this world (Rev. 18:4) and look to Jesus. Those who do will be rewarded (cf. Isa. 62:11) when He returns to rule over them (Lu. 19:27). The rewarded ones will enter their Master's joy (Matt. 25:21, 23), and share in His rule over the nations (Lu. 19:18-19). However, unlike with the first judgement of the raptured church, where all are saved (1 Cor. 3:15) when Jesus returns, those found fruitless are slaughtered (Lu. 19:27) and cast out (Matt. 25:30).

CHAPTER SEVEN

T he third parable of Matthew, chapter twenty-five, is that of the
sheep and the goats, also known as the 'Final Judgement.' Unlike
the first two parables, referring to the judgement of Israel, the last refers to
the judgement of the Nations, being the Gentiles. The judgement of the
Gentiles is according to their treatment of the Jews during the tribulation.

The Final Judgement
'When the Son of Man Comes'
(Matt. 25:31-46)

Concluding the Olivet Discord (Matt. 24), followed by the parables (Matt.
25), the focus is on the return of Jesus at the end of the age. The age refers
to the current time. There is a reference to two respective ages within the
New Testament, the present and the one to come (Matt. 12:32, 24:3). The
age to come speaks of the millennial dispensation, otherwise known as the
seventh day. This age is the sixth day, or millennium, paralleling the sixth
day of creation where God made man (Gen. 1:26-28, Ex. 20:9-11). God
created everything in six days (Heb. Yom, meaning a literal twenty-four-

hour period) and rested on the seventh day (Ex. 20:11), and the millennium to follow this age will be one of rest after Satan has been dealt with (Rev. 20:1-7). Again, the creation story parallels history, all six thousand years of it (cf. 2 Pet. 3:8, Heb. 4:1-11).

In sum:

- From Adam to Abraham is estimated to be two thousand years (two days)
- From Abraham to Jesus, time is estimated to be another two thousand years
- From Jesus' time to His return will be another two thousand years
- From the creation of Adam to Jesus last return to the earth is six thousand years
- After the six thousand years (six days), Jesus Christ returns and reigns for one thousand years (seventh day); the Millennium Reign.

When the earth and heaven complete their allocated seven thousand years in accordance with God's plan, this first earth and heaven will pass away, and a new world and heaven will be created, known as the eighth day (eight thousand years). The eighth day is a new day where everything is refurbished and made new.

The eighth day is not often mentioned, yet it is significant. Scripture provides some insight, mainly within the book of Leviticus (Lev. 12:3, 14:10, 23, 15:14, 15:29, 22:27, 23:36, 23:39), referring to worship and rest. The book of Numbers repeats Leviticus (Num. 6:10, 7:54, 29:35). Second Chronicles provides more insight by way of the eighth day representing completion, following the seventh day (2 Chron. 7:9, 29:17). Nehemiah states the same (Neh. 8:18), as does Ezekiel (Eze. 43:27). The eighth day is a new day, following the requirements and completion of the seventh.

Interestingly, on the eight-day, a Jewish male child was to be circumcised (Gen. 17:12, Lev 12:3, Lu. 1:59, Acts 7:8, Phil. 3:5), forever consecrated unto God through the sign of the covenant. Similarly, baptismal fonts in traditional church buildings are often octagonal due to the symbolism of the eighth day and baptism representing a new creation in Christ.

The eighth day follows the millennial dispensation where the earth and heavens pass away and are remade (refurbished) new (2 Pet. 3:10, 12). With the above-mentioned in mind, Peter urges his reader to live holy lives (2 Pet. 3:11), waiting for and hastening the coming day of God (2 Pet. 3:12, 13). Besides the book of Revelation (Rev. 21-22), Isaiah has the most to say about the eighth day (Isa. 66:22-23), following the seventh (Isa. 65:17-25). Jesus also alludes to it (Matt. 24:35).

Although Jesus' concluding statement, following the Olivet Discord (Matt. 24), refers to the eighth day (Matt. 24:35), His focus is on the events leading into the seventh, narrowing in on His return and the judgement. Matthew, chapter twenty-four, verses twenty-nine to thirty-one, followed by verses thirty-six to fifty-one, and the parables of chapter twenty-five concentrate on the judgement of the Jews and Gentiles. As mentioned previously, the parables of the virgins and the talents are aimed at the Jews, left behind to endure the tribulation.

The final judgement (Matt. 25:31-46) makes it more apparent, that the Jews are pinpointed with the specific wording, "As you did it to one of the least of these, My brothers, you did it to Me" (Matt. 25:40, cf. 45). The 'Brothers' are not characterised as either the sheep or the goats within the passage but are distinct, referring to Israel. Therefore, the sheep and goats who call Jesus Lord (Matt. 25:37, 44) are Gentiles, confessing Christ in the tribulation.

As mentioned above, the 'Final Judgement' (Matt. 25:31-46) speaks of the Jew's treatment by the Gentile Nations in the tribulation. Therefore, unlike the parables of the ten virgins (Matt. 25:1-13) and the talents (Matt. 25:14-30), the final judgement narrows in on the Nations. The theme of the previous parables declares a judgement of the Jews when Jesus returns. The final judgement declares a ruling of the Gentiles when Jesus returns. At the Second Coming of Jesus Christ, Israel will first be judged, and then the nations, followed by the surviving saints (Matt. 13:41-43). The righteous are rewarded after the faithless are condemned, leading into the marriage supper (Rev. 19:9).

When Jesus returns and judges the faithless, it is not that of the great white throne (Rev. 20:11-15), occurring one thousand years later, but rather one determining the guilt of the condemned. At the great white throne judgement, the guilty are sentenced, yet held in hades until then. The great white throne judgement, following the proclamation of the Jews, and Nations, one thousand years earlier, determines the measure of eternal punishment.

The one who knew God's will and word, yet did not do, and keep it, will receive a harsher sentence than the ignorant (Lu. 12:47). The more the one under judgement has been given, the worse it will be for them (Matt. 10:15, 11:24). Worse again will it be for the one who has fallen away from the truth, as Peter writes, "It would have been better for them not to have known the way of righteousness than to have known it and then to turn away from the holy commandment passed onto them" (2 Pet. 2:21). However, the worst judgement of all is reserved for those who have caused another to fall away through temptation. It would have been better that he was never born for such a one (Matt. 18:6).

Again, the premillennial judgement includes both the Jews and the Gentiles; however, Matthew, chapter twenty-five (vv. 31-46) concentrates on the Gentiles. The word 'Nations' (Matt. 25:32) refers to the Gentiles, who are distinct from Israel. The Greek word (ethnos, from where we get the English word ethnic) translated 'Nations', is also interpreted as 'Gentiles'. The prophet Joel (Joel 3:2, 13) addresses the same judgement, focused on the nations before Israel's decision. Joel's account is known as 'The valley of decision' (Joel 3:14). The valley of decision is not referring to would-be followers of Christ making a decision, therefore calling on His name, as some suppose, but rather God's judgement.

The time for committing to Jesus Christ has passed, there is no 'alter call' but instead, bloodshed (Rev. 14:17-20, 2017-18). When Jesus returns and judges the nations, two conclusions are given; one to the sheep (Matt. 25:32-40, 46) and the other to the goats (Matt. 25:40-46). Through the judgement of the nations, Israel will (then) know Jesus is 'their' God (Joel 3:17). But, for most, it will be too late (Rom 9:27-29).

Contrary to the judgement of the parable of the weeds, where the weeds are judged before the righteous (Matt. 13:41-43), the final conclusion states the righteous sheep on Jesus' right will be considered first, and when they are, they will be unaware of their good deeds (Matt. 25:37-38). During the tribulation, Gentiles wake up to the fact they have been left behind, repent, and commit to following Jesus Christ. They "Stay awake, keeping their garments on" (Rev. 16:15) until He returns at the end of the tribulation. During the tribulation, the repentant does good deeds, for which many will perish (Rev. 14:13). The labours of the righteous and their good deeds refer to sacrificially loving others, particularly those most at risk, the Jews.

Revelation chapter twelve reveals that during the great tribulation the Jews will be Satan's primary focus, and Gentile Nations, who "Keep the commandments of God and hold to the testimony of Jesus," will come to Israel's aid at their own expense (Rev. 12:15-17). During this time of trouble (Jer. 30:7), it will be difficult for the Jews, particularly following the antichrist's announcement that he is God (Matt. 24:15-21).

Following the judgement of the sheep, the goats on Jesus' left (Matt. 25:33, 41) are tried, according to their works (Matt. 25:41-46). It is important to note that good works did not save the sheep, but instead because they were saved, they did good works. On the other hand, the goats were neither saved nor did they do good works. Even if they had have done good deeds, they still would not have been saved.

Again, contrary to Matthew, chapter seven (vv. 21-23), where the lawless plead their case before being judged, in chapter twenty-five, the goats are afforded no such opportunity (Matt 25:41). Only after the judgement do they respond (Matt. 25:44), to which Jesus will repeat, "Go away into eternal punishment" (Matt. 25:46).

The goats pled their case by saying, "Lord, when did we not minister to You?" (Matt. 25:44). This suggests they did not know Jesus, the One they called Lord, due to not seeing the need (of His brothers), never mind responding to it. When you have Christ, you have the eyes of Christ, and likewise, Christ is seen through the eyes of those possessing Him (Matt. 6:22). To have the eyes of Christ is to see and know things unseen and unknown to others, although in part (1 Cor. 12:13, cf. 2:9). The fool does not know and cannot see Christ because the fool does not have Him (1 Cor. 1:18). During the tribulation, many confessing Christ (i.e., Lord), like now, who do not have Him, it will be evident by trying to seek to save (and improve) their own lives, even at the expense of their 'brothers' (Matt. 10:35-36, 24:9-12, Mk. 13:12).

During the tribulation, it will be challenging for most. Yet anyone refusing the mark of the beast (Rev. 13:15) will suffer more so, not being able to buy, sell, travel, or operate in any way within society. Famine will also be a global experience (Matt. 24: 7b-8, Rev. 6:5-6), particularly for those unable to travel and trade. The goats, who think they have Christ, may even be among those who resist the beast's mark (666); therefore, will suffer poverty over and above those with it. For this reason, their excuse might be, "We did not have enough for ourselves, never mind enough to share with others." On the other hand, the sheep who sacrificially share with the 'brothers' (Jews), out of their lack, perhaps remember the story of Elijah and the widow (1 Kgs 17:7-16), where the faithful widow ministered unto God's servants.

During the tribulation, especially throughout the last forty-two months, God will supernaturally sustain His own (Rev. 12:6, 14). God rewards those who sacrificially put others first. Again, none are saved by works, but because they are saved, they do good works, including laying down their lives for others, as Christ did for us. The deeds of the righteous are the evidence of their salvation (Ja. 2:26). Similarly, the unconcern of the goats for the 'brother' (Jews) in need (Matt. 25:42-44, 35-36) is also evidence for their judgement and damnation (Matt. 25:41, 46).

As a side note, the punishment of the goats was never meant for humanity, but rather Satan and his angels (Matt. 25:41). But because humanity has followed in Satan's footsteps, they too share in his end; that is, anyone whose name is not written in the Book of Life (Rev. 20:15).

Christ's judgement of the nations marks the beginning of His rule and reign on the earth, where the righteous, THEN, THEN, THEN (not now!), co-rule and reign with Him (Matt. 13:43, 25:34, Rev. 1:6, 2:25, 5:10, 11:15, 19:6-8, 20:4). Before Christ returns, true believers are subject to tribulation (Jn. 16:33), to be hated (not loved) by this world (Matt. 5:10-12, 10:22,24:9, Jn. 15:18). Anyone loved by this world is an enemy of God (Ja. 4:4, 1 Jn. 2:15). Being loved by the world should be warning enough, like popular 'preachers' who are praised and promoted by the likes of Oprah, these are likened to the goats, or even wolves (Matt. 7:15). Those claiming the wealth of this world, here and now, also fall in the same category of 'lovers of the world.'

In conclusion, Jesus' prophetic sermon commenced in chapter twenty-four, when "The disciples came to him privately, saying, 'Tell us, when will these things be, and what will be the sign of your coming and of the end of the age?'" (Matt. 24:3). Jesus answered the question by providing a list of signs, before stating the time. The time or season of Christ's return is narrowed in on with the lesson from the fig tree (Matt. 24:32-35), with an emphasis no one knows the day and hour (Matt. 24:36, 42, 44, 50, 25:13). Because no one knows the day or hour, all must stay awake (Matt. 24:42), be ready (Matt. 24:44), and remain watchful (Matt. 25:13). Those failing will be first left behind, and then still weakening in the tribulation, they will be shut out of the millennial kingdom (Matt. 25:12) and cast into hell (Matt. 24:51, 25:30, 46).

After the millennial kingdom, the righteous will go into the new heaven and new earth (the eighth day). The worthless, wicked Israelites and the goats will be resurrected for the great white throne judgement, resulting in being cast into the lake of fire (Rev. 20:5, 11-15).

The eternal destination of the good servants (Israelites), and the sheep (Gentiles), is the New Earth. Likewise, the destination of the wicked servants (Israelites), and the goats has also already been decided and was so before the foundation of the earth (Matt. 25:24, Eph. 1:4, Rev. 13:8). Before time began, God already knew His creation's response to the gospel - that said, the events must still take place first, providing equal opportunity to everyone to respond.

The mysteries mentioned earlier explained through Matthew, chapters twenty-four and twenty-five have been hidden since the foundation of the world (Matt. 13:35) and are now unlocked through the gospel for those with ears to hear (Matt. 11:15, Mk. 4:9, 23, Lu. 8:8, 14:35, Rev.

2:7, 11, 29, 3:6, 13, 22). Some, just a remnant, will respond and endure this side of the tribulation, and a few more during the tribulation, but by comparison, most will be 1). Left behind, and 2). Eternally judged. Let it not be you!

CONCLUSION

This series considered both the time and the signs leading up to Jesus' return. While Jesus addressed the signs before the time, in this work, the time was focused on the season for the things to come, signified by the rebirth of Israel. The rebirth of Israel in 1948 commenced the visible prophetic time clock for the end of this age. According to Moses, a man can expect seventy and eighty years on this earth, albeit with toil (Ps. 90:10).

Suppose we have understood the lesson from the fig tree (Israel's rebirth) correctly. In that case, the generation witnessing that miraculous event (cf. Isa. 66:8), where a dead nation became alive, again (Ezek. 37), seven years remain before Christ returns. Israel was rebirthed seventy-three years ago; therefore, the youngest person alive today 'witnessing' that event is seventy-three years old. If a man can expect up to eighty years of life (in general), then again, seven years remain.

Several times, as mentioned throughout this work, the tribulation period will last seven years. Once more, if eighty years is the general expectation of life on earth, in this age, with seven years of tribulation remaining, then the church could be removed (raptured) in the year 2022. In saying that, by no means I am attempting to know the day and the hour, only the season. Any, who claim such knowledge should be avoided. Jesus stated several times, "No one knows the day and the hour," yet still, many have claimed otherwise.

If the church is still on the earth post-2022, we will need to rethink our understanding of the lesion from the fig tree (Israel's rebirth) concerning the years applied to a 'Generation' (Matt. 24:34). Regardless of whether it be seventy to eighty years or otherwise, we know the time is now by the signs. The message, therefore, of Matthew, chapters twenty-four and twenty-five, is, "Stay awake" (Matt. 24:42), "Be ready" (Matt. 24:44), and "Watch" (Matt. 25:13). Whether or not you are caught up to be with Jesus before the commencement of the tribulation or left behind to endure the time of trouble, the same applies, BE READY!

www.ingramcontent.com/pod-product-compliance
Lightning Source LLC
Chambersburg PA
CBHW071414090426
42737CB00011B/1464